Merry Christmas!

To Cidny !

with Respect !

Merry Christmas !

from the Author

Giorgetta Duncan

12-15-2011

D1205910

# MICHAEL JACKSON

## We Are The Mirror

## BY JUJA D.

authorHOUSE®

AuthorHouse™
1663 Liberty Drive
Bloomington, IN 47403
www.authorhouse.com
Phone: 1-800-839-8640

© 2011 Juja D. All rights reserved.

No part of this book may be reproduced, stored in a retrieval system, or
transmitted by any means without the written permission of the author.

First published by AuthorHouse 6/13/2011

ISBN: 978-1-4567-6764-8 (sc)
ISBN: 978-1-4567-6766-2 (hc)
ISBN: 978-1-4567-6765-5 (e)

Printed in the United States of America

Any people depicted in stock imagery provided by Thinkstock are models,
and such images are being used for illustrative purposes only.
Certain stock imagery © Thinkstock.

This book is printed on acid-free paper.

Because of the dynamic nature of the Internet, any web addresses or links contained in
this book may have changed since publication and may no longer be valid. The views
expressed in this work are solely those of the author and do not necessarily reflect the
views of the publisher, and the publisher hereby disclaims any responsibility for them.

With love, I dedicate this book to all of you, the people of the world. Without you, without your generous contributions, this book would not exist.

A word about the power of opinion

*"If someone says your sister is a whore,
good luck proving you don't have a sister."*

Bulgarian proverb

# TABLE OF CONTENTS

# FOREWORD AND ACKNOWLEDGEMENTS

This book was a call for action. A strong calling from within compelled me to put together this book and provide a space for people's voice to be heard loud and clear. It was a call for service. Michael Jackson's death served as a catalyst for an enormous revelation about the power of public word and opinion.

Millions of people shifted their attention on Michael Jackson, staring at him, dissecting his entire life, his songs, his legacy, his children, his finances and every aspect of his being—some with love, gratefulness and awe, and others with hate, disgust, and rage. Even dead, he has continued to affect the lives, thoughts and opinions of others more powerfully than ever before. Michael Jackson lived a life torn between the immense joy of music creation, love, respect and appreciation on one side and the turmoil of accusations fed by media and people hungry for spectacle and "circuses" on the other. And then, I consider us, the people, a huge part of Michael Jackson's life because he cared about us and because we share the responsibility of creating his public image. We share the responsibility of creating who Michael Jackson is today for all of us.

The comments in this book, including misspellings and original punctuation (a perfect tool for checking one's own writing ability) are quoted verbatim. They are, in fact, a mirror in which each of us can see a reflection of our own lives, thoughts and feelings, and most of all our own words, words that have the power to give or take away, to inspire or disgrace, to create or destroy, for "death and life are in the power of the tongue: and they that love it shall eat the fruit thereof." (Proverbs 18:21)

With no time to lose, I called several of my closest friends and we started the book. I would like to give credit and thank my wonderful team, the talented and young Yani Dimitrov for his technical support, Betina Tsekova for compiling the material, John Gregory Stebbins for coming up with the name "We are the Mirror," my artist friends Nikolai Denchev for his inspiration and painting the surrealistic portrait of Michael Jackson and Marian Marinov for his creative expression and painting the covers of the book.

I especially want to thank my dear friend Phillip Velinov, for his ideas, knowledge of English, and enormous help in the creative and technical process of making this book a reality. Together, we had the vision of reaching the hearts of millions and providing the opportunity for all of us to see ourselves as co-creators of our own reality through the power of the words we speak. Thank you, Phillip, for believing in the book and me from the start.

And last but not least, I would like to say a big THANK YOU to my brother Pavel, who was my guest from Bulgaria during the month this book was created, for his patience, acceptance, quiet inspiration and joyful presence. Thank you for your encouragement, your brotherly love, absolute understanding and for allowing me to finish the book in one breath.

THANK YOU FOR SHARING,
"for out of the abundance of the heart
the mouth speaketh." (Matthew 12:34)

# INTRODUCTION

My dear readers, I am grateful for having the privilege to compile some of your thoughts, feelings, your love and appreciation, and some of your frustrations, grief and anger. This book is a memoir of HOW WE FELT when the "King of Pop," Michael Jackson, died.

Our goal is to document the entire spectrum of your opinions, comments and quotable passages. In "MICHAEL JACKSON, WE ARE THE MIRROR," we aim to depict a truthful and objective illustration of what the world thought and felt about Michael Jackson during the period between the day the pop star died (June 25) and the day of his memorial service (July 7).

Currently, the internet is the fastest and most direct way we can express ourselves, providing us with the luxury of anonymity and honesty without having to take any responsibly for our words.

The Webster's Dictionary definition of the word "**comment**" states "*1: a commentary; 2: a note explaining, illustrating, or criticizing the meaning of a writing; 3: a remark expressing an opinion or attitude,*" and an "**opinion**" is "*a belief based on what somebody thinks to be true or likely.*"

With these definitions at hand, I am convinced none of us really know the truth about Michael Jackson.

Being a person who enjoys beautiful music, yet not a music fan, I was shocked by the speed with which everything happened. Within an hour of Michael Jackson's death, the world already knew of it and began to react immediately. I started reading the internet postings about Michael Jackson and I got hooked. I was crying and laughing; I felt sad and happy, frustrated and overjoyed with love, thinking, "People have to read this!"

What really happened? Who was Michael Jackson for the world? I wanted to understand why people felt the way they felt and what drove some of them to buy tickets from London or Tokyo just to go to Los Angles and be part of his Memorial Service.

Reading this book, you will sense a powerful voice crying for a part of us that died with Michael Jackson, a part joyful, innocent and dear to us, a part that we, the people filled with hope wanted to protect but could not. We grieve for Michael Jackson, but even more so, we grieve for ourselves and our own lives.

What was my experience? On June 25, I felt profoundly sad, as if a friend had died. I had hardly listened to any of his music in the last two or three years. I stopped and wondered: "Am I a part of this mania taking the world by a storm, or is it something else?" Thinking about it, I realized that Michael Jackson's music had actually healed my heart a long time before when it was most broken and devastated. His music left a part of him somewhere deep inside me, a place almost forgotten.

The cassette "Off the Wall" was given to me as a present in Lake Charles, Louisiana with the advice, "Listen to him, he will make you feel better." I did not speak English at that time and had no clue who Michael Jackson was; naturally, he knew even less about me. Nonetheless, Michael Jackson's music had healed my heart. I started listening to him, going from a state of depression to a "better place," and the more I listened, the better I felt—loving him and dancing with his music. When I went back to Bulgaria, I took with me the video "We Are the World" (I love this song). There was an endless line of guests and neighbors who wanted to see it.

I have promised not to give my opinion about Michael Jackson in this book and to be absolutely impartial, and I certainly intend to keep my promise. The book is only a space where people from around the world share their thoughts about the extraordinary and controversial human being, Michael Jackson. It is a book about us, observing Michael Jackson's life, about our perception and reflection of our own lives. "WE ARE THE MIRROR."

We have used only a small fraction of the multitude of comments spanning the entire spectrum of human emotion. If you ever had an experience with Michael Jackson in person (positive or negative; inspiring or disheartening, whether it was a brief encounter, a lasting friendship or just a moment during a concert) and you want your story to be published, please share your experience at www.michaeljacksonreal.com

Thank you again for the generosity of your hearts and for sharing it with the world.

With all my love,
JUJA D.

# JUNE 25, 2009
# THURSDAY

*Michael Jackson, 50, suffers a major heart attack at home in Los Angeles, California on June 25, 2009. He is officially pronounced dead at 2:26 AM local time at the Ronald Reagan UCLA Medical Center. Jackson is survived by his three children, Michael Joseph Jackson Jr., Paris Michael Katherine Jackson, and Prince "Blanket" Michael Jackson II. Prior to his death, the musical superstar was preparing for what would be a series of 50 concerts titled "This Is It" starting July 13, 2009 at London's famed O2 Arena. News of Michael Jackson's death overloads web sites and the Internet nearly crashes.*

**shalala, Jun 25 at 08:18 PM**
Michael, I'm so deeply saddened to hear of your death. You were an extraordinary artist, I absolutely love your music. I know everyone here misses you, your music is on every radio station now. You have truly left an imprint on this earth. You will never be forgotten. Rest easy and god bless you.

**Mr. Bush, Jun 25 at 08:19 PM**
Mr. Jackson died of a cardiact arrest caused by his seeing a sale for boys pants that said half off!

**chandra, Jun 25 at 08:20 PM**
Your MOON WALK will be always remembered................!

**martin, Jun 25 at 08:20 PM**
Michael Jackson will always be one of the biggest influences of music forever,. Especially since the 1970's to now. He has touched us musically in every way possible. From music to video to dancing to just being the artist he wanted to be and everyone once to be. Micheal will always be remember for his music. We as people around the world have a forgiven any famous person for the faults and applaud him or her return to stardom.

**happy, Jun 25 at 08:21 PM**
another pedaphile dead, good

**M. Clark, Jun 25 at 08:21 PM**
It saddens me to read the judgmental comments of so many. However all of us have the right to voice our opinion. What we need to remember is that all of us fall short, in one way or another and all will answer for our actions. Life is too short to be judgmental. Let our character speak from the heart. Let compassion rule. Remember that those who show mercy will receive mercy and for the way we judge others, we will be judged. One fact is for sure, all of us will one day be in the same position that Michael Jackson is now, and what will others say about us?

**Stransky, Jun 25 at 08:21 PM**
Michael Jackson is a legend, who would have thought that he would die at the age 50 and not stay on for another 10 to 15yrs. He was a real legend and a ellusive superstar in the 80's to the 90's. I can remember growing up during my childhoods day s and would be listerning and watching his clips and fanatastic muzics. He will be remebered. Rest in Peace Mr. Jackson, even though there has been alot of painful critics about what you have done in the past,..you stand out and asked for forgiveness. And regarded as a supersta in the 20th century.......

**mike, Jun 25 at 08:25 PM**
There are some real ignorant morons out there. I wasn't a big fan, I did like some of his 80's stuff, and he does remind me of Elvis who also died in a tragic way. Both of these men were on top of the world and then later things would go very wrong for both of them. Goes to show that

happiness is indeed a tough commodity to hold on to. I hope that he has found peace.

**Rose L., Jun 25 at 08:26 PM**
R.I.P. MICHAEL JACKSON... you will always be remembered in my heart! I love your music! For all you haters you should ashamed of yourself! He was a great man! Rip

**kita, Jun 25 at 08:27 PM**
growing up in the 80's micheal jackson was a household name! i'm deeply moved by his lost! people God comes for everyone! be ready! love your love ones be happy with good health and live for today as if it was your last!!rest in peace mj!!!!!!!

**Maria, Jun 25 at 08:28 PM**
Personally i'm happy that he's dead. Karma always kicks ya in the butt!

**Not a Fan But..., Jun 25 at 08:28 PM**
....his music was part of my childhood & it feels like the end of an era. and.. To the people who come here just to bash him & leave nasty remarks, how would you feel if this was YOUR family member everyone was talking about? Regardless of anything else, he was still someones son, brother, father, uncle and friend and people are grieving for him. It doesn't matter what you think of him, THEY still deserve your respect.

**NoSorrow, Jun 25 at 08:32 PM**
He died the moment he stole childrens lives from them.
God took him before this tour started for a REASON.

**Katie, Jun 25 at 08:32 PM** R.I.P mj i luv♥ ur muzic. & i no deep down u werea great person & u shouldn't have cared what deez hataz out hear hav said cuz they prolly waz juss liez. Take care ill miss u!!

**brett, Jun 25 at 08:32 PM**
i remember being in grade school and id stay up late on fridays to watch friday night videos in hopes they would play billie jean-one of the greatest songs ever

**chuck, Jun 25 at 08:34 PM**

His family lawyer has just appeared on cnbc and Fox and believes prescription drug overdoes was the cause.

**John, Jun 25 at 08:34 PM**

U will truly be missed Micheal, My daughter & son felt soooooooooooooo sad for u don't care what the world have to say u r the best nobody knows what happen only God knows, RIP miss u.I will always love & remember u. See u in heaven.

**Hunter, Jun 25 at 08:34 PM**

Holy Freakin Crap;; I Honestly thought he was going to live till he was 120 Poor Mikay

**Rhonda, Jun 25 at 08:35 PM**

For all those who use the name of God and are pleased to see someone pass because of things you THINK they may or may not have done. I will keep you and Michael in my prayers because last time I checked God was our judge and he and only he is the one we will answer too.

**Rhenu, Jun 25 at 08:35 PM**

We will pray for ur soul to be rest in peace.The world missed u MIKE. U STILL ALIVE BY UR MUSIC.Love you.....

**Mari, Jun 25 at 08:37 PM**

Uhm, I am really disgusted.I just watched Larry King Live, and they showed the picture of them trying to revive Michael, with his eyes shut. Honestly that is something I didn't want to see, and I doubt his family wanted it blasted all over the news. Way to for doing a vultures job and swinging in before the flies do. You people are disgusting, and I hope the family sues seeing you "don't even know who the source is" according to one of your reporters that was on Larry King Live. Have better taste, write about how he will be remembered for how he touched lives, not blast his dead face all over tv.

**shane, Jun 25 at 08:37 PM**

hmm....Mary jane dies today huh??...thats sucks..i already had my ticket to his funeral in hell..the one they having right about now.I am pretty sure satan had his spot picked out ages ago.I liked his dance moves though...but to tell the truth I would sleep alot better knowing one less gay on earth.zzzzzzzz

**Stacy, Jun 25 at 08:40 PM**
Michael Jackson, may your soul rest in peace. You will be missed by those who cherished your talent in music and for being the greatest music pop star ever. Yes, Micheal may have acted a bit stranger than usual but no one will ever make me believe he messed with little children. To all the haters out there, I dare anyone of you all who has never sinned to cast the first stone! You were not there so how would you know what really happened! God do not like ugly! Michael gave people hope and the inspiration to become a singing superstar just like him. I love u MJ!!

**bre, Jun 25 at 08:41 PM**
I AM SO SORRY 4 THA LOST OF MICHEAL JACKSON!!!!!!! I LUV U I AM YOUR NUMBA 1 FAN!!!!!!!!!

**Debbie, Jun 25 at 08:46 PM**
All you hateful imbeciles - YOU WILL GET YOURS.

**Ee, Jun 25 at 08:53 PM**
Good music. Bad person. Go figure.

**Kamisha, Jun 25 at 08:58 PM**
Love this guy! Crazy how at a time like this, I still here reporters and the news press still commenting on The crap that happend in the past or better yet, that they don't even know if it realy happend! Guess People will be people!

**joyce, Jun 25 at 08:59 PM**
Micheal Jackson was our Elvis. He Will be missed dearly, but he lives on in his great music. I feel now he's at peace and is singing in heaven. Thank you Micheal for all you have brought to this world. Your job has been accomplish. Gonna miss you.

**nell, Jun 25 at 08:59 PM**
im going to miss him alot. he had a pretty tough life but was an enormous influence on so many people.

**judy, Jun 25 at 09:00 PM**
Michael you will be missed. Those of you who have bashed Michael and intending to bash him need to look at your own life before you throw the stone. Who's prefect? We all have done something wrong.To the family I know you will miss Michael but try to remember all the good timed you shared and from this day forth spend as much time with your love ones show them how much you love them.Peace and God be with you. HATER stop judging and show some love you'll find life to be much happier for you.

**John, Jun 25 at 09:00 PM**
Look on the bright side, children are safe again.

**Anonymous, Jun 25 at 09:03 PM**
I am just so going to miss him!!! No words to say!!!! My grieve goes beyond anything!!!

**smilie12, Jun 25 at 09:02 PM**
The same "overstated" label can be said for Elvis Presley. He was a fat neurotic drug addict without many good sounding songs in his later years.

**carly, Jun 25 at 09:05 PM**
man i'm only 9 and i miss him like crazy well at least he's on peace up there walking with God i was eating at Joes Crab Shack when someone got a text and then i found out music by michael came on and i almost cried i didnt eat my food and i spilt ranch i was a mess without him alive

**Jonathan, Jun 25 at 09:05 PM**
At some point in his life, he probably touched all of us in some way with his music, talent, or his unique blend of passion and courage. We'll miss him.

**Brat, Jun 25 at 09:05 PM**
Leaving aside his personal issues, the man had talent. He was a very lost soul who hopefully now is at peace. I dread the next few weeks as the vultures will descend and the media feeding frenzy will be horrific. In a way I suppose its fitting, he lived his life under the glare of the spotlight. Why should his death be any different? The ones I feel sorry for are his children, hopefully he was smart and had a will in place that will see to their well being without the three ring circus that a custody trial would become.

**p-man, Jun 25 at 09:06 PM**
not relevant? Michaels music is some of the most influential and essential music out there. i hate most pop music but his work is something i can really get my teeth into as a musician. Michael was a great singer and performer, one of the best. its just such a shame he had to destroy himself with all his surgery. rest in peace MJ. you'll definitely be remembered.

**Ima, Jun 25 at 09:15 PM**
Poor ol' Michael...he was the goodest, most bestest, most wondermus, most greatest, coolest, most grooviest, most magnificent, extree special, brilliantest, most outstandingest...

**Tammy, Jun 25 at 09:22 PM**
Now your at rest with the world now you will answer for all your worldly sins.. I hope that your innocents that your were said to be is true. We will all miss your music and dancing and the crazy reports.....Gods peace be with you.....We who loved you will pray for your soul and your family..... Go ROCK Heaven... I'll see you there!!!

**Oy, Jun 25 at 09:25 PM**
Explain to me why we are dedicating this much time to a molester?

**chaz, Jun 25 at 09:35PM**
he did more in 50 years than i did in 78 years r.i.p.

**maria, Jun 25 at 09:36 PM**
I am in shock...he might have went though his problems..but i grew up

with him...grade school dances with his pin on my chest ...he was the best....there will never be a artist like him again

**Greg, Jun 25 at 09:36 PM**
He probably was the greatest musician ever, with endless talent; however if he didn't accept Jesus Christ as his Lord and saviour, he is now in Hell ! No ifs or buts about it.

**Jim, Jun 25 at 09:39 PM**
Michael Jackson was a man of extremes; from his ever whitening skin (seems he refused to be black) to his multiple surgeries, only to end up with a ridiculous pointy nose. Had a chimp for pet (maybe it was more than a pet), only one silver glove, a Disneyland like house, slept with little kids which got him in trouble with the law more than once and strained his relationship with his sister. But, all in all, he was a good musician and contributed to the music world with a unique style.

**KH, Jun 25 at 09:43 PM**
at first i thought it was a joke that michael had died, but sadly,its true. all i can say is R.i.P Michael you are in a better place now ... HEAVEN:)

**Ashley, Jun 25 at 09:47 PM**
Have some respect, people! Whether you liked Michael as a person doesn't matter. He was one of the GREATEST entertainers EVER! RIP Michael. Your music will SURELY live forever!

**maria, Jun 25 at 09:51 PM**
never can say good by! is the best song, and still my favorite!

**ktct, Jun 25 at 10:00 PM**
Wow. I can not decide which leaves me with more sadness: 1. The death of MJ; 2. The death of innocent until proven guilty, and, finally the death of spelling, grammar and punctuation.

**who r u, Jun 25 at 10:01 PM**
man,u people act as if he is a god...i feel really bad and i cant believe it but im not sad that he is dead..im sad because his life was not a life he was

happy with and plus he didnt know jesus christ, and is now tormented. im feel so sorry for him.i cant say rest in peace...i wish i could....

**freewheelin, Jun 25 at 10:02 PM**
Ive been a DJ for 35 years and I respect the man for his talent and feel his private life is his cross to bare. Only GOD can judge him. RIP MJ

**Ailene, Jun 25 at 10:04 PM**
R.I.P. Michael, you were a one of kind musician and that will over time, overpower all the nasty things people have said.

**Debbie, Jun 25 at 10:05 PM**
I agree, If you didn't like him don't leave a message. Respect his family and friends. What ever your thoughts on Michael, he will always be THE GREATEST!!! LONG LIVE THE KING!!! I LOVE YOU MIKE R.I.P. YOU WILL BE MISSED!!!!!

**lj3000111, Jun 25 at 10:09 PM**
michail he was a grate singer and danser ppl thay tell me that he was a pervert and i downt think so michail was a senger , danser , artist , and a fun prson in his one way. wen he was living every buddy made crool coments and remarks and now wen he is deid thay deside to cut the giy some slake gess what he cant here tham now so cut the crap and dont triy to make up for lost time becus it is to late fell sarry and gilty but the way you thot of him be for will never chang so give it up . p.s. thank u giys and gerls that like him from the begining and im sarry i miss him to one of my idls michail Jackson

**Debbie, Jun 25 at 10:10 PM**
This about Michael. get with it! Damn! A man is dead. Where is the respect? How can people be so damn cruel. HATERS!!!!

**Antonio, Jun 25 at 10:11 PM**
Our thoughts and prayers go out to his family... A great entertainer.. You will be missed Michael.

**chelsea, Jun 25 at 10:12 PM**
you all are pathetic...thoses alligations are not proven and what if he

didnt do it..then all this was for nothing..bless that poor man..may he rest in peice...regardless of tabloids he was still an icon and made and impact in many peoples lives...so why dont you stop calling him a child molester and think of something better to do with your pathetic lives.. this man had a family and kids that will miss him very much..along with his fans...i honestly think he deserves some respect...he was an amazing artist can't you at lest give him credit for that people...GET A LIFE... you will be missed Micheal

**Catina, Jun 25 at 10:19 PM**
Michael Jackson is gone. I can Hardly believe it. The industry is losing so many of entertainments' icons. I just take comfort in knowing that to be absent with the body is to be present with God. So rest in peace Michael. You will be missed but never forgotten.

**D, Jun 25 at 10:23 PM**
I think as a special tribute to one of the worlds greatest inspiration and stars in his own right, we protest and stop buying tabloids the tabloids that exposed him to be a monster and destroyed him. Let's get together, facebook, myspace whatever, I stop buying tabloids,

**Southern Comfort, Jun 25 at 10:23 PM**
My heart goes out to Michael's family ,friends and fans.He was a music icon of my era.His music will live on.Who are we to judge,our maker is the only one that should judge Micheal.May he rest in Peace,I am saddened and I will miss him .He brought his music and dance for all to enjoy!!!

**Karen, Jun 25 at 10:24 PM**
I believe I speak for many of us born in the early sixties that Michael Jackson, at the time known as a part of the Jackson Five, was a distinctive and notable new era in music. It was a fresh pop rock that distinguished his music from the traditional rock and roll of the sixties. His music made us feel all the emotions of a lifetime and for that we both thank him for his hard work and dedication additionally we express our condolences as he will be greatly missed.

**melanie, Jun 25 at 10:25 PM**
to those of wo who insist that Jackson was never guilty of child molestation... would YOU pay 10 million dollars to an accuser if YOU were innocent??

**Richard, Jun 25 at 10:29 PM**
Long live Michael Jackson. Confused, weird, talented and simply brilliant. Changed music video and dance forever. Remember this day forever. RIP

**Christopher, Jun 25 at 10:30 PM**
Michael Jackson was so huge all you had to do was say his first name and people knew who you were talking about. On my way home this evening, every radio station I turned to played a tribute to his legend. His was a musical legacy that will never be repeated. A child star that became a musical icon and all of us, all of us will truly miss him. I cannot think of any other artist that both young and the old can relate to. He will be missed dearly by us all.

**Zera, Jun 25 at 10:32 PM**
i will miss u even though i am still little i love you R-I-P pest in peace

**Cynthia, Jun 25 at 10:37 PM**
My condolences to Michael Jackson's family. What a shock. I was not expecting two celebrities to pass away in one week.

**Adam, Jun 25 at 10:39 PM**
This has been a sad sad day, and week in the entertainment world. First Ed, now today Farrah and Michael. So so sad. Thoughts and prayers to all the family, friends, and fans,

**megr, Jun 25 at 10:42 PM**
AMen"I can't remember if I cried.When I read about his widowed bride,But something touched me deep inside
The day the music died."

**Mardi, Jun 25 at 10:43 PM**
Michael, humanitarian, legend of the 20th & 21st century; you will be missed dearly.

**Adam, Jun 25 at 10:44 PM**
Very well said! A legend, a icon. Michael will never forgotten. I feel like today is like the song "American Pie"

**Bearman, Jun 25 at 10:44 PM**
Whatever your thoughts on Michael, it was shocking to see he had died... as well as Farrah. Created a cartoon in honor of them if anyone wants to check it out.

**joejoe, Jun 25 at 10:51 PM**
I can't stop crying, Michael Jackson represents a time in my life that was so special his music and message effects my soul.

**gingermeg, Jun 25 at 10:51 PM**
I want to say sorry, for the way you were treated by this world Michael. RIP

**me me, Jun 25 at 10:54 PM**
Rest In Peace..I Love T The Song Thriller..I'll Miss You.!

**harry, Jun 25 at 11:00 PM**
Micheal, I am sorry for not being a loyal fan. I should have stood by your example of humanity and not let the naysayer give me cause to doubt. you have given so much to those kids who thought nothing was possible due to sociatal status. I will do my best now to honor your memory, but for now...R.I.P. I will miss you.

**jrrrz, Jun 25 at 11:01 PM**
the children of the world are little safer now.....

**mike, Jun 25 at 11:06 PM**
Well, I don't know if he did molest that kid or not....Hmmm...I wonder why the father did take the money instead of having him prosecuted.... Interesting point. I don't know if there is a God. But if God does exist,

and he is reading some of the idiotic posts on this board, man, he has to be shaking his head and wondering where he went wrong... Unbelievable. If I ever become stupid like some of the idiots on this board, I hope that my heart stops beating.

**SB, Jun 25 at 11:09 PM**
Very sad that both Michael and Farrah lost their lives today. (Only good thing might be the Gosselin's will not get all the attention.) The world lost real celebrities today..... and they will be truly missed.

**80's fan, Jun 25 at 11:10 PM**
In my mind, Michael will always be cool and black.

**will, Jun 25 at 11:11 PM**
i wonder how many of you really new him to judge him since you have also been judge by others maybe being innocent , we will never know the truth. ( respect others, stop hateing )

**archie15, Jun 25 at 11:11 PM**
micheal jackson was the gretest pop sensation I have ever heard though he has bad things he has done in life ,on his roll but I pay my tribute to this great singer.

**Colez, Jun 25 at 11:17 PM**
A dark day today as it pours down where i am, in shock & unsteady... This man was an inspiration to many many people and he will truely be missed. Although his legacy will continue to run beyond oblivian.. His compassion you can see in his eyes, may we not remember the troubles and speculations about his past but remember the "WOWING" factor he had over many of us with his magic musical talents/performances! A Musical Genius that will be remembered forever A sad day for many! R.I.P Michael

**Mitul, Jun 25 at 11:17 PM**
I grew up on his music.he was no..he is the greatest cultural iconic hero ever.

**Cranston, Jun 25 at 11:17 PM**

My, my, my................. the freaking media is going to be relentlessly harping on Jackson's death for eons! OK, so Michael Jackson has died. Good people die everyday, some horrific deaths, but how much recognition do good, everyday people receive? Some not even an obituary. Well, it's these "high profile" celebrity deaths that stop the presses. The television media in particular must drop everything to stay "grounded" and ram this content down our throats for weeks if not longer. Enough already!

**moonwalker, Jun 25 at 11:18 PM**

ts very sick and sad that people come and post their negative comments on these boards. If you wanna hate, find yourself a "hate" board, i'm sure they are out there. Alot of people like myself will continue to listen to his music and respect the entertainer he was. while i will agree that in his last years, he became very strange and odd, it doesnt change his music or his legacy. he will forever be "the king of pop". the hateful comments are disrespectful and unnecessary. Its very sad that people come on here and say vulgar things just to get a rise and start an arguement. If you dont like michael jackson, i'm sure you can find something better to do, than make vulgar comments about a pop legend. Rest In Piece Michael! We will never forget you

**Ceretha, Jun 25 at 11:18 PM**

Michael I absolutely adored you, and played your thriller album/cd for 20 years. Its a great shock, deeply missed. Thanks for your brilliance.

**Tmadelyn, Jun 25 at 11:23 PM**

I was born the year THE JACKSON FIVE was first on the airwaves. Michael's music has been a part of my whole life. I cry each and everytime I hear "BEN". Everyone will remember him in their own way, but through everything he did in his music was true to his life. His change in appearance didn't ever strike me as strange behavior, he simply wanted to show the world he believed in world peace, love, and that it doesn't matter if your black or white. Love and grace to you Michael.

**Edwin, Jun 25 at 11:24 PM**

I'm no his big fan but I was crying when i heard that. How could i be?

**will, Jun 25 at 11:26 PM**
every one has an opinon with out ever really knowing.. some of you haters should take a look in the mirror, what do you give back to us here on earth besides your dirty ( attitude) judge since you also will be judge!! god bless your soul michael. Thank you

**chuck, Jun 25 at 11:29 PM**
As time passes so will legends.....

**mjj4eva, Jun 25 at 11:43 PM**
i cried ever since 6:25pm til 11:30 PM. all i can say is: The best there is, The best there was, and the best there ever will be

**Booskii, Jun 25 at 11:44 PM**
I cant believe that there are ppl that dnt like Mike Mike and that there are ppl that can jus hate on him like this give him a break. Miss u Mike X's and O's. Some of yal should think about what yal are sayin.

**cami, Jun 25 at 11:45 PM**
I am so terribly saddened by Michael's death. I am 63 years old and didn't grow up with him. However, I'm an old hippie who loves his music and videos. I never believed any of the accusations against him. "Dearest Michael, may God hold you in the palm of his hand and give you peace. May you never be lonely again."

**MJFan, Jun 25 at 11:46 PM**
It is so sad that people believe everything that is reported on the news or tabloids. Here it is on the day of this man's death that instead of saying prayers for his family people are on here posting juvenile comments. What proof did we ever have that he did or did not do those things to those children. None of us were there. I think we need to look at our own faults before we start judging others. How many us have been blamed for something we did not do? My point exactly.

**to stephen, Jun 25 at 11:50 PM**
Why dont you go warm up a can of soup for a hungry child instead of posting here? Not EVERYTHING in life is about hungry children. besides i think we pay enough in taxes already.

**Mark, Jun 25 at 11:57 PM**

In 1977 we lost a Rock Roll Icon Elvis at age 42. Twenty Eight years later we lost a POP Icon in Micheal both of these Icon fought from being alone but had a amazing gift to lift people spirit through their music during some terrible events on American soils. Let remember them as God Angels . Mark

# JUNE 26, 2009
# FRIDAY

*Doctors complete an autopsy of Michael Jackson's body. A cause of death is not established. Further tests will take an additional four to six weeks. Speculations continue to link his death to an overdose of prescription painkillers. Fans around the world mourn the death and celebrate the life of Michael Jackson.*

**Darrell, Jun 26 at 11:21 AM**
Good ridance Michael...does this mean we won't see LaToya Jackson & Diana Ross ever again? Everyone knows Mike, LaToya & Diana were the same person. Young boys everywhere are can breathe a little easier today. Catholic Priests thought this guy was a FREAK!!

**Ehblancz, Jun 26 at 11:22 AM**
It's slooooooooowly sinking in, Michael Jackson is dead. Despite my trepidations about his personal life, I love his music and was a big fan in the 80s. He spent 45 years of his life in the spotlight, hopefully, now he can rest in peace. Join me and other fans over the next few days at www.runarounddiva.com as we celebrate the life of a legend. Let's send this "bright star" home in the right way.

**Thundercat1945, Jun 26 at 11:29 AM**
Actually his best performance was when his hair caught on fire.

**MASHONISIN, Jun 26 at 11:33 AM**
To the family of Michael Jackson.He may be gone but not forgotten, our

love for him will always be in our hearts. take it one step at a time and may the lord be with you on every step you make in life. Michael brought joy to everyone young and old, hearing of his death shock the world but we know his spirit will always live on and his music will always continue for many years after life. love always

**Jacqueline, Jun 26 at 11:36 AM**
This is how I will remember Michael. I feel like part of my childhood has been taken away.

**MJ lives, Jun 26 at 11:41 AM**
I think MJ took a look at his bank account and had a heart attack. He realised he's bankrupt.

**StArKrOsSeD5387, Jun 26 at 11:42 AM**
I must say that when I found out about Michael Jackson, I cried for a while! I mean, he was a big inspiration in my life, and through all the bs... I'm still going to remember him before all the alligations... when he was just Our King of Pop. I'll miss you Michael Jackson!

**Bobbamm, Jun 26 at 11:47 AM**
The hands down greatest entertainer of all time..You are forever loved and will be forever missed..I know that gods choir is raising the clouds of heaven and joyous on this heartbreaking day.. my name is khandi from new york and i'm glad to have experienced his majesty

**Stephanie, Jun 26 at 11:50 AM**
I will have to agree with my father and music journalist Jim Farber (whom the movie Almost Famous was loosely based on). Sometimes the craziest people can be geniuses. Jonathan Winters would be a good example,a fantastic comedian who spent time in a mental institution. However, in Jackos case I think that his mental instability came from childhood physical and mental abuse. Joe Jackson was a nasty S.O.B. . Michael not only changed pop music (with the help of Quincy Jones, respectively) but the way American culture was in the 1980's. Every kid in the early eighties did the Moonwalk. Teenage boys wore that red jacket with the diagonal zippers. I just wished that he was not looney toones. Spending millions f ucking up his face, his nose. Letting boys sleep in his

bed? Wow. If the molestation charges were not in full effect in the late 1990's, if he did not dangle one of his kids outside a window, he would have sold new records.

**mom52, Jun 26 at 11:53 AM**
Let's be brutally honest here. If this person wasn't famous he would have been in jail years ago. He is a predator, a phedophile and a child molestor. He is where he belongs now.

**Jackie, Jun 26 at 11:53 AM**
You always will be a sweethearth, dearly loved by the world. This is a big lost. thanks for your music by the way has a mesage heal the world, look yourselve in the mirror a be a better person. We love you. R.I.P

**G.N., Jun 26 at 11:57 AM**
Even God has a most wanted list and guess what! We are ALL on it! Michael Jackson has done alot of good things in his life for alot of people. I feel sorry for you if you can't see that. I remember going to a dance some years ago and I met a guy who was feeling pretty low. Michael's song was playing " Man in the Mirror". We should ALL really listen to the words to that song he said. Thank you Micheal Jackson. I know I will miss you. God bless you in this life and all others

**emily, Jun 26 at 12:02 PM**
I am real fan of Micheal Jackson, & have been since I was 8 years old in second grade.I am now 34 years old.I grew up listening to him and am in complete shock that Micheal is gone. My heart really and trully goes out to his kids and his family. Micheal will truly be missed.

**Bill, Jun 26 at 12:05 PM**
Micheal Jackson will live forever in our minds. What a Triller he was.

**SEXYCHEYB, Jun 26 at 12:06 PM**
Michael Jackson is the single most popular entertainer in the world. I trust that just because the press has said so many negative things about the past issues that he has had, it does not stop you from saying a prayer for him and his family. Life is way to short to dwell on minor things that we have no right to comment on anyway. The only person that can

judge him is GOD... Trust that he is up there singing and dancing in the presence of the people that went before him and love him. REAL TALK.

**Jim, Jun 26 at 12:07 PM**
I cannot say I was a big fan, (but think he was a major talent),though I loved "Off the Wall" and "Thriller". I wish that Michael had been able to find some peace in his life as his later years seemed mired in one controversey after another. RIP

**Mira, Jun 26 at 12:08 PM**
We lost the Pop Genius who seems to be the loneliest man on Earth when he died according to the people close to him. MJ was a sensitive soul who never had a childhood. This should be a wake up call for the entertainment industry. LET THE KIDS GO TO SCHOOL,PLAY WITH FRIENDS,SING IN SCHOOL CHOIRS AND ON FRIENDS' PARTIES.DO THEY NEED TO ENTERTAIN US FROM THE AGE OF 10-11 AND EARN MONEY? WHY DO WE HAVE THE LAWS AGAINST CHILD LABOR? Michael would be still alive if he was aloud to live a normal life.

**EssiePeaches, Jun 26 at 12:18 PM**
I fear Michael Jackson was murdered by someone not educated in medicine injecting him with pharmaceuticals. I fear Michael Jackson was murdered.

**Mary, Jun 26 at 12:19 PM**
Tbh Michael deserved to die. He was a horrible dirty child molester . A monster who's face looked disgusting. Ive neva seen anything like it b4. absoloutly disgusting. I used to love michael jackson. Now i am glad he's gone. Where he belongs...Hell i feel sorry for his family

**Talia, Jun 26 at 12:21 PM**
I'm sorry but I agree with mom5, if he wasn't as famous as he was he would have been in jail. I absolutely believe that he is a child preditor and although he did have some good songs I feel very bad that his death is overshadowing farrah fawcett's tragic death. She deserves to be

remembered for her strength, courage and lovely personallity. Michael Jackson in his later years turned into a strange individual.

**Mary, Jun 26 at 12:22 PM**
Good ridence u child molester. He was a ugly peice of work. Poor plastic surgeons :( they'll hav no 1 else now . U belong in hell michael jackson.

**Sick people here, Jun 26 at 12:27 PM**
talia- plenty of FF articles you could go post on. Give people who actually admired his mark on the music world a day to not be badgered by individuals such as yourself.
Mary- there's a special place in hell reserved for YOU.

**a Fan, Jun 26 at 12:30 PM**
To Mary and Talia. You are disgusting individuals with no heart. I don't know if he was any of those things,
but if he was I don't care because he was not near my child and I'm judging him based on his career, which was incredible. He was a troubled soul but it's only up to GOD to judge not you. you are nobody to judge.

**blacknmeskin, Jun 26 at 12:36 PM**
R.I.P Michael Jackson...I love you so much. May you now be at peace and leave this hatin azz world. All the negative comments about you don't mean anything. That damn kid just need money for his poor family and didn't know how to ask. You beat that case so tell them in your words to Beat It!!!! You did it big! R.I.P King of Pop

**Kelly, Jun 26 at 12:38 PM**
Mary and Talia- you must have been molested as children, because you seem to be very angry. You must also have a crystal ball to be able to determine that the rumors are indeed FACT.

**Rashonda, Jun 26 at 12:42 PM**
U know it is sad that in this time of mourning that some SICK folks can only focus on the negative the truth of the matter is he was a EXCEPTIONAL artist and he has a family that has to mourn his loss right now. Mary and Talia who are you to judge and wish someone to

hell you are NOT GOD!!! You should focus on where you will be when you close your eyes and leave this earth.

**Slave2Blade, Jun 26 at 12:43 PM**
whether or not you liked or disliked him, he had an incredible career that spanned many years, thanx to his pushy father...I personally feel that he wasn't the "cleanest" soul in the universe, but his family and many people cared for him and are mourning his loss...for them I am sorry.hope the people that felt they were victimized by him sleep better at night.a loss no one will forget.

**sara, Jun 26 at 12:43 PM**
i am totally shocked by the horrible things people are saying! Damning MJ to Hell is NOT your place! last time i checked there is only one who has the right to judge and that would be god, so unless you're him i wouldn't go there. that being said, yes he got throwed off, there are tons of people who do. we really have no idea as to what happened to him behind the sceenes in his life, what he went thru. and we don't know if any of the accusations actually happened or not. there are tons of rumors and law suits all the time; only the people that were actually there know what really happened. Reguardless of if it's true or not it is terrible to speak so cruelly of someone after they passed. imaigine if there were a group of people that disliked you for whatever reason, how would your family feel if they heard people rejoicing your death. i say people stop being so judgemental and terribly cruel or it may be you who ends up in hell!

**Becca, Jun 26 at 12:52 PM**
I hope that all of you that are dissing the Michael Jackson realize in some part, that NO MATTER WHAT, Michael Jackson was a music icon and Legend. His family and children have suffered a great loss and dont desreve to hear there loved one hated at this time. Yes, every one had there opinion and at this time you should keep it to yourself. Michael Jackson was a wonderful human being who brought alot to this world. Music, first and foremost. You may not like him, but famous or not, he was cleared of all charges and maybe some of you (Mary) should just except the fact that there are some real shady people out there that will extort money from anyone and they will say anything. Leave your negative comments at bay and let his family, friends and fans morn in

peace. I'm pretty sure Michael isn't in hell, but in a much better place than where we are. OJ is famous and look where he is??? Michael was, is and always will be innocent!!!! R.I.P king of pop, my kids will know the real u

**peaches, Jun 26 at 01:00 PM**

all you people can go to hell.michael jackson was the great singer,song righter,and dancer, you and every one else are just jealous, that you didnt have his fame. so if you dont like him that is your choice but let him reast in peice.

**m-1, Jun 26 at 01:01 PM**

Michael - thank you for "BEN" my favorite song - and I want to say that I think Michael was sad his whole life, and that the only happiness he found was through his music, and his children. As far as the cruel comments posted everywhere, God is the only judge - and he is a loving and forgiving God. Rest in peace Mike - no more sadness or cruelty. God will wrap you in his arms. Condolences to your family.

**Kriley824, Jun 26 at 01:03 PM**

I am not a "teeny-bopper", a generation X or someone younger than *Gasp* 50. I grew up with the Jackson 5 on tv and on the radio. I watched Michael Jackson change over the years. Did I understand all his plastic surgery? No. Did it really matter? No. He was still a great entertainer. When we lived in Hawaii, my husband and I took our 5 year old son to see his concert at Aloha stadium on the only US stop on his tour in January 1997. It was awesome. We oldies enjoyed it as much as the younger kids.He's gone...but his legacy will live on. RIP Michael..

**Dbakernjreal, Jun 26 at 01:19 PM**

Keep your friends close - keep your children closer. Famous kids belong to their parents not the hanger - oners who want a percentage of what they earn. Family is important and being separated from his parents and siblings put him in the position of having no one around who really cared. What a Pity!

**GUEVARACAL, Jun 26 at 01:21 PM**
Did you all forget that he was into little boys ?? Or do we just forget that ???

**Angelbyedays, Jun 26 at 01:30 PM**
GUEVARACAL How could anyone forget what Micheal was accused of? The same media people that put Obama in the white house are the same media and people that won't let anything die out. The fact is He was a troubled man and look at his childhood he never had one he never matured he didn't have a chance, His fan's gave him the love he craved from his father and that is why his fans were important to him. I'm not excuse him we all have sinned and we all have to face God but who are we to judge? No matter what Micheal did in his life only God, himself and the accusers know for sure what happened the rest of us just speculate, No matter what anyone thinks of him He was an american ICON and he was a true talent and no rumors or facts can change that.

**Antonella, Jun 26 at 01:32 PM**
He was the BEST of the very BEST no one will EVER come close to his music much less the way he danced MAY GOD BLESS HIS SOUL ETERNALLY ~

**ty, Jun 26 at 01:35 PM**
I'm just bummed about MJ passing away. What an amazing talent. It's so unfortunate that he wasn't surrounded by people that had his best interests at heart. I'm glad that he's finally at peace. It's a shame that so many people are using these message boards to say negative and hurtful things. I can only say that it's never good to put such negative energy out into the world it definitely comes back to you. His heart was so huge, open, and giving and unfortunately that also allowed for terrible things to enter into his life. My prayers are with his children and loved ones during this difficult time.

**LEONA A. 4U, Jun 26 at 01:38 PM**
MICHAEL JACKSON THE ONLYONE , HIS MUSIC HIS DANCE, NO,ONE CANT DANCE LIKE MICHAEL OH SING LIKE HEM .LIKE WE SAID IN SPANICH DESCANZA EN PAZ MICHAEL JACKSON,

**CogJm4, Jun 26 at 01:39 PM**

to the idiot that wrote about the Billie Jean video, you can tell that there is an adult in the bed. That body is to big to be a 5 year old child. LEAVE MJ ALONE AND REST IN PEACE!!! Lots of LOVE,Jeannine

**cookiecrumble, Jun 26 at 01:42 PM**

Cranston, not even two days into this death, and you're already annoyed about it? Filter out anything wit Michael jackson in it and get the hell off this page. If this was your father or brother, you would not be saying this crap at all.

I was crying for days about this, RIP michael jackson we love you till death. for your music and your contributions to charity, we thank you.

**Beatlesarebest, Jun 26 at 01:43 PM**

My favorite song he sang was with the J5. It was "Who's Loving You". Vocally, that song is a masterpiece! Especially for a child singer. He was AWESOME! I was 5 when they came out with "ABC", and I've loved almost EVERYTHING since! Thank you Michael. You sacrificed so much just to make people happy.

**amcfarland, Jun 26 at 02:54 PM**

This is an awful lost to the world, MJ was such an awsome entertainer and humanitarian. Yes he had his share of troubles and issues in life, but who hasn't in some form of another. He was a genius and will be greatly missed throughout the world. Prayers go out to the family at this time, may they turn to the God of all comfort. RIP MJ..Who's Bad..He's Bad....

**Erica, Jun 26 at 02:55 PM**

my goodness cant you negative people take it some where else. i am tired of hearing bad things about m.j. the man died and all u have to say is good bye and we hate you GROW UP people....... have some respect for his family they are suffering a lose and you people say little boys can breathe easily WTF.... mj you will be forever missed and loved

**Margaretthemelon, Jun 26 at 03:01 PM**

we all love yo u michael jackson!!! your music is amazing!

**David, Jun 26 at 03:16 PM**
Im only 21 but I grew up on his music too. I can remember being 3 or 4 years old standing in front of the tv trying to keep up with Michael. Hes a legend that will live on forever. Hes the king of pop baRIP Michael Jackson. May God take you into his loving arms away from all the hate of this world.

**GetAGrip, Jun 26 at 03:24 PM**
Why are so many people unwilling or unable to see the truth through all their tear-stained god-like worship and adulation. Is fame, celebrity, and some semblance of artistic talent all it takes for the most heinous acts and behavior to be forgotten? The Cult of Celebrity has gotten out of control in this country, particularly when the celebrity is dead. Commend and celebrate his music if you like, give him due credit for his impact on popular culture, but please, stop deifying this troubled, and troubling human being.

**Teri, Jun 26 at 03:26 PM**
Because of my older brothers and older sister I grew up listening to the Jackson 5. Then growing up in the 80's while in high school I began listening to Michael Jackson and I've loved him ever since.

**Anonymous, Jun 26 at 07:55 PM**
Mj was not only a musician but an icon...and for those who think he was a molester can be the most bigit small minded person....nobody knew what happened at that ranch...and if he was such a molester..WHY WOULD MORE KIDS GO THERE????!!! GET IT RITE!!! RIP MJ

**Mrfinn9, Jun 26 at 08:03 PM**
Despite what the most recent impressions of the man....We know all the words to these songs. We lost a great entertainer today. It's kind of odd but this is the first icon of my youth to go that I really feel sad about. What a great singer/songwriter. I will miss having his presence and his potential for greatness.

**Bikerat57, Jun 26 at 08:18 PM**
My generation (baby boomers) may have thought Michael Jackson freekish or at least very eccentric, and didn't listen to his music because

of their bias. Like so many genises, it is only after they are gone that their true art begins to be recognized. He was the pop artist of the century in my mind..there may never be any better. Rest in pece Michael..you have earned it many times over.

**CartmanFan76, Jun 26 at 08:18 PM**
I feel like a part of my childhood is gone

**CBGale2, Jun 26 at 08:22 PM**
Burn in hell you child molester!

**Ivy, Jun 26 at 08:33 PM**
Dear Allie, If you had the smallest bit of knowledge you would see the truth. I have studied most of my life, trying to understand how the human mind works. When you look at how hard his life was. His father was a very abusive man, not just with him, but with his entire family. According to how things are processed and dealt with in the human mind, he would have never become a child molester.
He would have in fact turned out like his father, if anything. Someone that would get their kicks by beating someone else to feel dominate or better about themselves, not a child molester. He never had a good childhood. As he got old he just wanted to be a kid and finally had the means to do so. Michael was far from being like his dad, he was always a good person. His only crime was giving too much, to people that never deserved his charity to begin with.They got pissed off that he was no longer going to be providing for them, and they wanted more (Since they got used to living with Michael???s money). Michael Jackson had given so much of his money throughout his whole life, just trying to make this world a better place. He gave hope to people that didn???t have any to begin with. I know that in your mind you must think I am a little crazy for saying what I have said. What you don???t know is that this is all coming from someone that has been molested as a child, by a step dad, until the age of eleven. Back in my day there were just things that one was afraid to say, not like it is now. With that said, I believe with all my heart that he never did the things the media claimed he did. Trust me I do want child molesters to PAY, but Michael just wasn???t one of them. He was in fact the most caring person this world has ever had the privilege to know.One day the truth will come out and his name will be cleared,

and seen for what he was, a great humanitarian. God bless and keep him! With all my heart RIP and sleep eternally with the angels looking down on us. You will never be forgotten!

**Purplefire04, Jun 26 at 08:40 PM**
FOR ALL THE PEOPLE TELLING HIM TO "BURN IN HELL" As he said in one of his songs "LEAVE ME ALONE!!!!!"

**Iengar, Jun 26 at 08:41 PM**
michael jackson left an indelible mark on the world with his pioneering music and will be remembered for many decades after his death which is more than you can say for the small minded people who are leaving nasty comments

**Jacobsensl, Jun 26 at 08:46 PM**
I pray that you haters are never put in the position Michael Jackson was. He was famous and people wanted his money. There was never any proof of his "molesting" as you put it but there were many hands out for his money including the woman that "loved Him" and gave birth to his children. We have no idea what kind of life he lead as a child but we do know he was in the spotlight since he was avery young. We may not understand his need to hang out with children, but it is not for us to judge. He may have been trying to ge backt the part of his life that was lost. I think the only thing he is guilty of is wanting his childhood back. The only one who ever has known his real anguish is gone now and I pray that he is wrapped in the love that he so badly wanted on this earth. Michael, may you rest in peace.

**Concern, Jun 26 at 08:53 PM**
My sincere condolence, goes out to the entire Jackson Family. It is sad to know that a very talented young man just starting to live at the age of 50, despite all of his Millions, Talents, and Successes, still LIVED a LOST and LONELY LIFE and could not LEARN how TO LOVE HIMSELF FIRST but tried to find it in all forms of worldly things, instead of PEACE in JESUS CHRIST, may his SOUL REST in The SAD THING is that he used his Pain, Brokenes, Suffering, and Lonliness to make himelf successful, but he also had ato pay the piper to without doubt the negative publicity that came along. In his Siblings cases, they too were able to

become successful, despite their traumatic childhood. I pray that they are seeking the right type of counselling during This his demise, to heal the wounds that they've suffered during Childhood, because they never seem to go away, and quoting Michael "I'm looking at the man in the Mirror, I'm asking him to change his ways, No message can be any clearerGod Bless

### Michelle, Jun 26 at 08:55 PM
Michael was truly gifted, he will be missed. Pray for his family. And yes Allie there is a God and He has stated we are ALL sinners that can be saved by His grace, through His Son, Jesus Christ. So unless you know for a fact that she accepted Jesus Christ as her Savior, she's not in Heaven, but in Hell. Put your Farrah remarks under Farrah's moments.

### LvTurk, Jun 26 at 08:58 PM
One of my favorites was "Rockin Robin" but I can't remember a single song he performed that I did not thoroughly enjoy - he was the best & his works will live on forever. I am from the 40s & therefore the 50s/60s music affected me most. So from the Jackson 5 to his great personal works I had the pleasure of it all (original/fresh/exciting). I wish he could have had a longer life but he certainly achieved to great heights in his musical, artistic-stylistic & star quality ways. He apparently suffered in his last years and we, his fans, along with him. So, that part is over, but we wish his family well and the ble ssings and well wishes will surely help relieve the pain somewhat-in time. Our sincerest condolences-clear sailing!!! Turk

### Qkweenb, Jun 26 at 09:29 PM
YOU KNOW........SOME PEOPLE'S LIVES ARE FULL OF HATE, RAGE, NEGATIVITY, HYPOCRISY, AND UNHAPPINESS THAT THEY WOULD RATHER SPIT ON PEOPLE'S GRIEF AND OPINIONS INSTEAD OF JUST BEING QUIET. WHY DOES EVERYONE ON THIS FREEKIN EARTH WANT TO DO GOD'S JOB AND JUDGE PEOPLE?? IT DOESN'T TAKE A ROCKET SCIENTIST TO KNOW WHAT GROUP OF PEOPLE ARE DOING THE BASHING.....THEY HATE EVERYONE THAT'S NOT LIKE THEM, AND HOW PERFECT THEY THINK THEIR LIVES ARE BY TRYING TO HIDE THE TRUTH FROM ALL THE NEIGHBORS! IT IS AN UNEXPECTED AND SHOCKING DEATH....... REGARDLESS OF THE HISTORY.

**tmulenga, Jun 26 at 10:30 PM**
You know what,i grew uip listening to Michael Jackson's unbeatable voice. My dad was the biggest listener of Michael's music. Till this day I still listen to this entertaining music. I think that the way his voice is when he sings is so intresting, it is intresting because if you hadn't noticed;no one in the world can pool off the singing voice he dose. I can't belleive Michael Joesph Jackson died. After all these years somebody just can't die like that. I have his movies and stuff.Those might be worth alot of money$$$ in 10 years

**bridgette, Jun 26 at 11:40 PM**
I feel so sorry for those three kids,but I don't feel sorry for the rest of the Jackson Family because they helped to create the screwed up person Michael Jackson was. They enabled him and turned their heads to what he did to children. You don't pay out twenty five millions dollars to a child's family if you did nothing. When he did that, instead of going to trial to prove him innocence, he lost me as a fan. The worse part of this, is he brought three kids, that he supposedly loved, into his freaky world. He had them walking around in scarves over their faces and masquerade mask in public. These kids wouldn't know normal if their lives depended on it. They are going to be the trophy at the end of a custody battle. Whoever gets the kids, get the future royalties off his estate. The Jackson family is a sad collection of people who lived off of Michael and his hard work. Now they will probably live off of Michael's kids. Michael's pain is over, but unfortuantely it begins for his kids.

**RKD8971, Jun 26 at 11:56 PM**
Wow! What a day! I loved Micheal Jackson when I was younger but he turned weird! That being said, He was Absolutely "the King Of Pop"! What an awesome entertainer he was!! OMG, the posters and albums on my walls........... I am very saddened by his death. He will always be remembered!!!!!!

**Burkemarlboro, Jun 26 at 11:56 PM**
The man was good looking I will never understand why he messed with the way he looked, His music was the best I have never felt sch sadness over a actor passing away

# JUNE 27, 2009
# SATURDAY

*Michael Jackson's body is released to his family. No official funeral arrangements are planned at this time. Fans continue to mourn the death and celebrate the life of Michael Jackson around the world.*

**mandipandi321, Jun 27 at 01:39 AM**
even though michael has some controversarys he will always be known as the king of pop and for his talent he had many good song but i know i will always remeber him for thriller and his moon walk r.i.p. michael jackson the world and i love you

**Rita54, Jun 27 at 02:54 AM**
Know one will ever understand you Michael because their is on one like you or who can compare to your singing capabilities, your dancing, your style, your goodness. I know your remarkable gift from God has shown the world something they will never , have again! The child who lived inside of you can now come out and you will be a star that shines forever for everyone to see!! You were truly a gift from God!!!!

**bwkopper1, Jun 27 at 03:00 AM**
Though MJ had deep family problems, for which he broke away from, or tried. He was very much a talanted soul. He try'ed to find comfort and exceptance through many individuals which I beleave lead him on a path of self-destruction, due to his lack of security and a self desire to please others. Shame, shame on those who deprived him to truly be the King on Pop. And truly be a great MAN. I shall miss the MJ of the early

*Juja D.*

days. These comments are from a FAN who is 55, and remember's the beginning's of the Jackson 5. GodBless and rest His soul.

**ChristC, Jun 27 at 03:36 AM**
Well if he would have just left his nostrils alone. Possibly he would have allowed enough oxygen up to his brain. Poor Michael had some good music, but it just never sounded the same once he pinched off his nose permanently.

**Bohdey, Jun 27 at 05:05 AM**
MJ was indeed great. I wish he did not end up this way but i really love him sincerely.

**piratesbaby911, Jun 27 at 05:26 AM**
MJ, a legend that came for a perpose and left for another perpose. His come was for us to listen and love his music while trying to dance like he did. His other perpose of leaving was for us to remember him and always dance to thriller, billie jean, beat it and more. MJ was the King Of Pop, and always will be.Like they say, " There will never be another Michael Jackson"

**SIDDHARTH, Jun 27 at 05:34 AM**
MJ was truly the king of pop. look at the fanfare after his passing away. look at he sold out concerts tht cud never happen. he truly was and will always be the' KING OF POP.' way to go MJ.

**shimmi, Jun 27 at 10:14 AM**
michael jackson,s was the most auspisioues person in this in world . he had passed away from us but would be live in all hearts who were the fan,s of him , he cant die coz of his all life income charity to poor and peace of world its cant do any other star in the world also he gain the lots of world records with every moments of his life no can compete him ,can't beat him by his popularity , he was the king of every recpective area by heart , by riches , by his popularity

**shimmi(2), Jun 27 at 10:18 AM**
god give him the best place in haven as well coz of his sincerity with the

world people , as his all earnings involve with the charity, pray for him for his haven.

**allgood, Jun 27 at 10:36 AM**
he was a wonderful soul.he;s in heaven now we will love him always' can't believe he's gone.but he's with god & jesus.love you MICHAEL JACKSON& FAMILY!!! THE ALL GOOD.S

**Dione, Jun 27 at 10:39 AM**
I??m shocked!!!! I loved Michael, your songs were and Will part of my life!!! I??ll miss you, Michael!!! So long!!!

**Jadecrystal27, Jun 27 at 11:10 AM**
We'll most definately miss this ICON!! God Bless you Michael, and thanks for the years of wonderful music.

**blackie, Jun 27 at 11:22 AM**
Hi Christian from the time i learned about the Jackson5 as a group until they went their separate ways and after,each and every one of the siblings are and will forever b talented. Michawl has always been my favorite becose he had more spunk,he took Elvis Presley/James Brown and rolled them both up into 1, that's how you get Michael Jackson, was and will 4 ever Bad!!!!!ABC,One More Chance,Don't stop, Thriller,I'm Bad, The Time,Man in The Mirror,ect......all his music

**Lsexygal1960, Jun 27 at 12:12 PM**
Michael you will be deeply missed.Even that you had alot of problems in your life you were still the same person deep down inside.And when you hit those prely gates sing your heart out!!!!!!!!.

**Trones470, Jun 27 at 12:17 PM**
The loss of Michael Jackson is truly devastating. He will be remembered always by his fans. There are countless songs that will always bring me back to a special time in my life, just by hearing the first note. Rest in peace dear Michael ...you truly are the "KING OF POP" and no one can ever take that away from you!

**G.O.D., Jun 27 at 01:30 PM**
Michael was a person like you and I. He only had alot more money. Yes he suffered due to all accusations but his suffering is over. Of course he is in heaven with no more sorrows. Now go on with your lives and let him rest in peace.

**wow, Jun 27 at 01:45 PM**
Good list about Michael at shrinkblog. Makes you realize the scope of his talent and influence

**sanaz, Jun 27 at 01:53 PM**
I like his dance and specially his dance it was amaizing (moon walk) but about dark side of his life i don't know what to say.may god put a mercy on him.

**Dawn, Jun 27 at 02:29 PM**
Michael is part of "Gods Rock-n-Roll Band" along with the rest of the musicians that left us. He is happy now, God Bless you Michael for all the talented gifts you have left us to remember you Thank you for your album you gave me personnally after your show with your brothers at Madison Square Garden...Love you, Dawn.

**bugahdug, Jun 27 at 02:58 PM**
I noticed amazon's top 10 in music, the first 9 were MJ, last was something else, no doubt that has changed now.

**acn1359, Jun 27 at 02:58 PM**
Michael Jackson will forever be that angelic child who sang about a rat to me and when he danced with such funk and grace I was bewildered very much amazed the songs he wrote performed and sang no one will ever compare to Pops mesmerizing king my heart bereaves that mournful date God took away a most loving soul to escort Farrah Fawcett and accompany Ed McMahon in heaven

**Ashley, Jun 27 at 04:42 PM**
Poor elmo,you need to see a psychiatrist. Rest in peace Michael,you are loved and will be missed by millions.

**Bluemonringsp571, Jun 27 at 05:06 PM**
Michael leave us with so many wonderful memories with his music. The amazing fact is that he left this earth with so many many fans of all ages. His legacy will live on, through his music. And although we are now surely deprived of his continuously creative art; I say to you now, MJ you will be missed, but I hope that you finally have found your peace in Neverland in the sky.

**juneeva, Jun 27 at 05:07 PM**
I love michael jackson as i was listening to his music i cried it made me feel like i really knew him also made me feel like i lost someone in my family he was a great man i didn't here not 1 curse word in his music may MICHAEL JACKSON rest in peace

**Tracy, June 27 at 05:17 PM**
Wow!..sorry, but I don't think that MJ's Mom or Pop's are the right people to have anyones kid's. Just look at the not so wonderful job they did with their kiddo's..I would love to see Janet step up and take them though...she's seems to be the only sane one in the whole bunch..if they are given to Grandpa they would not have a chance at all...all bout the money for him and just look at how much he loves being in front of the cam now..only going to get worse, and look who else are running to be on TV...Big Al and Jesse Jackass..makes me sick! Poor MJ never stood a chance to be normal and now their going after his kid's..C'on Aunt Janet, do the right thing baby girl.

**Roxy, June 27 at 05:17 PM**
Did Lisa Marie Presley ever consumate her marriage to her transexual wannabe husband Michael Jackson???

**Diane, June 27 at 5:18 PM**
Michael is LOVED. He may not have used the best judgement in all circumstances, but I know that he did the BEST he could, given the circumstances. So many people were out to make him look BAD! The profit in it for them was just too tempting. It's those EVIL people that should burn in h-ll...namely that eastern Indian man who also "interviewed" Lady Di, then wrote a book making her look not quite so pristine either. HE should walk away from journalism for good, they

all should, until the lesson is learned that it's all about SUPPORTING our fellow human beings..! Self-righteous, self-centered, GREEDY A-hole. Those "interviews" were so twisted, & so in essence a LIE within themselves. People. Do NOT believe those reports they put out. Do NOT put another dime in those bottomless pockets. Do you know? Michael was a GOOD person, who tried to HELP the World. He did so much GOOD!!! Let's never forget that. & Talented to the depths...

**katy, June 27 at 05:20 PM**
Wow, should any of you be judging anyone!? let the man r.i.p. or try to. We still have his fucked up family to continue passing judging and rude comments about.

**Jon P., June 27 at 05:24 PM**
does anyone know if jacko was saved? i mean did he ask jesus into his heart and accept him as his lord and savior of his life? There is nothing that anyone can do for him now , i just hope he found jesus before he died

**Tom, June 27 at 05:30 PM**
Hmmm...lets see...does this affect me at all? Nope. Does it affect any of you? Nope. So who cares? Plus, shouldn't this be posted in that racist Black Voices section?

**adamp, June 27 at 05:31 PM**
THE SKELETONS ARE GOING TO START POPPING

OUT OF THAT CLOSET!! JUST HEARD THE KIDS AINT HIS!!! LOL!!

**Brandy, June 27 at 05:34 PM**
Come on people there is no reason to be so cruel, we will never know for sure if he did the bad things he was accused of as there will always be rumors. However why don't we set back and let God do his job! There are none among us who have never done anything wrong!

**todd, June 27 at 05:35 PM**
He could've hung up his musical career to become a Catholic priest

**JJ, June 27 at 05:34 PM**

He was a sick man. You people are just being "kind" because you don't want to seem like the bitches you are.

**Tom, June 27 at 05:36 PM**

I wonder if the government is going to bailout his debts too

**Bill, June 27 at 05:37 PM**

I wonder if he's getting molested in hell just like he molested little boys on earth?

**Charlotte, June 27 at 05:50 PM**

TIA & BONNIE; Wonderfully, wonderfully put. You are the class acts I was talking about. BILL - you ARE NOT a class act.

**charlotte , June 27 at 05:51 PM**

TO JW: Yet another "class act" - in comparison to the others. Where were some of the individuals on this venue when they took SPELLING? God bless us! P a t h e t i c!

**laura, June 27 at 05:51 PM**

Look- everyone knows by now that Michael was in financial ruins. He apparently wasn't good with hiring the proper people who would do "right" by him. It's obvious that Michael gave way too much to random folks especially those families who would let their children hang out with Michael (do a little research on Latoya and you will read mountains of information on Michael & the way he splurged his money). Michael was very generous with helping charities (that is a fact) he also spend a lot of money on BS monthly. The fact of the matter is, Michael did things his way and rightfully so- he worked extremely hard to do so. Now with that being said- Michael also owed many many people- credit was Michael's favorite thing to do it appears. We can digest everything and anything about Michael- truth of the matter is, Michael was an extremely talented person. He will forever live in my heart. I never attended any of his concerts but I always appreciated his music and his dancing talent. I wish the Jackson Family the best- I especially wish Michael's children the very best- they will forever miss their dad.

One last note: I never ever cared for Elvis. I did not care for his style of

*Juja D.*

music-not now not ever, nothing personal, just my opinion & thoughts.
Love you Michael- God speed!

**Ashley Ray, Jun 27 at 05:54 PM**
I think Kristine Hoffman needs to shut the f**k up and show some
respect =] r.i.p Michael Jackson

**DevilOnTheRun, Jun 27 at 05:55 PM**
You've tried to heal the world..but it's sad world couldn't heal you. RIP
MJ.

# JUNE 28, 2009
## SUNDAY

*The BET Awards are filled with Tributes to Michael Jackson from numerous stars including Beyonce and Stevie Wonder. An announcement for a recording of a tribute song to Jackson is made. Fans around the world continue to mourn the death and celebrate the life of the singer.*

**Jjwowzr, Jun 28 at 01:30 AM**
I can remember back when I was nearly 3 years of age when I use to walk around the house singing "You Are Not Alone" and doing Michael Jackson's dances throughtout my years. If you think about it, a lot of dances, well most dances are created from him. I bought his 'Number Ones" album back in January 2009. I am still a fan. I can talk to the 'Man In The Mirror'. Mauzh love to all of his fans and especiall to his family.

**Matrixcl55, Jun 28 at 02:02 AM**
Now the $$$$ vultures come...Jesse Jackson, Al Sharpton and Joe Jackson sit your a$$ down. The man isn;t even in the grave and now you old has been-wannabee's coming swooping in for a cash call... Where you fools last Sunday or before this tragedy? The man needed help and no one said NO...Perhaps poetic justice or just like Elvis... At least the pain is no more and we can all see " IF YOU WANT TO KNOW WHAT'S WRONG WITH KIDS...JUST LOOK AT THE PARENTS". Parents are supposed to protect kids instead of living their "sorry" live vacariously through them. And Jesse, Al and Joe Jackson...sit your money grubbing a$$$$ down. You shoukd have had this conversation last Sunday with Michael instead of today. Oh, I forgot,

39

you didn't think you would get paid if he was alive. RIP Mike...you were truly an inspiration to my generation. In fact you were a beacon during the civil rights/affirmative action struggle for so many of us. THIS IS THE GREATEST GENERATION folks....

**Smile18235, Jun 28 at 02:09 AM**
I remember when I was a kid back when Elvis had passed away, I cryed, he did some dance moves that weren't very well liked at that time, but then came Michael Jacson and he just threw him self into his music and dance and We as people have learned to except it. we must remember that he had a really horrible childhood and was a child himself as he got older. My Favorite all time video/song would have to be "THRILLER". So here we are we lost to legendary KINGS. My thoughts and prayers go to his family and especially his children...what a terrible lose to our generation once again..R.I.P Michael Jackson you will be sadly Missed by all your fans.<<<<3

**Matrixcl55, Jun 28 at 02:10 AM**
If you want to make the world a better place.... just "LOOK AT THE MAN IN THE MIRROR"...... Now let's listen and enjoy the music and get off our butts and do something positive for the world. RIP MJ..... your music made the world a better place.... So much pain for such a precious soul....... No one understood or gave a damn....... HUMAN NATURE!!!!!

**HAMPSHI, Jun 28 at 02:19 AM**
How many deaths will it take???.....John Belushi, Elvis Presley, Nicole Smith, Michael Jackson and how many others, BEFORE these Drs. STOP dishing their dopey pills and meds. out like candy???? Yet no one wants to "talk about it". WHEN WILL THEY WANT TO TALK ABOUT IT????

**RJosh3, Jun 28 at 02:32 AM**
How can "I'll Be There" not be on the list? I LOVE that song! But of all of them,"Thriller" is definitely my favorite. RIP Mr. Jackson. You made a lot of us looking to our own mirrors over the years, and I thank you for that. Bless your family. Dancing and singing with the angels now.

**Ihavefaith18, Jun 28 at 02:53 AM**

He may have had problems but people should not disrespect the dead like that. At least his memory will live on to the generations to come. I dont what he did are didnt do next time you want to judge someone take a look at your self. MJ was who I grew up listing to and the Osmonds I will never forget him rest in peace MJ. He's not my king God is my king but he was a good singer and he had some moves. Its not all his fought what ever happened in his life. Love you MJ

**Sixpassmidnight, Jun 28 at 03:35 AM**

i was a tender age of 6... seeing Michael's video to black and white... and remembering it sticking with me even to this day... he was a great inspiration to me ... and i'm sure many can agree that he only brought us hope and joy... and truly was a voice for change... .. .. we must not remember the died for the bad... but only in the good... who are we to judge... no one has ever been made perfect.. and i'm sure if any one of us, were a world iconic figure, too would be explained by gold diggers by any means... and its sad .. may he rest in peace... and his memory too be remembered in good faith...

**sixpassmidnight, Jun 28 at 03:38 AM**

two errors on my previous post...dead not died... and exploited not explained darn auto thing

**Tamlagordy, Jun 28 at 04:02 AM**

Michael had a very troubled life. He had money but money doesn't buy you a perfect life. I enjoyed his music very much in fact my favorite cut by him is "Off The Wall". So please be kind to the departed as he never hurt you. He was a troubled soul and I hope he finds peace up in Heaven that he couldn't find on Earth. Thank you for the music Michael.

**pie, Jun 28 at 04:03 AM**

Michael and Latoya are one tin the same person, money and sociopathic behavior is fire and gas side by side. get over this air bag with holes ,

**Thickcocogirl79, Jun 28 at 04:10 AM**

I don't know the Jacksons, or Michael... I don't know if he was a pedophile... I know that later in his career, he was eccentric to say the least, and very "weird". At the same time, he made amazing strides in music, and made some of the best music ever!! I grew up with him, watched the Jackson 5v cartoon, danced to his songs, EVERYTHING. I really feel that people are quick to judge, when they have no real idea of what's going on. Hate him, or love him, he was an amazing musician, and have accomplished things in music that most artists dream of doing. He was weird, did A LOT of weird things, but who knows what that guy went through. I'm still in disbelief.... never thought he would've died the way he did. I just want people not to believe what they're spoon-fed by the media. He was a decent man, that got lost in life, may he rest in peace!

**chilli, Jun 28 at 05:58 AM**
sounds like black and white issues that god killed Michael and Farrah went to heaven. that was the dumbest s it i have ever heard.I think you are mad because you re a b

**sara, Jun 28 at 10:58 AM**
i just want to say again that there is only one who is in the position to judge and that is GOD, so unless you're him~keep it to yourself.

**acn1359, Jun 28 at 12:40 PM**
just beat it don't stop till u get it up I'm talking bout the man in the mirror I'm asking him 2 master wait no message cud remain any clearer if u want 2 make the world a better place take a look at yourself and master wait only a genius cud create such lyrics no not just a genius but a patron saint thank u god 4 lending us saiint michael in order to prove my devotion to him i will be his greatest fan by having my foreskin tattooed with his image like any true devoted fan would be honored to do a true fan brands themself no higher devotion than that and now i understand 4 saint micahel if i wanna b a star in something i got to be staring something and he will be with me always and i will bestow his glory like any faithful servant among him and his glorious angels thank you god 4 lending us saint michael your holy son brought us the gift of pop n was persecuted like your son now he is safe with you you shared us your greatest gift n we smeared him when will we ever learn mayb never):

**ONTHEGL, Jun 28 at 12:44 PM**
I blame his close family members and his close friends and the Doctor's

for his untimely death. They all enabled him ot get what ever he wanted. Why didn't they at least make atempts to help them. Just like Elvis..... Anna Nicloe..... Wether the medications were good for him or not they gave them to him.. What happened to sugarpills????? Fake pills! I loved his music, and I will listen to his songs for the rest of my life. When he had children stay over and slept with them, why didn't someone say NO, THIS IS WRONG!!! Just because you are a STAR there is stlll RIGHT and WRONG. I bet his family wishes now that they would have said NO more often. Michael may you rest in peace. A fan forever....

**Virginiamoon10, Jun 28 at 02:25 PM**
I respect Michael Jackson the way he was, Of all singers he could have went to gangstar rapping and using a lot of foul language, but he was a true classy artist in all his music you never heard any ugliness are disrespect towards mothers or women in general, or of any gangster miss doing, Heres to you MJ for being an all time Classical entertainer, I wish tho you had stop with all the cosmetic changes you looked your best in Man in the mirror and Thriller, But sometimes we just can't seem to be pleases with our selves, I wished you could of loved yourself as much as we loved you just the way you were, as far as judgement on any rumored miss haps, we are not to bear false witnessing are judge others, and that I pray you found peace with in Gods good Mercy, may you live on in peace and joy and find finally joy within yourself

**joyce, Jun 28 at 03:43 PM**
There will never again be anyone with as much talent as Michael Jackson. He was truly a dynamo. I saw him in concert 1 time and I have never in my life seen anyone with more energy than him. Sure he got weird in recent years, but who wouldn't having gone through what he's gone through his entire life. He had his childhood STOLEN from him at a very early age. I feel that his dad is partially responsible for his death. Mary, she who is without sin cast the first stone. You sound like a very evil, bitter person. He was acquitted, remember? That means found innocent. Are you forgetting about the one kids mother who got her kid to lie to extort money from MJ? You're a democrat, aren't you. I just can't see a Republican being that evil.

**Ricky, Jun 28 at 03:50 PM**
I was a big fan of Michael's Thriller, Bad and all the music from his childhood. I performed as Michael on TV in the European "Shooting Star" competition and and just uploaded "She's out of my life" as a tribute to his inspiration in my life, it's not a great recording, but he made me remember that music is the food of love. Ricky

**Carol, Jun 28 at 04:26 PM**
First Of All I Feel For The Jackson Family. I Grew Up Listen To Michael's Music. As For Mary And Talia What Is Your Problem He Dealt With His Problems When He Was Alive So Why Not Leave Him Alone Now That He Is Gone. As For Farrah Seeming To Be Left Out The Difference Is She Was 62 And We All Knew It Was Coming. With Michael It Was So Sudden And No Warning As To It Happening. If You Had Watch The New You Would Have Seen That So For All Those That Want To Put Him Down Still Since He Is Gone 3 Words For You All GET A LIFE

**jodie, Jun 28 at 05:04 PM**
michael jackson was one of the favrite pop stars ever jackson was my star no one could ever change how much i loved jackson even though he changed his face heeps of times that was ewwwwwwwwww rip michael jackson

**Erica, Jun 28 at 06:55 PM**
one bad apple-in the bible it says u should not pass judgement only god can so. i was not saying that he did not do those things did i??? nope i didnt, the fame and his goods songs didnt cancel his crime i know that

**JaberV, Jun 28 at 07:18 PM**
Not anyone knows if the charges on Michael were real..Why would any parent let a child hang around a grow man..And most of all if someone did that to my child there is not enough money in this world to keep my mouth shut or my hands off the person that did that..These parents have brain washed the children to say these things..these parent need to be thrown in jail for trashing michael's name...He was a great paerson did alot for this world and try to live the life he never had as a child..Maybe if is own father would not of nick named him big nose maybe things would

of been different for him...He had a every sad strange life growing up....
Rest in peace you will be missed by many...

**ccashm, Jun 28 at 08:28 PM**
No more sorrow, no more pain...Just keep on singing to sweet Jesus again
and again. Your spirit will never die as long as your song is on the lips
and minds of all of the nations you have united with your immeasurable
talent. Now you can rest Michael Jackson, your legacy has been etched
in stone.

**JoanneVL, Jun 28 at 08:12 PM**
Why isn't the theme song to the movie "Free Willy" on the list?I always
thought that was the one song which gave an entirely new twist to the
meaning of those two words in the title thanks to Michael Jackson.

**Brightskies5, Jun 28 at 08:24 PM**
Michael our real life Peter Pan gone forever. This is so hard to believe
and will reverberate throughout the months and years to come - just the
same way it was when Elvis Presley suddenly was taken from us. This is
so unfair and it makes me think that something could and should have
been done to make sure that Michael would NOT have been subjected to
the same circumstances with all the different pain killers just like it was
the case with Elvis. Who are these people who call themselves "doctors"
having been selected and given high status to make sure that the stars
they serve receive the best care money can buy? Apparently that does
not seem to hold true as we are all witnessing AGAIN! This is simply
unacceptable and unforgivable that Michaels personal physician did not
put a stop to the Oxyontin, Demeral and God knows what else Michael
was taking right under his doctor's nose. History has repeated itself with
another senseless "murder".

**Bjomountsi, Jun 28 at 09:46 PM**
I personally loved MJ and am really saddend by the loss-however i believe
if the media left him alone and stopped bothering him-Maybe he would
NOT have gone the way HE did-SO theyre PART to Blame-for this
TRAJIC LOSS-For THOSE who want to knock him down-EVEN
AFTER HE IS NO LONGER WITH US_THEY should Look in
there OWN Backyard-LET THE MAN REST IN PEACE_NOW

HE IS IN A BETTER PLACE WHERE HE WILL HAVE PEACE_
NO ONE CAN BOTHER HIM EXCEPT GOD HIMSELF.HE IS
THE KING OF POP AND ALWAYS WILL BE_NOONE WILL
TAKE HIS PLACE_He is GONE TO SOON_I also am suspicious
of the Doctor that was there while he died-The Jackson family has
EVERY RIGHT TO WANT ANOTHER AUTOPSY HIS DEATH
IS SUSPICIOUS TO ME_What do you think MJ FANS CR fom
Massachusetts.

**Rockmyworld1954, Jun 28 at 10:35 PM**
Whatever demons Michael Jackson faced throughout his life, he was a
creative genius. His music will live on and on. I have been a fan since the
first time I saw The Jackson 5 and thought how adorable he was.

**GBROND23, Jun 28 at 10:46 PM**
All of his music sucked! He sounded like Mickey Mouse, and his sister
Janet is a dead ringer for Minnie. King of POP?? The only thing he ever
popped were little boys...

**MJP0858, Jun 28 at 11:13 PM**
Michael Jackson may not be the most overrated artist of all time but it's
close. His dance moves were not original. Ever heard of Jackie Wilson?
Most of his best songs were written by other people. And there weren't
that many of them to begin with. A promising career (highpoint) with his
brothers and a couple of decent albums does not make Michael Jackson
an icon.

**Bscakita29, Jun 28 at 11:18 PM**
there have been two great loses in the music industry in the last 50 years.
there has been the great lose of Elvis Presley and now the lose of Michael
Jackson. through all of the BS people threw at him he was still the king
of pop and will truly be missed. what a great entertainer the world is a
dimmer place without his brilliance. my heart goes out to his family and
we miss you already King Michael.

**MJP0858, Jun 28 at 11:20 PM**
3 decent solo albums and a career with more holes in it than swiss cheese
doesn't make someone the King of anything. Paul McCartney makes

Michael Jackson look like the King Of Hype. His best, most long-lasting work are the songs he did with the Jackson 5. i will be proven right as the years go on.

**Bscakita29, Jun 28 at 11:27 PM**
mjp0858 your comments show your ignorance. paul was a great group entertainer as part of the beetles. his solo career has never and will never reach the heights of michael jackson's career. even paul had great respect for michael and would probably not appreciate your comments. so maybe you should gain some knowledge about that which you speak before making ignorant comments.

**LadiRabbit, Jun 28 at 11:30 PM**
WHERE'S YOU ARE NOT ALONE... SMOOTH CRIMINAL.... DIRTY DIANA???COME ON NOW PEOPLE. LETS GET IT TOGETHER. HE HAS MANY OTHER SONGS THAT ARE BETTER THAN THOSE... PERSONALLY I DONT LIKE HIS JACKSON 5 SONGS. WASN"T A FAN WHEN HE WAS A LITLE KID I"M A 1990 BABY.. HIS VOICE WAS A LITLE ANNOYiNG BUT I RESPECT AND LOVE EVERYThiNG HE GREW UP TO BE ESPECIALLY UNDER THE CONDITiONS OF HiS ******* FATHER!!! HE NEEDS A GOOD ASS WHOOPiN ALOT OF MiCHAEL. DOWNFALLS WERE BECAUSE OF HiM & WHAT HE PUT HIM THROUGH AS A CHILD!!! RIP TO THE ONE & ONLY KING OF POP

**Garn407, Jun 28 at 11:30 PM**
This is one list I agree with. Good calls. Gotta Be Startin' Something is a great song and you just don't hear it get the credit Billie Jean and Thriller do. Those songs have been so played to death I don't even list them as favorites anymore (though they are genius). Hey, all you naysayers with a bone to pick with Michael, I don't care what your opinion of his life are, as you are entitled to your opinion. But the man is dead and he left a legacy like no other. If you don't think he had talent, clearly you aren't familiar with his career, and are showing your own ignorance. And I'm saying that with a clearly open mind. At 52, I've watched him since the begining and after, oh, fourty or so years of this watching, I am more than qualified to speak. He was phenomenal. You people, on the other

hand, don't know the meaning of the words compassion or respect. Save your negative comments for a more appropriate time, as I'm sure you'll have your chance to trash him in the near future. For...

**Everette2003, Jun 28 at 11:33 PM**
as a nation we are shameless in our comments. love him or hate him. it is what it is. michael is the king of pop. who gave you the right to judge anybody? we need to read our bible more .that right we don't believe in that either. rest in peace mj you were the best in your game. and the rest of you you know where you can rest in......

**pjcandyfields, Jun 28 at 11:34 PM**
I loved "BEN". Always brought tears to my eyes. After learning of Michael's demise, on my way home from school "BEN" was all I could think of as, as my eyes teared up on the train. Michael Jackson was truly a genius and will be missed by all!!!!!!!! My heart goes out to his family especially Janet and his mother.

**GeordieBC, Jun 28 at 11:44 PM**
Ben - I agree. And I"ll Be There has gotten a lot of play time too.

**MJP0858, Jun 28 at 11:55 PM**
Bscakita29 - Michael had great respect for Paul, too, as he bought the publishing rights to the Beatles catalog many years ago. But how can someone be the "King Of Pop" when his career has so many gaps in it? Elvis, Dylan, Sinatra, Paul M. to name just a few never stopped recording or making movies or doing concerts their whole lives. Bob and Paul are still doing it and they are in their 60s. They have written hundreds of songs and are still touring all over the world. The coronation was way too premature.

# JUNE 29, 2009
# MONDAY

*Michael Jackson's death triggers a global outpouring of grief. He is the topic of every front page headline. The three major US evening news networks—ABC's World News, CBS Evening News, and NBC Nightly News—devote 34% of their broadcast time to Michael Jackson.*

**Kristine H., Jun 29 at 08:27 AM**
I think this is stupid it has been 5 days that he has died and no body wants to hear about it anymore

**lorena, Jun 29 at 10:29 AM**
mj is the best in the hole world. but he died now he will not have pain on his back because he is now with god . I wish he is happy and all of his fans will miss him so so so much and he was very nice . And it was nice too that his house was called Neverland like Neverland of Peter Pan I new that his favorit movie when he was a kid was peter pan .

**corncake97, Jun 29 at 11:03 AM**
Although i am only 11 years old right now, my mom lived in the time with Michael Jackson. Once I heard one of his songs, I fell in love with him! My mom told me that she had never gone to one of his concerts, and now she won't have the chance. But she also told me that people, at his concerts, used to faint, pull their hair out, and do other un-imaginable things. I wish the Jackson family tons of peace,

*Juja D.*

**RaRa, Jun 29 at 12:30 PM**
I didn't see this particular show "18 Key Moments", but what made it so supposedly bad? Or was this just "baiting" for comments, since he passed away suddenly last week? Shame on you.

**Sonal, Jun 29 at 12:38 PM**
MICHAEL JACKSON was and will always be undoutedly the best singer dancer performer but above all a great human being and to lose him like this just doesn't feel right and for me his just taking a long break from his stressful life....hav a beautiful dream MICHAEL and rest in peace in our NEVERLAND (heaven)

**HoneyPrettyFly, Jun 29 at 01:03 PM**
MICHAEL JACKSON WAS ONE OF THE GREATEST MEN ALIVE HE REACHED OUT TO THE WORLD N ALL HE WANTED TO DO WAS MAKE A DIFFERENCE.. NOW I MAY ONLY BE 19 SOON TO BE 20 BUT HE WAS HUGE... I KNOW ALOT ABOUT HIM... I FOLLOW HIS AUTOBIOGRAPHIES...I LISTENED TO HIS MUSIC..I EVEN CRUSHED ON HIM....HE WAS THE GREATEST <3 NOT ONLY WAS HE A FASHION ICON, BUT GREAT FATHER, SON, BROTHER, FRIEND.. N HE WILL GREATLY BE MISSED...!

**klawtubu, Jun 29 at 05:30 PM**
MJ is better off than in this world of bigots and hypocrites, people who compare him to Elvis watch out, the bigots don't want him to be compared no way, shape or form to the King of Ripoff.

**acn1359, Jun 29 at 05:38 PM**
Michael Jackson the king of pop loved us enough to share his lollipop boy was it delicious now the taste is bittersweet like the tears i cry cus god has taken away a saint to escort an angel to comfort a genius in heaven he was persecuted for being overly affectionate dead now resurrected in our hearts and minds closed eyes cant see but when opened see love gods greatest love of all a child will teach them the ways of all aspects of entertainment by his stripes we are healed by gods greatest love

**jackie, Jun 29 at 05:44 PM**
how can anyone be allowed to get in debt to the tune of $500 million dollars??guess that's what comes from being a star.us common folk panic when we owe a few thousand.someone should have put an end to his being allowed credit years ago. there isn't a person in the world that should be extended credit until they have paid off most of their previous bills. all jackson would have had to do is lower his standard of iving to that of a normal person.for someone that grew up so poor in the city of gary, indiana he sure was a poor example for the young people. and it's too bad that he never took the time to honor gary and give back to the place that made him what he became.

**sassafras, Jun 29 at 06:00 PM**
Michael's death is sad and untimely, but I believe ones deeds finally catch up with us. His musical genius is undeniable and will endure for a long time, and as with most stars whose lives had ups and downs, he will be thought of with fondness and compassion.

**Jennifer, Jun 29 at 06:01 PM**
I think its wrong to talk about dead people the way that some of you are... if you were that popular and died im pretty sure that you wouldn't want anyone talking about you the way that you are talking about Michael! Whether or not you liked the things he did during his life he was still human and the last time i checked humans are not perfect and make mistakes. So before you start talking badly about him think about what you want to say and think if you would want someone saying that about you when you die. You're not perfect and I'm not either just let the man rest in peace!!!

**Allison, Jun 29 at 06:16 PM**
Sunday's NY Daily News reporter said in a column that Michael Jackson should never have gone to trial on those charges. They were trumped up. Not to mention the vultures ruined his reputation. Now there are some who want to pick his bones too!

**sharon, Jun 29 at 06:18 PM**
Michael Jackson's music is timeless. Love ya, Michael

**Rob NYC, Jun 29 at 06:19 PM**
Johannes is right. He was man who died. If a musician who you never met before changed your life and was your hero, you are a joke. He was an entertainer. He died of a drug overdose. Now move on

**wisdom, Jun 29 at 06:19 PM**
I will go into my 401-k and take out over $25,000 to purchase some mike jackson items.He was the greatest.

**bernie, Jun 29 at 06:25PM**
I Love Michael - but I'll never look at pop/rock stars again without thinking they do drugs......even Madonna or girl singers.

**Cheri, Jun 29 at 06:31 PM**
What if he wanted to die and be remembered like Elvis. I mean if he would have died of old age do you really think he would be getting this much media???? They are already saying he will make more money after his death than he did alive. $700+ million will make a pretty good living for his children. I think it's some what odd that he predicted his own fate.

**juniper, Jun 29 at 06:34 PM**
No,,,, matter how MJ died, his Mom lost one of her children, I hope she wont let the money be her main focus, she has to think about Michaels children...........

**MJ, Jun 29 at 06:36 PM**
Hey all my beautiful fans this is Michael Jackson. I'm not really dead i'm just hiding under your childs bed playing hide in go seek. This is just a publicity stunt to boost up my up coming concert.... umm one moment please.. I'll have one of those pink ones they look so pretty.
Love,Michael Jackson

**kayla, Jun 29 at 06:38 PM**
really? were you in the bed with them?

**CHRISTIANNA, Jun 29 at 06:39 PM**
You know, there are people out there who say, " He didn't molest any

children, or He wasn't convicted, and then there is the most important one, No mother would take a pay off from someone who molested their child" Well, in this sad world, unfortunately there are mothers who don't give a damn about their children and will do anything for money no matter how hurt their child is or tramatized, they will do what they have to do. I know of 2 diffrent child cases going on right now where MOTHERS have allowed their children to be around sex offenders at which cost one child her life. Thank GOD the other little girl was saved before anything happened to her or at least we don't know that nothing has happened to her sexually or mentally, but she is home safe with her grandmother, someone who loves and cares about her. This is a sad world, and to think that because Michael Jackson is a legend and the "king of pop", he wouldn't molest a child because he loves children so much, that is an understatement. He may not have been convicted, but only he and the children he possibly molested knows the truth. and IF them took a pay off to keep quiet about the whole situation with their children, they are sick and in the long run they will go to hell for it and I am sure their children will hate them as they get older.

**cathy, Jun 29 at 06:40 PM**
I will Not Miss him. he's a freak

**M.J the pedophile man, Jun 29 at 06:42 PM**
I hope they dont let those boys I diddled near my grave.I hate the smell of piss. M.J

**M.J king of poop !, Jun 29 at 06:50 PM**
Hi it' me, Peter Pan the pedophile man.I am so nervous and edgy I think I am tweaking from not having my daily dose of demerol. Satan says I will get over it once I start working in the furnace.I told him I was Peter Pan and that I dont work only play with kids wink,wink. He said peter Pan is a pussy and that made me sad. M.J

**sbhappe34, Jun 29 at 06:54 PM**
His estate could be like Elvis, he only had about $400,000 when he died. Good management look what it is worth now. Course the ex wife was behind it. I don't think there is anybody that sharp in the family to listened to the right people. The poor children will just be exploited

and momma Jackson made a mess out of the children she had. They are the most heart breaking of all of this. Do they have a chance. Pray pray pray.

**Yvonne, Jun 29 at 06:55PM**
So What!!! Who don't leave bills behind. Leave Michael Jackson alone. He is in a better place than we are, as you can here. All you guys are miserable tricks. (smile) FOOLS.

**mona, Jun 29 at 06:57 PM**
I wish I was a lawyer to defend him when the media nailed him.how brutal it is to charged for being a criminal before you prove innocent,put your hands in chains that breaks your heart before bruising your wrist especially if you are in your career where .you put yourself for others. what a nasty rules we have.what a nasty corrupted courts

**David, Jun 29 at 07:03 PM**
The real is truth is nothing any of you say makes a difference on these boards, not even what im writing right now matters the slightest. Thats the truth...........pointblank.

**jane k, Jun 29 at 07:06 PM**
i don't believe michael ever molested anyone. i remember 20 years ago the Los Angeles police department saying there were about a dozen (what would prove to be fraudulent) allegations against jackson per month. and before child molestation became the prevailing accusation, his alleged criminal activities involved everything and anything.it is generally acknowledged that child molesters will go to incredible lengths to conceal what they do. michael's problems arose because he openly admitted that he had children sleep over. i think if he was guilty someone could have come up with damning evidence. there was certainly financial motive.

**anjlwme2000, Jun 29 at 07:06 PM**
George dear.....who told you he died the same way Elvis did?? just curious

**MARIBETH79, Jun 29 at 07:07 PM**
I Michael was so broke why had he not liquidated his rights to the Beatles

music which he was brilliant to acquire? This is juat another stunt by his family

**Dan, Jun 29 at 07:07 PM**
Enough with Micheal Jackson. His lifestyle and beliefs led to his own demise. His day had come and gone, time to move on.

**msucowgirl09, Jun 29 at 07:07 PM**
*sigh* even though i didn't really grow up in the reign of michael, i discovered his music when i became a teenager. he has inspired me choreographically and has contributed a lot to the music industry. people are so cruel, why would you even bring up his horrible history? i hope people dig up your past after you die!

**Ron Adams, Jun 29 at 07:09 PM**
I think that Jackson was in love with chlidren's pee-pee's what a scum bag ---They'll make room in hell for that low life bastard

**Doug, Jun 29 at 07:12 PM**
GOOD RIDDANCE !!!!!

**blah, Jun 29 at 07:13 PM**
MJ is in hell right now ...........................thats all i know.

**ou8150, Jun 29 at 07:18 PM**
the Jackson family are whores. MJ supported them for years, now they will cash in on his estate's future earning. All is forgiven and they always loved. Give me a break. Whores

**antman, Jun 29 at 07:23 PM**
boy thats why the word is so messed up,don't hate on the man ,let him rip.all you haters need to get a life and grow up, if you didn't like him then what the hell are you writing on this page,
Boy its a shame the way that people hate on others,all that you heard was the bad things,and they never told of all the good things mj did so plz grow up and let mj rip im out

**Bob, Jun 29 at 07:30 PM**
I am disgusted because there were more people then Micheal Jackson that died last week and I don't think it is fair that they only put his death past any others and not only that Our Men and Women in the middle east fight each day and you think that the media keeps reporting about every little detail about them and their deaths NO and so enough is enough broadcast the news and quit draging out his death. He is gone and so should the reporting.

**italia, Jun 29 at 07:42 PM**
i just want to say i will miss Michael if he did that to a child than god is the one he has to deal with . i grew up off of Michael and its amazing how he is worth more dead than alive and it appears his fans love him more now than they ever did i live in harlem and i went to 125th street at the apollo and there is 2 blocks filled with boot leg cd,video and i must say t shirts that are so beautiful i just wish the exploitation of him and the monetary gain here is unbelievable i thought the obama frenzy was unbelievable but you got to see it to believe it his music is every where geez if this was around the time when jesus died would we be in a frenzy..........stay away from drugs they kill but then again he died of a broken heart the media built him up and tore him down...pray

**ruggit, Jun 29 at 07:44 PM**
When was Jackson's last hit? He was a has been. All the Superstar talk by his family is just a ploy to up his value. Noticed that Jesse and Al slipped into the mix to see if there was any racial plunder for them.

**Connie, Jun 29 at 07:49 PM**
I'm listening to Michael Jackson Radio right now and I'm convinced he was and will always be the most talented performer in our time. Please let him rest in peace. He never had peace when he was alive.

**Luke, Jun 29 at 07:50 PM**
LOOK People he is no F--king KING of anything. never has been Just another drugie who over dosed We only have one KING and he looks over you every day. and it sure ain't MLK either he just happen to have the name

**oilfieldworker, Jun 29 at 07:52 PM**
tired of all the news about mj death remember we also had other stars that died the are not getting the same coverage. rip mj

**OLI, Jun 29 at 07:54 PM**
MARS, are you s..... or what? Don't compare anyone with Jessus. You are so ignorant; you don't know M.J. bibliography! NO one will ever die again for our sins.

**Truth_Verdad, Jun 29 at 07:58 PM**
The truth is, he did it to himself! ... More truth to this is; when I see the news, and hear all the Black people praise him saying his is the Black Elvis, when no one remembers the late 80's and early 90's when he said he was ashamed of being Black, so then the transformation began! ... His family and Black people were stunned by what he did next! ...He changed his nose, he changed his skin so he can become white, and then he said he wanted White Children ... Don't deny it, you've all seen the TV, you've seen him and his white children! ... Yes he had talent, but let's not forget his past life style, and the TRUTH!

**Kathy, Jun 29 at 07:59 PM**
This sad genious had to end this way. Almost like Howard Hughes and Elvis. The Bull crap about the outpouring of love from his family and friends makes me mad. The man died alone but for the PAID doctor that sat next to him as he slept. So sad, where were these close friends? Could they have saved him?

**Lexi, Jun 29 at 07:59 PM**
His death has literally stopped my life. One of the only good parts of my childhood has died with him. It is so unfortunate how the media treated him, not just through suspect accusations, but every other aspect of his life. Thankfully now he has transended the fishbowl life he could never escape. My thoughts will forever be with him, and his spirit will live on in my heart. I will love him forever, as will my children to come. I will miss you always, the Great, the ONLY and the unfortunatly late, Michael Jackson.

*Juja D.*

**Lee, Jun 29 at 08:01 PM**
The news coverage of MJ has been extremely overdone. A paragraph or two on the day he died would have been more than sufficient. Fortunately, there was no news anywhere in the world over the last 5 days since his death and so the major networks repeated hour after hour of the boring details of his worthless life.

**sandra, Jun 29 at 08:03 PM**
Yes, MJ, was really always good at what he did. singing ~ dancing ~ buying women to have his kids ~ and molesting little boys. When he was still Black, he was Great, but when he bleached and got plactic, he got Sick.
Such a shame ! I do wonder if he ask God to forgive him!

**pat, Jun 29 at 08:12 PM**
AN AMERICAN legend has passed and regardless of the situation and how people feel he influenced dance culture and gave a lot of happiness to a ton on people , I WISH MORE people could do what he has done and will do for years even in death , he joins all the great people JOHN LENNON, JIM MORRISON, JANIS JOPLIN, ELVIS , wow what a band they have in heaven

**BonnieU2, Jun 29 at 08:39 PM**
The "racial discrimination" hucksters and $vultures are coming out of the woodwork! Trying to grab whatever publicity or money they can, just like all the parasites who lived off of him when he was alive. The man got whiter every year, married two white women, and left behind three white children. And now, just like OJ Simpson who rejected his own race, they are claiming "Michael was ours! A Black Man" and no one should talk about his bizarre appearance, behavior, or drug addictions! What a joke!

**BonnieU2, Jun 29 at 08:44 PM**
Sorry, Pat: JOHN LENNON, JIM MORRISON, JANIS JOPLIN- all in hell....John Lennon said the Beatles were "bigger than God" Jim Morrison & Janis Joplin, both drug-addicted, completely self-centered and had no interest in God or Heaven.

**dstreettalker, Jun 29 at 08:55PM**
He sold more than 3/4 billion albums. Let say that he got $2 per album at least that a 1.5 billion, add the concerts and shows and related articles sold, you are easily looking at least 2 billion or more this man made when he was alive. He obviously was never broke. For him to owe that amount of money is suspect at best. There is the likelihood that MJ had some stash in places people don't know about. When it is all said and done, a few billions will be available for viewing,

**steve, Jun 29 at 08:57 PM**
This was probably some type of conspricacy. MJ had been supporting his family and associates for years. It looked like this latest comback would fail, and only pay off his creditors, so they had him killed to take his estate and future estate earnings. Just like Elvis, whose relatives made millions after he died, so will MJ's relatives. Blood is thicker than water, but money is thicker than blood. RIP MJ. Your only falt was you trusted too many people.

**Erica, Jun 29 at 09:06 PM**
okay, seriously!—All of these negative comments first off need to check your facts before you make ignorant comments like that! Most of what you all are saying is false and they have proved that to be so! He was studied and interviewed by psychiatrists that said not once did he portray the mindset of a pedifile. What he did portray was the mind set of a 10 year old. Someone that was as esentric as MJ, we need to look at thier childhood. He never had a normal one, was basicly abused by his father, and much more troubled to continue to write. He was aquited on all counts against him. And did you ever think that things like that would be made up in order to gain money. And he may have left financial debt, but he did and i quote "Jackson's money woes may be solved through smart licensing arrangements." more money is going to be made to his name through his death then in his lifetime, trust me his financial woes will be solved soon in due time. And one final thing if you dont care about the news on MJ or dont want to hear it anymore,ect. then why are you taking the time out to read the article and comment on it. Seems like you care a little to me. And go outside and play a sport or something and stop watching tv then if it bothers you so much. This is going to be in the media for a while, so deal with it somehow! He was a very talented

man and will be missed! He gave us some great music and did a lot of good for whoever he could! He was listed in the 2000 edition of the Guiness Book Of World Records for breaking the world record for the "Most Charities Supported By a Pop Star". It states that Michael Jackson has supported 39 charity organizations either with monetary donations through sponsorships of their projects or by participating in their silent auction.

**e, Jun 29 at 09:09 PM**
my opinion michael jackson was the greatest singer and performer. no one could hold a candle to his dancing. i will miss him so much. i don;t believe all the garbage about him touching children. it was all about people trying to get his money. he was an easy target because of the way he changed his face. he looked yes, strange after so many face and nose surgeries, so people talked crap about him and the tales on the tabloids got weirder and weirder and the ones who didn't like michael jackson are the ones who believed it. if there was an ounce of truth to any child being touched by michael do you really think a judge would have awarded him custody of children that were not his natural children?? a michael jackson fan forever!!

**SayWhatGirl, Jun 29 at 09:15 PM**
"He will make more money in his death than he did in his life"Doesn't everyone? lol.

**Art, Jun 29 at 09:17 PM**
Another strange little man with talent. Remember his music and forget the guy. Move on, people....

**KJ, Jun 29 at 09:20 PM**
"BonnieU2" get YOUR facts straight!!! John Lennon NEVER said they were bigger than God. He said that, at that particular time, the Beatles were probably mentioned more than Jesus. Never did he say they were better or more POPULAR than Jesus!!! I'll also bet my bottom dollar that he did FAR more to improve the world during his lifetime than you will EVER do in yours!!!

**TONI, Jun 29 at 09:34 PM**
MICHAEL WAS A GREAT ARTIST IN THE 80'S...GROWING UP IN THE 80'S WAS MAGICAL AND EVERYONE WANTED TO BE LIKE HIM...WHO DIDNT RUN OUT AND BUY "THRILLER"...SAD THING IS HE SEEMED TO BE IN ALOT OF EMOTIONAL PAIN...WHAT PERSON IN THEIR RIGHT MIND BUTCHER'S THEIR FACE LIKE HE DID.....HE MADE OVER 700 MILION DOLLARS BUT HE IS LEFT WITH A DEBT OF AROUND 500 MILLION...REPORTS SAY THAT HE KEPT USING HIS HOUSE AND BEATLE RIGHTS FOR COLLATERAL, THOSE PEOPLE HAVE TO BE PAID BEFORE ANYONE...THE CHILD MOLESTATION CASES HURT HIS CAREER ALOT, WHO WANTS TO SUPPORT A PERSON THAT DOES THAT, EVEN THOUGH HE WAS FOUND INNOCENT THE SECOND TIME AND THE FIRST TIME HE SETTLED OUT OF COURT...THEY SHOULD JUST LET HIM REST IN PEACE...I LOVED HIM IN THE 80'S BUT IN THE 90'S I LOST INTEREST IN HIM AND HIS CRAZY LIFESTLE.

**robert, Jun 29 at 09:36 PM**
Beezo3, because you are so educated, will you tell us about your use of the letter "k" as used in your sentence. I'm dying to know, as you had just berated Johannes, on his spelling. Petty isn't it, and who cares , right.

**TRC, Jun 29 at 09:37 PM**
You're an idiot - MJ was acquitted of that charge, so it's slanderous to say it. It's clear that he was a little "freaky," but to be disrespectful of someone who has passed...it's just gross.

**Erica, Jun 29 at 09:38 PM**
your an idiot get your facts straight before you state your opinion! better off without him they are going to be going through legal battles for a really long time.. and just lost the only parental figure they new.. and you dont know anything about him or what he did or didn't do .. so shut the hell up!

**Jodi, Jun 29 at 09:38 PM**
Yes he was on drugs....I haven't lived his life. What we would think as a "smooth ride" perhaps it isn't?
I just think it's unfair to judge, if you haven't walked in one's shoes. ....
On the other side, reality will you..."you Reap What you Sow"It is what is is....

**Breana, Jun 29 at 09:43 PM**
"Before he died, interest in Jackson collectibles was on the decline as fans voiced their disgust over the child molestation allegations against him." BULL S**T. His fans never "voiced their disgust," his fans KNEW HIM BETTER THAN THAT and VOICED THEIR SUPPORT. It was the ignorant mindless, media obsessed drones who where "disgusted" because they believed whatever they heard and didnt care to think for themselves. DONT YOU DARE pretend that we all believed those rediculous allegations. And DONT YOU for a second wrap his fans together with those opposed to him. We stood behind him from the begining and we will stand behind him now.

**Lynn, Jun 29 at 09:46 PM**
Okay, so Debby Rowe gave up the rights to those kids, obviously for a price. She should not be allowed to get them back. However, have you seen the pictures of those kids. They are white. Lets not forget MJ was a black man, those kids do not have any of the features of a black father and a white mother. Maybe a DNA test is in order. And MJ's parents did not necessarily do a good job with the 9 kids they had, why give them 3 more to screw up.

**Ally, Jun 29 at 09:48 PM**
Michael Jackson was really the King of Pop and he was always famous and he lived his life to fullest so god bless his soul .People gather up for these kind of incidents but they never gather up due to the economy now and how we as middle class struggle and suffer so much financialy . No one ever complains or gather out why Californians have to pay more taxes , why the gas prices are going up and why so many people dont have insurance and are sick at the same time???

**Jodi, Jun 29 at 09:51 PM**

I don't think Michael Jackson was a "hero" he was a genius... having said that, he wasn't like you or me whom walk threw life making a living, we all make. He was different...It goes to show (sadly) He was human after all...

**don, Jun 29 at 09:58 PM**

Oh , found not guilty, so was OJ, and Robert Blake. Poor Michael was raised wrong, so was Jeffry Domner. He may have made good music, but he was still a child molester. Why else would you pay 20 million for someone not to testify?? I saw a clip where he was at a concert in France , with a small boy in his lap, they should have arrested him right then !! And Joe?? Yeah, my boy died, by the way I've started a new businness . What a idiot !!

**Shelly, Jun 29 at 09:59 PM**

...did he molest you have you ever seen him molest anyone. Judge not

**Jodi, Jun 29 at 10:02 PM**

See here is the problem....
I was on the debate team in high school. Having said that, I was suppose to look at every view. I see every view....Some ppl are idiots ( I would never tell them so)

**Erica, Jun 29 at 10:11 PM**

hey Lynn just letting you know a white woman and a black man can have a white child and display caucasion attributes...like i have said people can share their opinion but please be educated if your going to share it! if you don't know your facts keep your opinions to yourselves.

**MAGPIE, Jun 29 at 10:13 PM**

It's so sad to lose a GREAT ENTERTAINER,Michael had such compassion for people. He started it all!! (Live Aid concerts,( we are the world) HE GOT TO THE HEART OF US ALL!! I know i will miss him and every time a song come on i will get a little teary eyed, we all got up to Dance every time we hear his music~~~ please remember That!!

*Juja D.*

**Steph, Jun 29 at 10:14 PM**
All you judgmental people make me sick. You the sickos. I don't care who it is, you don't talk about someone like that when they aren't here to even defend themselves. You never know what someone goes through unless you walk a mile in your shoes. I wish your life could be put under a microscope you hypocrites. Everyone would find out how stupid and ignorant all of you are. I hope you are judged 100 times more then Michael! Because god doesn't like ugly and you will be satans butt buddy if you don't watch it.. R.I.P Michael! No matter what, you were a human being with feelings and none of these people here including myself knew you personally. I hope they are paid back ten fold what they dish out. Uneducated retards...

**mercy, Jun 29 at 10:15 PM**
WOW WHEN DID GOD MAKE YOU ALL JUDGE AND JURY YOU ALL WILL HAVE YOUR TURN IN FRONT OF THE LORD!!!!!!!!!!!!

**Lisa, Jun 29 at 10:35 PM**
How could anyone in their right mind give custody of any children to Katherine Jackson. She allowed her wicked , opportunistic, greedy, husband to beat his children into submission so that they would perform and take care of him financially.

**pstrshubby, Jun 29 at 10:41 PM**
Once again a lot of people have to trash someone that has died.Remember people."Let him without sin cast the first stone". also "YOU" that are always blogging hateful comments remember this. Over 200 years ago "Thomas Jefferson" said. " No foreign enemy shall drink from the banks of the Ohio River,No enemy shots will be fired in our country,no foreign land shall take over us,we will be taken over from within."Do not blame Bush or Obama,the blame lays with us,we are already being taken over from within with all of our hate towards each other.

**lISA, Jun 29 at 10:41 PM**
I agree. Grant it he had good music however people are making him out to be a hero. If my children were young and not grown I would have to make them aware that this is not a man to be idolized. He did not live

a good life. I feel sorry that he lived the way he did, and died in such a manner, but enough is enough already. Farrah Fawcett showed true courage and should be commended, but we hardly hear anything.

**Dean, Jun 29 at 10:51 PM**
I read M.J.'s will, it read " TO ALL MY FRIENDS AND FAMILY, I LEAVE YOU ALL MY DEBTS.

**Tanya, Jun 29 at 10:56 PM**
M.J might be the King of Pop but, King Jesus is the KING of us all. Everyone including you must died and answer to the HOLY ONE. No amount of money can buy it. M.J. was a true icon for entertainment. I heard him talk about GOD in his trail. That whats going to get the King of pop into the gates where the KING of all the ROCKS should want to be.I hope to see him there soon

**Michael, Jun 29 at 10:59 PM**
All set with Michael Jackson and the whole damned bunch of them.I'd much rather read about Farrah Fawcett anyway...

**Joyce, Jun 29 at 11:07 PM**
Let the man rest in peace he is dead an gone an we must
all go on with our live's my heart goes out to his family each an everyone of them may God bless the family of Michael an watch over them at a time like this i'm very sorry for there loss.

**Steve, Jun 29 at 11:14 PM**
He was a pervert, and frankly...I won't miss him.

**paulm1, Jun 29 at 11:31 PM**
the news said he had a shot of demerol and began to breath funny. that means he overdosed on the medication. he went into respiratory failure which is an od.

**ADMR, Jun 29 at 11:39 PM**
What's Done in the Darkness, Always Comes to Light - What a Mess.

*Juja D.*

**terrie, Jun 29 at 11:47 PM**
If you are Americans, than America is in trouble. We have failed a lot people. Judging and can't spell or complete a sentence. RIP MJ

# JUNE 30, 2009
# TUESDAY

*U2 dedicates the song "Angel of Harlem" to Michael Jackson while performing their first show of the U2 360 tour in Barcelona, Spain. Bono sings verses from "Man in the Mirror" and "Don't Stop Till You Get Enough" at the end of the song. Jackson fans continue to mourn the death and celebrate the life of their beloved singer around the world.*

**Danielle, Jun 30 at 12:09 AM**
Look People...........you're born......you live......you die! Get over this death of Michael Jackson. He was no king.......just a mental case that like young boys. Has everyone forgotten all the things that he has done to the children..........dangling one over a banister.......molesting young boys! What is wrong with this world today! Stupid people idolizing someone like that!

**Liz, Jun 30 at 12:22 AM**
I believe this man was trying to relive his childhood the one his father took away from him when he was alittle boy. It seems like he was just a dollar sign to many people especially his family! He probably bought neverland just to have someplace where he could retreat and be the child he never was, only relating to children because they understood him and taking him for the kind, gentle soul he was. All of these allegations about molesting children seemed to be just another way of getting money from him. If all of the lawyers, Doctors, so called friends and family members thought he was overdosing on medications why didn't they try to help him? Because they were to busy counting the money he gave them. Now

everyone will want the children because they see dollars signs again. Why don't they take into consideration that he was their father no matter how strange he seemed how wierd he acted, he loved his children and they loved him dearly. Only now will they see how cruel the world and the people in it are when the newspapers bring out the photos and crazy stories about him, and not the wonderful things he did for people and the wonderful music and talent he brought to us. Hopefully God will spare them from the cruelness of all this and things to come . Rest in peace Michael, if you can.

### SiMPLi3xMEE, Jun 30 at 12:39 AM

i love michael jackson and im 16 years old the first time i remember knowing about him and his music was when i was two years old and my older sister and her best friend were in the living room watching MTV and thriller was playing i was watching it and that night i went to bed and i had the most scariest dream about it i woke up and he was on my wall talking to me i ran out the room into my parents room so scared lol. but despite that i loved michael jackson he had and will always have and hold a special place in my heart he changed music and the world so all the haters keep hating because thats what made him even more famous. he went through a lot of crap that some can and cant relate to verbal,mental,and physical abuse but through it all he came through and did his damn thing michael no matter what anyone has to say about even though ur gone i'll be the one to back you up.

### Kathy, Jun 30 at 01:16 AM

Michael Jackson is dead. Let him rest in peace. It's time to move on.

### tommy, Jun 30 at 01:30 AM

You Michael worshipers will eat your word when you see the toxicology report, it will show drugs. Don't forget he got sued by a pharmacy in 2007 for 101,000. Anybody else ever owe that much for drugs? I did not hate MJ but the man paid off a family instead of defend himself against charges of being a pedophile. Would any of you do that or would you want to keep your good name? What he did was the closest thing to admitting guilt. I am glad I never worshiped anyone like you nuts have.

**jwb, Jun 30 at 02:14 AM**

one less pedophile, freak and weirdo to worry about..the little boys are safer now.

**JD, Jun 30 at 02:21 AM**

He was a man who was an "awesome" singer and dancer. I can still remember where I was when I saw his "Thriller" video on MTV. He was a man who had many "issues" as attested to by his own words in interviews about his childhood. I wish he didn't, but he did. As far as his contribution to society; I don't see much other than entertainment. He spent $89,000 on a chess set (recorded during an interview while shopping in Las Vegas) when he already had a "nice" one at home. He may have given much to charities and other things that I am not aware of??? His spending of money was possibly a "fill in" to meet a need. If he didn't sing and dance well, we wouldn't have give him the time of day. I feel for Michael Jackson; I feel that he was a victim of fame and greed; and now I hope that he made amends with his creator and can rest in peace. I pray for his family; specifically, his children. May God's grace rest upon this family and their futures. We as the public need to let them do this peacefully. We have many other issues to be concerned with right now in the world. God Bless you all and let's move on.

**betty, Jun 30 at 02:28 AM**

i didn't like elvis and i don't like mj either. i think Farrah should stand in the spot light more, she was a true and beautiful person that had a long struggle in front of her, bur she never gave up to drugs, sleeping with little girls. some of you are buying up his music after he is gone, where were you when he really needed you to bail him out of debt, if he was ever in one. i don't think Michael's mother should have his kids,she never was there for him what makes the family think she has changed. DOLLAR SIGNS SAYS IT ALL.

**Dottie, Jun 30 at 03:58 AM**

Michael Jackson will always live on in our hearts, It was shocking to here he pass on, No matter if the news is good or bad people are always going to talk about him forever.Micheal did a lot for people and sick children and a lot of those people go around and spread lies about him and he still kept helping . That shows what kind of person he was a caring guy.

*Juja D.*

**SLYEST FAN, Jun 30 at 04:09 AM**
YEA HE DID A LOT OF THINGS LIKE SEXUALLY HARASSING
SMALL BOYS EH? YEA RIGHT

**SLYEST FAN, Jun 30 at 04:05 AM**
I am Black and African. I liked Michael in the beginning. Best musician ever. I spent hours trying to dance like him as far back as before Cds and Dvds ever came to existence. I don't think there will ever be anyone to match him. We all have a right to do whatever we want with our bodies: tattoos, piercings etc but when u start distorting the part of ur body that is used for breath, then something is wrong. When he started working on his nose i knew he will not go far. He could have worked on his dick, balls, hands, etc but not the nose. He could get a green dick, blue balls etc but hell not the nose. Then we have lost all family values that we now turn to drugs. When i look at my kids, even the most sophisticated pain killers cannot replace the pain killing effect i feel when i am with family. When u start making kids using strange absurd means, your fucked up. I guess he was planning to shag an alien or donate sperms to an alien from outer space to make alien et kids. People, lets be realistic. Michael fucked up right to the end. His doctor is not to blame for anything.
1) when you hire a doctor at 126k a month then your system must be f***** up real bad.
2) i would not kill the goose that lays the golden egg... So just quit looking at the doctor. I hope Michael's soul rest in peace. I guess he planned something strange to be done to his body. Maybe incinerated put in a jar, take to outer space and then throw it out to float in the atmosphere without gravity... Well just a quick reminder before i leave: Michael is in for a surprise when he gets to the other side. All the plastic surgery will disappear, he will have BLACK SKIN and a BLACK AFRICAN NOSE!!!

**Robert, Jun 30 at 04:48 AM**
goodness the comments today are sadly lacking in education I think. Bridget you lost a few zeros there he's $500million in debt, but his Beatles ownership is worth that they say. Guan I really think he might be dead, the debt isn't bad compared to assets, and his new look is so bad I'd want that gone. But I agree with others, when does the news return, or has the World stopped with him?

Michael earnings hasn't stopped yet, and won't for 20 years. Guan I do think he's dead, but not so bad his new look was only good for the grave. I agree with others wheres the news, or did the World stop because he stopped?

**Robert, Jun 30 at 04:52 AM**
he'd love that all the little kids playing his leggo

**aintweenie, Jun 30 at 04:59 AM**
The king of pop has met the prince of darkness.

**Rob, Jun 30 at 05:02 AM**
yes I agree but that father using him didn't hurt the other siblings and send them nuts did it? I think Hollywood affects them must be the smog off the hills?

**sally, Jun 30 at 06:14 AM**
It is ingorgant people that caused MJ so much hurt. He believed the good in people and finds out how evil and hurtful the public can be. He was target for easy money.He wanted to "Make the world a better place for you and for me" I will never believe he would hurt anyone especially a child. He was an abused child. Shame on people to criticize.He gave his live to entertain the world. Be kind his family is suffering a great lose and don't hurt his three children by being an idiot. I will miss him he gave the world a gift of talent you will never see again.My prayers are with him and his family. His father is still an idiot.

**MIGWEB, Jun 30 at 06:21 AM**
What can you say about MJ, he was larger than life...a true showman, and a terrific singer, my heart goes out to his family/friends/ and all those fans who will miss his persona. Wow, we always lose the great ones too early..MJ may you rest in peace, the saying must be right "God needed an Angel"..God Bless...

**Mike H., Jun 30 at 06:27 AM**
Let me ask something... Why does the Black community think Michael Jackson is the icon for them? Michael spent his life and money trying to look white... Face lift after face lift, skin treatments to dye his skin, hair

treatments to straighten his hair...He wanted to look like Elvis.. Michael was very talented and gifted, why did he want to live as a white guy?

**rzhill, Jun 30 at 06:37 AM**
look at all the young boy's parents, they don't have to worry about their little boys now!!

**Lisa, Jun 30 at 06:40 AM**
I have never seen more ignorant comments in my life!!! MJ was a great artist, but a very troubled person. Someone posted that if he couldn't sing and dance what would he have done....probably would have been a human being. I can't imagine having all that money, and still not having enough. He was a caricature of a "person"...not real. I also wish some of you rocket scientists would stop writing in "textspeak"...mybe u dmb shts don't know nything lse.

**joyce, Jun 30 at 06:47 AM**
Anyone who would let him accumulate that kind of debt deserves to lose every penny.

**Leo, Jun 30 at 06:49 AM**
JOE JACKSON IS A PIECE OF CRAP! IT WASNT BAD ENOUGH THAT HE BEAT THE HELL OUT OF HIS KIDS WHEN THEY WERE YOUNGER, BUT NOW HE USES HIS SON'S DEATH AS A PROMOTION TO HIS OWN NEW RECORD LABEL?? YOU 80 YR. OLD PEICE OF CRAP, MY OPINION IS: THE WRONG JACKSON DIED. YOU ARE SICK AND SHOULD BE ASHAMED OF YOURSELF!

**Lisa, Jun 30 at 06:51 AM**
To Mike H., He didn't want to look like Elvis, he wanted to look like Diana Ross!!!

**raynabow, Jun 30 at 06:52 AM**
Keisa-Kee...You should have spent less time listening to Michael Jackson and more time working on your spelling. My second grader can spell better than that...come on now!

**Michael, Jun 30 at 07:33 AM**
I read that Michael Jackson is going to be stuffed and tour city to city in a circus.

**jake, Jun 30 at 07:42 AM**
I can assure you that MJ had plenty of money tucked away in trust accounts for his children and for himself, there will be no lack of money, granny knows of these trusts which is why she is bucking for custody, Look at Elvis, died with less that 300k, ex wife PP turned his death into a cash cow, worth more dead than alive, go figure.

**joe w., Jun 30 at 07:55 AM**
Michael was a child molestor first,a preformer second,and a good dad to his kids ,as long as he didnt get naked and cuddle with them in bed.I could never get Billy Mays' gadgets to work.Farrah had nipples you could hang a winter coat on.I'll take a bald Farrah ,TY.

**CAZ, Jun 30 at 08:15 AM**
You guys that dont like MJ had to click on the page to get here and read the comments, Then you spend time writing your names ,email addresses and crappy comments { i guess your lives are so sad that bad attention is better than non }Now let me put this in simple terms that all you anti MJs will understand -IF YOU DONT LIKE THE GUY DONT CLICK ON THE LINK-Geesh

**PEACE, Jun 30 at 08:31 AM**
Michael Jackson's enormous talent gave the world a glimpse of God's infinite greatness! God indeed works in mysterious ways! The GREATEST COMEBACK of all times – skyrocketing sales of Michael Jackson's music and videos AROUND THE WORLD to bring eternal joy and happiness to the planet! Michael, your mission on earth has been accomplished supernaturally, way beyond your wildest dreams! You can truly rest in peace FOREVER now!

**jblxxx, Jun 30 at 08:46 AM**
Ok he was a great performer and all that but he was also a clown who was fond of little boys. alright already let's move on there is more important things to worry about, like south korea and the uprest in iran and the

war in iraq , and noone is protesting or worried about it but yet you have a whole bunch of idiots mourning this freak.

**rsrjrs, Jun 30 at 08:54 AM**
Let's not forget this man is a child molester. Thats just one less preditor we need to worry about.

**Danny, Jun 30 at 08:56 AM**
Michael would not win on "So you think you can dance", and he would not win on "American Idol". He was just an average entertainer. His real genius was hiring Quincy Jones.

**Rontruth, Jun 30 at 09:02 AM**
I liked Jackson's "We Are The World" back in the 1980's. I liked his song that insulted the CIA. After all, they killed our 1960s heroes, President Kennedy, who tried to stop Vietnam war, left Castro in Cuba: all hated by the CIA. Come to think of it, Michael Jackson hated war and hunger also. He died suddenly. So did JFK. Hmmm. The phone call to 9/11 made by someone who said a "cardiologist was with Jackson when he died." Was Jackson a cardiac patient, and no one knew about it?

**Nate, Jun 30 at 09:03 AM**
get over it!!! But, what about that old Joe Jackson?? Is he nuts?? Goes around grinning, stating Debbie Rowe will have no say so? Sharpton better advice this stupid "father" better. He needs a dose of reality..he's still abusing his son by "riding" once again on his back, wanting to open a new record studio?? And the brothers and sisters, a tour in Jacksons memory?? Yah, right, they need money is all and a dead Michael is supposed to be their "cash cow" They are all nuts!! Let the man be 6 feet under before you go around grinning, opening record studios and planing a tour to get some cash into their pockets!! What a bunch of idiots,,,no wonder Michael was detached from them, who can blame him? Those poor children, Joe Jackson surely thinks of them as his cash flow as well. He needs yo go back to las Vegas, stay there..and Debbie Rowe could not be worse as a caretaker of HER children......

**kandygrl1994, Jun 30 at 09:09 AM**
I know it's sad and all that Michael Jackson died. He was a great

entertainer, and Thriller is one of the best music videos ever made. But I'm really tired of hearing about him and I feel bad for Farah Fawcett. The woman died of cancer and all we can talk about is whether a wacky entertainer died of an overdose or not.

## Dorothy M. Y., Jun 30 at 09:13 AM

Dear Michael and the Jackson Family,
I'm sorry you left us at such a young age, I myself am 72 yrs. old. I remember that young group "The Jackson Five", I loved all of you then and I always have. I'm tearing as I write this to you and your family. I hope now you can get some rest. We always expect perfetion and service from all of the people in your industry, we never put ourselves in your shoes, all we know is that you are expected to give us what we want. When things go wrong we doubt, suddenly the love and trust we had for the person in question. No matter what happened in your life I always knew that you were innocent of all of the charges. What you do in your private life is between you and your GOD. Tlhey crusified you for years as they did many others, Elvis, Princess Di, Anna Nichole, and you. The tabloids and some of teh news media should be held accountable for some of the negative news they report, (expecially now, things haven't even been proven yet and they are all over the news with mis -information,I'm sorry that I am a part of this society that lets people be treated this way. You gave so much of yourself and gave so little to yourself. I don;t feel that you ar a genius I think you are greatness, you will be remembered at least by me for the rest of my life as the one who taughrt the world how to love and how to give and to have work ethics, you never gave up you went on until the end. I don't have a favorite song because I think that all of your songs including the The Jackson Five's are ever lasting. I pray that your children whom you loved so much will be spared the drama that so many family's have experienced in the past. Ari Onassis's daughter and other children who lose their parent or parents. I hope the court takes a deep look at the way these children are being bargained away. The mother gave up her wrights when she let you buy the children Its like an adoption when the parent gives up her or his wrights they are out of the picture. As for the nanny taking custody for the children who ever heard of such a thing. The parents and family are more responsible for the children then anyone else would be. I know I was raised by my aunt who was a

wonderful human being (she was in her late 60's, I was 11 going on 12, she lived to be 99 years). The children know their grandparents, aunts, uncles, cousins and friends. We use to be for protection of our children but now anything goes. Everyone is after the money. The courts should put whatever monies the children receive from the royalties and whatever money comes in trust for the children and only allow money for food, cloths, education and medical expenses to be used from the estate. Who ever gets the children will have to provide a place for them to live and what ever else they want to contribute to the children. That's when you will see who is for the children . Who can take care of them free of charge except for the above mentioned. There should be receipst for every dime that is used and there should be estate planners who (more than one) who can direct the children's estate. The father had hangers on's don't let this happen to he children. Its time someone spoke out about this now. Remember if it hadn't been for the parents " The Jackson Five"would have not existed. Michael may GOD Bless your soul and spirit and shine favorable on your children and family. The only other time I felt like this is when I heard the news that President Kennedy had died, and when I lost my love ones and again when I watched the crusifixion of Jesus. Remember man creates all suffering and GOD heals. A fan and admirer. You will be missed.
Respectfully,
DM Y.,

**Dean, Jun 30 at 09:26 AM**
Dorothy ..you might want to consider getting a life of your own.

**Chuck, Jun 30 at 09:34 AM**
Since Obama was such a fan, perhaps a bailout is in order? Its only 1/2 billion--chickenfeed these days, right?

**Casey, Jun 30 at 09:40 AM**
I hope everyone understands what this man has done for music. He is an icon. I was so disgusted with everything that has been said or accused that he did. It actually made me not think as highly of him at one time. You know the media is great, but it's also not so great. It can sometimes lead you into believing something that may not be as bad as they portray it is. We are all human, we all make mistakes, we are all

sinners. Some of us can be Hippocrates at times. Whatever you think personally about the man is fine, it's a free country remember? However, you can never doubt his musical accomplishments. Musically, the man was/is the KING. He will be very missed. And by the way, Billie Jean was the best , with Thriller being a close 2nd!!!!

**Bo, Jun 30 at 09:41 AM**
Good riddance. That child molesting pervert should have been castrated and locked away years ago, and you people still sing his praises. "there are none so blind as those that will not see"

**Leeka, Jun 30 at 09:41 AM**
AN BIG PAPA THAT GOES TO YOU 2 JUST BY READING YOUR COMMENT YOU HAVE NO LIFE YOU UNTALENTED MORON !!!
AN BO JUST SHUT UP U HAVE NO CLASS AT ALL . WHAT YOU NEED TO DO IS SIT DOWN SHUT UP AN MAYBE EDUCATE YOURSELF!!!!!!

**Don, Jun 30 at 09:47 AM**
Why White Media always stand in judge of African American? Where are the Black Media? It all seems very very Bias and one sided.You never see black stand negative in Judge of White Stars. Just a private thought! Dam!!!!!!!!!!!R.I.P. MJ

**DJJCREW, Jun 30 at 09:50 AM**
THE Mans dead an your calling him a junkie your probably the junkie. YOU HAVE NO CLASS TALKING ABOUT THE DEAD IN THAT MANNER . WE ALL KNOW MJ WAS TALENTED . SO SHUT YOUR TRAP !!!

**arminh, Jun 30 at 09:57 AM**
What planet are you all from? The sicko jacko molested kids, I dont care if he can sing. So if you think he can sing, does that give him the right to molest kids? He is a sicko, freak. Eternity will be very long down there.

**Linda, Jun 30 at 10:01 AM**
MJ ruined his name all by himself. He was a very talented pedophile who has died. Let's move on.

**Don, Jun 30 at 10:02 AM**
You people need help! You're very SICK!!!!!!!
No one ever hold the Media accountable for anything, Do you know you own the airways? LoL'o much hate in America!Amazing!!!!!!!!!!!!!!May God be with ya.R.I.P MJ

**Linda, Jun 30 at 10:07 AM**
Thanks, "Don," I was waiting for someone to play the race card. Only question is, what was he? White or black? Seems to me he was ashamed of being black so bleached his skin to white...and don't give me the sad story about vitiligo....that happens in spots, not all over. So should the "white media" defend him or the "black media?"

**Jesus M., Jun 30 at 10:08 AM**
Michael Jackson was a great human being in the news all they talked about was his record sale and supposably child molestation. Like Michael's father highlighted. he use to give a lot to the people that needed. he was one of the celebrity that use to donate the most to hundred of causes writing numerous songs for dose causes like "We are the world" We don't have the right to judge him. judge yourself before judging him. i am writing my second poetry book and i am going to dedicate a poem to him. he deserves it. in my first book i wrote one for Aaliyah. That poem is in my book "Pure, true feelings" my new book will have a poem dedicated to the king of pop. may he rest in peace. if u want to buy my book "pure, true feelings" you can get it at barnes and noble.com or amazon.com May god bless you all sign,
Jesus M.

**Bud M., Jun 30 at 10:08 AM**
Well. I don't know about you people, but I sure would like to date Marilyn Monroe again. (Would've liked to last week also.) LOL

**Lars, Jun 30 at 10:08 AM**
he was a child molester!

**King of Pop, Jun 30 at 10:08 AM**
I love it when people throw the first stones, yet why aren't you worried about the brick house built all over you. It is very sad and embarrasing that this is what the world has come down to. Cynical and Sarcastic SOB's. It's because of these individuals that the media act like vultures and attack people, whether stars/ politician, whatever still human. May you rest in peace Michael, some people are just too stuck on stupid to realize such a great loss. Please, lets just focus on the positive things that Michael did, like raise money for the starving kids in Africa and other parts of the world. Ask yourself something, when was the last time you did something without expecting something back. And to think that we are supposed to be the dominant raise that thinks. Very sad, sad indeed. Go ahead keep the media like vultutres.

**Debbie, Jun 30 at 10:15 AM**
Good Morning All, I enjoy reading all the feed back, but please, If you are complaining about another poster, Please Put down their name so we know who you are yelling about. Im sorry MJ Died, I enjoyed his misic & his dancing. But he had alot of people around him, that I'm afraid, were also using him. But thanks to Video we can still enjoy his talent for years to come.

**Reason, Jun 30 at 10:17 AM**
None of you people know what really happened with MJ and the accusations against him. Celebrities are targets for big payouts and often it's easier to just pay the accusers than to fight them and deal with all the negative publicity. Clearly the public will believe the worst regardless of the truth. None of you posting has all the facts and yet this man has been found guilty in the public eye. This is a perfect example of how a little knowledge is dangerous. I have to admit that I have wondered about him, and if he really is innocent of the charges, then it is truly a shame. I cannot imagine being accused of something so horrible and having to live with it as an innocent. It would haunt me, and therefore I will not judge him without having all the facts. For someone as uniquely gifted as he was, he spent a lot of time trying to make or buy his own happiness... how unbelievably sad. Rest in peace MJ.

**Randy, Jun 30 at 10:25 AM**
Where has Debbie Rowe been all this time and why has she not been involved in the kids' lives? Also did Michael Jackson impregnate Ms. Rowe or was she impregnated by other means. It appears that the children bear no genetic resemblence to Mr. Jackson prior to his appearance change in the 1990s. And we know that physical attributes of one's off-spring certainly comes forth whether it is skin color, hair texture, etc.

**honeez, Jun 30 at 10:26 AM**
"MARS" Michael was a just a man michael jackson was
not our messiah !!!! Jesus already died for our sins, its a done deal!!!! are you insane mars????

**Maria, Jun 30 at 10:30 AM**
I have to admit that I was one of those who thought he was guilty of child molestation, but I changed my mind after watching many interviews in recent days. I think he was just a man/child who really loved kids - and some money hungry parents saw him as their meal ticket. They had to coach their kid to lie in court, and the kid couldn't remember what to say. The first family who got $20,000,000 opened the door. He paid them off to get rid of them so he could get on with his life, never imagining others would do the same. Remember, he was found not guilty in that incident. They were, and are, disgusting human beings and I thank God they didn't get a nickel - and had to pay for an attorney on top of it. I can't imagine growing up in the spotlight like he did, with a very mean and strict father who saw his children as his way to cash in on a lavish life for himself. By the way - all of you kids on vacation hanging out on your computers - GO OUTSIDE AND PLAY.

**Liz D., Jun 30 at 10:39 AM**
Decades of drug abuse is probably what weakened his heart and caused his death.
I can just imagine what this funeral is going to look like.
That's what is holding it up, they're lining up the entertainment for the "event". ACK
His father is a disgrace, his son wasn't even dead that long before he's before the cameras promoting himself and his newly formed company, and the great entertainers he's recently signed up.

**Carolyn, Jun 30 at 10:42 AM**

All he wanted to do was sing and dance. It is not easy to go on stage and be so popular. Let's just look for the good in him for a change. He never hurt anyone. He had a gift and we were lucky enough to have been able to have him entertain for his and bring us his music. There is so much negativity and now he cannot fight it any longer. That was the problem. I believe you can turn to the Dr. for this. I think he did a great job protecting his children from the media as he knows what they can do. Michael looked great in his last rehersal pictures. He still had the "Michael stance." He was Michael Jackson "the performer. Thanks Michael.

**Bill, Jun 30 at 10:49 AM**

Michael was a great entertainer. I don't judge people I don't know personally. Some of Michaels troubles can be traced directly to his father. This young man had no childhood. I was looking at an interview the news was doing with Joe Jackson he didn't look too broken up about his sons death. He was smiling. I guess he was thinking about all the money he will be getting from Michaels Memorabilia. I'm sure when it is his turn to go no one will miss him.

**Nana6, Jun 30 at 10:56 AM**

It's a shame that when Micheal Jackson was alive that he didn't feel the public's love as it's being showed now! If he was not guilty as the courts did acquit him, then why didn't the public embrace him with this love when he was alive? I am a believer in God and do believe that he did things that where unGodly. But it is not my right to Judge a human for what was done on Earth. Only God judges! I feel sorry for the family's loss and for his Children loss and pray that God give's his mercy on his sole and offer's him the right's to enter the Heaven above. God' be with you "Micheal". And the Jackson family!

**vanessa, Jun 30 at 10:59 AM**

ANY DEATH IS SAD, BUT YOU ALL ARE TALKING LIKE YOU KNEW HIM PERSONALLY! i BET NONE OF YOU WERE TALKING KINDLY OF HIM A FEW YRS AGO WHEN HE HAD MOLESTATION CHARGES FILED AGAINST HIM. YES HE IS DEAD LET IT GO MOVE ON, HES NOT THE FIRST HE WONT BE THE LAST TO DIE.

**Lola, Jun 30 at 11:00 AM**
Oh, please, bury the man. I am so sick of hearing about him. He is dead, thank god. His children are safe now. I won't miss him. He is not Elvis or God. Just bury the mf and let us get on with good television.
You are right, I will miss Billy Mays much more.

**Regina G., Jun 30 at 11:11 AM**
I can't stand that celebrity reporter, who is doing nothing but sensationalizing the death of MJ. This smug bitch has made her a career on dogging MJ. For her to say, she is so concerned about his kids, and then suggest to the supposed sperm donor of these kids, to come forward, to collect some of MJ money for support, is heartless and completely irresponsible. She hates MJ, calling him an drug addict. MJ is not the only celebrity to have taken drugs, but she just won't let up, giving lurid details of his body, his weight, his peach fuss on his head. Calling him pitiful. No she is the pitiful one, because her whole pathetic existence is to trash MJ. Get a F****** Life.

**Michi, Jun 30 at 11:14 AM**
I will miss Michael Jackson dearly! He was my idol, and not only was he a great entertainer, he did a lot for charities, did ya know he did the most charity, than any other celebrity! He had a bad childhood growing up, and he also, stated he was very lonely!! So no one should state; "move on" how insensitive, and uncaring some people up here can be, the ones that say move on must be very jealous, and cold-blooded, you stupid ass jerks! ! ! ! I love Michael Jackson, and my heart goes out to his family; especially his mother, and kids! ! I WILL MISS YOU SOOO MUCH MICHAEL!!!!!!!!!!!

**Donna, Jun 30 at 11:26 AM**
All of your negative comments are sick, all of you have skeletons in your closet, my view is Michael Jackson was great, entertain all his life and did a damn good job at that. I grey up with Michael, the summer they made ABC , the world was in an uproar about it. All your people with your negative remarks are probably youngsters that don't recognize music when you hear it. The Jacksons are going through thier grief, be kind, be nice, because you are going to have yours to go through, and I'm sure

that you won't get any recognition like he has. If your can't say anything nice don't say anything at all. RIP Michael.....

**Cat, Jun 30 at 11:33 AM**
I liked his music when he was black!

**Nancy, Jun 30 at 11:37 AM**
Can't help but wonder what Michael's contributions might have been had he not been saddled with having to live under the weight of all these allegations.
As far as that's concerned, as the mother of three children, had one of my children been molested, no cash amount would have "settled" it. I can't think of a parent that feels differently. I think these charges were drummed up by oportunistic adults willing to sacrifice their childrens integrity for a large payday.
Michael, I'm sorrry this world couldn't provide a better forum for your talent. Perhaps the next world will.

**John, Jun 30 at 11:39 AM**
Michael Jackson did have talent. He could sing,... and he could dance. But he had to be a total idiot when it comes to common sense? Did he receive any education at all? You wouldn't think so by the way he acted, and spent money. I can only hope that his assets will be confiscated to pay back at least a part of the debts he owes.

**liz, Jun 30 at 11:41 AM**
They were doing an interview on CNN with someone right after he died, and the person was asked something along the lines of "Why did Michael like children so much?" He said he had asked Michael the same question and he replied "Because they're the only people who will tell me the truth."
There is a lot of truth in that statement, and people don't need to think he was some sort of freak. He was a very talented man, but he never had a childhood. That is probably why he was the way he was. I don't believe he molested anyone. The one boy said his father made him say the molestation took place, and it was a way out of the poor house for his family.
Judge not, lest ye be judged.

**Fred, Jun 30 at 11:43 AM**
If millions of people find this pathetic guy somehow worth idolizing, there is not much hope for us. Except for the"smell" of money, he would have been just another street gutter creature.

**Denizio, Jun 30 at 12:00 PM**
Death; great career move

**Deb, Jun 30 at 12:03 PM**
I think its a shame that since MJ has died poor Farrah's death has been pretty much forgotten.

**Boatdog, Jun 30 at 12:07 PM**
New record deal with his Doctor is coming soon.
"Waco Jocko won't be Backo" takes 30 minutes to boot-up and then plays "Killer"

**punkie71657, Jun 30 at 12:19 PM**
Michael died on Thursday, June 25. He has been dead for 5 days. Why have they not buried him or announced funeral plans? It take black people for ever to bury their loved one's. White's bury their loved one's in 2 to 3 days. When is his funeral?Catherine is a nice lady but she is to old to be raising children. She will be 80 on her birthday. The court should award them to their biological white mothers. Maybe the kids can have a normal life. I like Michael when he was younger before the plastic surgery, bleached white-skin and the Mexican hair implant. Best of luck to his family. Janet Jackson will file for bankrupt as she take on Michaels financial burden.

**Metal Tiger, Jun 30 at 12:29 PM**
I'm not a big MJ fan, but I have to credit his success as a performer. Sadly, however, he fell victim to his own success, and probably didn't listen to any counciling from anyone who cared enough about him to try and help. Alot of entertainment giants vall victim to themselves. Ozzy Osbourne should have been dead for years (NOT that I would ever wish that upon him, don't get me wrong), and is still cranking out music...sort of. Michael should have tried to rein himself in, but couldn't for whatever reasons. It's

a shame, because he probably could have done bigger and better things than he did accomplish if he had. However, R.I.P., Michael.

**ladywiccan47, Jun 30 at 12:35PM**
You must admit he was a great entertainer, but he did lead a weird life. Showing up for court in his p.j.'s didn't really help. Didn't like the man, wouldn't walk across the street to see him walk backwards on the stage or grab his privates

**bobby, Jun 30 at 12:36 PM**
question are you people out of your freggen minds he lived he died just as we will you would think he was god instead of a singer, dancer, ----child molester

**Lindsay L., Jun 30 at 12:44 PM**
Hey Freaks, I'm next....and by the way..."Billy Mays was Addicted to OxyClean, not OxyContin..."

**PEACE, Jun 30 at 12:55PM**
As they say, your words are a manifestation of what is inside you, and continuing to speculate (you don't know the truth) and spew venom only reveal that you are hurting inside. Seek to find out what it is in your own life that you need to resolve, and refrain from speculating and spewing venom against others for what goes around comes around, your turn will surely come, judge not lest you be judged, remember God is the ultimate judge, and, in case no one told you, you are not God.

**Wofman, Jun 30 at 12:55PM**
What a circus. Now they are going to try to blame the Doctor Murry in Michaels death as if nobody in his family knew he was taking drugs. This guy was on performance and precription drugs for many years. Michael Jackson turned into another Hollywood Excess Nut Case as so many of them do This man was not happy with himself as he thought he could be another Elvis that is why he had to marry the kings daugther and dumb ass Al Sharpton and now Jesse Jackson family spokeperson should have all stayed home to stir the pot. The only ones I feel sorry for is Michaels kids--------------The Wolfman-----------------

**lUCKY, Jun 30 at 01:00 PM**
kEEP IT CLEAN AND KEEP IT REAL!, YOUR DEATH CALL MIGHT JUST BE A MINUTE AWAY. SO TAKE THE TIME TO REFLECT OVER YOUR LIFE AND ASK YOURSELF WHAT COULD YOU HAVE DONE BETTER THAN MICHEAL DID, AND GO DO IT BEFORE IT'S TOO LATE. MAY HIS FAMILY AND FRIENDS BE BLESSED BY HIS PASSING, BECAUSE HE WOULD NOT WISH OTHERWISE FOR ANY ONE. IT IS NO EASY STREET LIVING IN THE PUBLIC EYE. DONT WORRY HIS DEBTHS WILL BE PAID, BECAUSE HIS NAME WILL NEVER DIE THE WAY HE DID. PEACE TO HIS LOVE ONES NOW AND ALWAYS.

**PEACE, Jun 30 at 01:05PM**
MICHAEL, WE DEEPLY MISS YOU! Our loss is unfathomable and we are overcome with grief, but we take comfort in knowing that you can truly REST IN PEACE now, forever surrounded by all the love and happiness that you deserved while you were with us. Feel the outpouring of all the love from this Universe to you now, though much too late! WE LOVE AND THANK YOU FROM THE BOTTOM OF OUR HEARTS for being here for us over five memorable decades, generously giving to our needy, talking to us through your music and videos, and bringing us joy and happiness during our youth and the various stages of our lives, even as you endured undue persecution. As your mission on earth, you became an inextricable part of our lives all across this planet to deliver a message from above that will live on in all your music and videos, from generation to generation, until the end of time. WE WILL ALWAYS REMEMBER YOU...YOU WILL LIVE IN OUR HEARTS FOREVER!

**Mary, Jun 30 at 01:07 PM**
So sorry for Michael's mom. A10 million drug bill at one drug store WOW how many drugs did this poor boy take. A body weight of 110 lbs.

**Maxine M., Jun 30 at 01:09 PM**
I'm 84 and I've enjoyed listening to many songs by Michael. He was such a handsome young man before he decided on all the plastic surgery but that didn't affect his singing. I'm concerned about his children; I'm

sure their grandmother will give them a lot of love and tender care. Hopefully, she will tell some of the "hanger-oners" to take a hike, e.g., Jesse Jackson and many others. We Christians need to pray for the family and especially the children.

### Rahmel, Jun 30 at 01:13 PM
He is loved by blacks and white an its a dam shame that you didn't know that lets not make this a black and white issue admit it you'll never be as great as he was hater RIP MJ

### PEACE, Jun 30 at 01:18 PM
Michael Jackson's ENORMOUS TALENT gave the world a glimpse of GOD'S INFINITE GREATNESS!

### Turk, Jun 30 at 01:19 PM
The "man" was a walking freak show who molested little boys.

### Christina, Jun 30 at 01:24 PM
My heart goes out to Farrah Fawcett's family and Michael Jackson's family. It just goes to show you that we don't last forever on this earth. We should love one another and take life as it comes day by day. Live it well and treat people good because you will be judge one day in heaven. So think about that when you are saying bad things about people. Only god can be the judge of us.

### PEACE, Jun 30 at 01:33 PM
Michael Jackson passed away while he was working hard at what he enjoyed doing, preparing for his comeback to bring joy and happiness to his fans. But God works in mysterious ways as He granted Michael the GREATEST COMEBACK of all: Michael Jackson's music and videos are now playing ALL AROUND THE WORLD, bringing His message from above along with eternal joy and happiness to the entire planet! Listen to the message in his songs! Michael, your mission on earth has been accomplished supernaturally, way beyond your wildest dreams! You can truly REST IN PEACE now, forever surrounded by all the love and happiness that you deserved while you were with us. WE DEEPLY MISS YOU...WE WILL ALWAYS REMEMBER YOU... YOU WILL LIVE IN OUR HEARTS FOREVER!

# JULY 1, 2009
# WEDNESDAY

*Michael Jackson's last will is filed by attorney John Branca at Los Angeles County Courthouse. The guardianship of his three children is given to his mother, Katherine Esther Jackson, and Diana Ross is chosen as a successor guardian. Twenty percent of his fortune as well as twenty percent of money made after his death is to be allocated to unspecified charities. Contrary to previous news reports, the Jackson family officially states there will be no public or private viewing at Neverland. Plans for a public memorial for Michael Jackson are underway.*

**SherryP, Jul 01 at 12:36 AM**
"Oh baby give me one more chance, to show you that I love you...won't you please let me...back in your heart" (Michael Jackson's "I want you back") Fitting words for what he would be saying 30 years later in his life. You never left my heart, Mike. I know some of your fans abandoned you, but most of us did not. We've always been here, right by your side. And we knew that, whenever we call your name, you'll be there...with an unselfish love and respect for us. Whenever we need you, you'll be there... God love you and keep you. Thank you for sharing the precious soul that God lent to you for such a short time...

**Chuck, Jul 01 at 12:47 AM**
I have met Dolly on a couple of occasions, and she is as real and sincere as she appears here and on television. She also gives one hell of a concert herself. I never embraced MJ's music, and always thought he was just plain strange, but if Dolly thinks he was wonderful, then I trust her

completely. I don't even want to contemplate what this planet will lose when she leaves us. It's too horrible to think about.

### MsLelav1, Jul 01 at 02:56 AM
I would like to say that MJ willl missed and I send out my regards to the family. The only problem I have now is that why we as his fans did not honor him before this sad time. The old saying "GIVE ME MY FLOWERS WHEN I CAN SEE AND SMELL THEM". He will never be forgotten and he has made a difference in the world today. R.I.P. We luv uLady V....

### Jithints, Jul 01 at 06:29 AM
The king is dead.The living legend have passed away. Cant believe his death. There is none in this world to replace him. HE WAS THE GOD. WE WILL NEVER FORGET U.

### Herculeswv, Jul 01 at 10:52 AM
This is a great top ten list, but where is the heart wrenching "She's Out of My Life"? That one tears me up. Billie Jean is my all time favorite b/c I can't listen to it w/out picturing the infamous moonwalk that I watched in amazement when I was in the 6th grade. I am also very fond of "Dirty Diana" b/c it was one of the few times that he looked very sexy to me.............no disrespect intended about his looks. BTW, that's an aspect of his life that fascinated me just as much as the general population, but I have decided to focus on his God given talent instead of what we considered to be his oddities & indescretions. I can not judge for I didn't live his life.............a life void of a childhood.............one that was frought w/ abuse. I can only pray that he found peace and comfort and that he knows that he single handedly changed the culture of pop music. Thanks for pumping my heart, touching my soul and enlightening my mind.

### scooter, Jul 01 at 11:58 AM
Instead of bitching about peoples spelling why don't you get off your fat ass and do something about the schools that taught us to spell this way. Other wise let us say our peace without all the BS.

### Tradeatoz, Jul 01 at 12:05 PM
Socrates was poisoned and Jesus was crucified again on Thursday June

25th 2009.....nothing has changed in thousands of years....but God has not given up hope...he will continue to send his Sons again and again....

**Michael123, Jul 01 at 01:25 PM**
Michael Jackson has broken Billboard chart records! He has captured 9 of the top 10 spots in the Top Pop Catalog Albums chart. Amazing, right? Read the full story at to find out more about the incredible feats Michael has accomplished after his death.

**harry, Jul 01 at 01:52 PM**
I will always love you Michael!

**Philip, Jul 01 at 02:39 PM**
What about Farrah Fawcett and Ed McMahon? Where are their covers? Always Overshadowed by Michael!!! Tsk......

**Lana, Jul 01 at 02:56 PM**
Deep, cleansing breaths, Phillip. Can you honestly say that Farrah and Ed had the same impact on popular culture as Michael Jackson? I don't think so.

**rest in peace mike, Jul 01 at 02:38 PM**
let mike rest in peace. dont throw dirt on a deceased man's name unless his name is hitler or bin laden (my spelling is probably wrong). mike changed music and music video forever, the greatest musically ever to do it. da kid allegations were disturbing, but was proven in the court of law?? no. allegations were dismissed due to lack of evidence. ANYBODY THAT LIVED THE LIFE MICHEAL DID (BEGINNING TO END), WOULDNT HAVE EM ALL EITHA.

**Robert, Jul 01 at 03:00 PM**
To the people who are complaining about Farrah not having a cover: While Farrah impacted pop culture and will never be forgotten, she only was a impact in the 70s. While, Michael "The king of pop" was an impact in the 60s,70s,80s,90s,00's. So I do think he does ever cover he is on.

**Nancy, Jul 01 03:36 PM**
Michael Jackson was a humanitarian....He has donated MORE THAN

300 000 000 DOLLARS to charity. Media Never mention that...His songs say more than enough about what he stood for, songs like Man in the mirror, heal the world, and we are the world came from his heart.. This man where so unfairly treated by the media and people who wanted his money. He worked so hard to help children and the poor. Nobody can ever take his place. He is not just an artist but a humanbeing who where too naive and sweet for this world. We love you Michael and we miss you more than words can describe. The world where a better place when you where here with us. I feel so sad for MJ, he always cared about people's opinions of him.He wanted ppl to know the true MJ so badly he practically begs for our understanding in his song childhood.He owed us nothing, but gave us his all.Truly an amazing person I can't blame God for calling him.Such a good person who only wanted to make the wold a better place.This world was so cruel to him it hurts my heart to know how much pain he had to endure, but he never once Complained. NOT ONCE! He never stopped doing good to others. I just can't stop crying, this is so sad and my heart is broken. Why did the world take him for granted? Does anybody understand that we lost a national treasure? A man that was unique, he was so kind down to earth and shy..Fame never changed him.He was too good and sweet for this world. We will NEVER hear ore see this kind of talent again.HE IS GONE FOR EVER and that's why I am so sad.I wish I could have seen him happy and top of the world where he deserved to be before he left this world. He had just turned 50 and he should have been celebrated with the biggest party in music history. Instead he was at home alone with his kids. Nobody cared about him when he was alive.. Sony and Tony Motola can go F*# themselves they never stood by him when he needed them the most, but where always there when he was on top of the world. MICHAEL WHERE PROOVEN INNOCENT, but nobody cared about that. and the media just hyped up lies to sell magazines and earn money. WE MISS YOU MISS YOU MICHAEL ! He always dreamt about making charity called USA for Iraq, that would have been beautiful. Omg I am just bursting out in tears now. He was so unique, we love you so much. Thank you michael for everything you did for the world. OMG you where so unfair treated by the world. How could we have hurt you so much? We always took you for granted, and now we will never experience your presence and beauty again. You where the sweetes and most caring

soul! WE MISS YOU AND LOVE YOU ALWAYS PRINCE OF
PEACE KING OF MUSIC!!

**E.Blogger, Jul 01 at 04:52 PM**
Neato. I will look for my mangled copy (postman always squishes it thru
the mail slot). Poor Farrah is probably on page 30-something.
Anyone suffering from MJ news fatigue yet?

**crispy, Jul 01 at 05:08 PM**
Those of you who want all 4 covers can have my copy. I am sick of Michael
Jackson coverage. On the other hand, I'd rather see him than another
pointless Twilight cover.

**Awesome! Jul 01 at 05:36 PM**
Someone famous died, so let's exploit his death by making as much
money as possible from it! We'll offer 4 different covers of the dead
guy, and we'll be able to sell 4 times as many copies of our mag! (But we
shouldn't make more than 4 different covers, because people might start
to suspect it's nothing more than a cash grab...) Man, celebrity deaths are
amazing for business! I wish they'd die more often.

**Shannon, Jul 01 at 07:18 PM**
I'd introduce you to stupidity and ignorance, but it seems the three of
you are already well acquainted.

**No, Phil, Jul 01 at 07:24 PM**
You're not the only one who is disappointed a tribute to his prepubescent
boy diddling, dangling-babies-off-balconies wacko white person phase is
missing.

**BDB, Jul 01 at 07:24 PM**
I am seven years older than MJ and I can remember seeing THE
JACKSON FIVE for the first time on the tele. It is very hard to describe
my feelings when I first heard of his passing. I felt as if it was a family
member who had passed, where I think of them morning, noon and
night. I pray his children will have the support they need to cope. My
prayers are with the family and truly, especially, the kids. God Bless.

**John D. C., Jul 01 at 07:58 PM**
Didn't He Amend His Will Last Winter And Leave The Beatle's Songs To Paul McCartney.I Think The News Is Missing This Angle Of The Story.

**james, Jul 01 at 08:38 PM**
To the cook. Its obviously you aren't of African American descent and didn't grow up on michael jackson music. Also it's obviously apparent you aren't educated enough to use better language than you did. I pray for his family, and children. He will surely be missed by me and my friends. I am about his age. We dont know when we will die. I just thank god for his contribution of music in my life.

# JULY 2, 2009
# THURSDAY

*Debbie Rowe officially states she will fight for custody of Paris and Michael Jr., the children born during her marriage to Michael Jackson. Madonna salutes Michael at London's O2 Arena. The Material Girl gives an emotional tribute at the venue where Jackson was scheduled to perform 50 concerts. Thousands of people across the globe make arrangements to be at Jackson's memorial service at the Staples Center in Los Angeles, California on July 7, 2009.*

**Temeculadog, Jul 02 at 12:33 AM**
Michael Jackson on earth you did good, i hope on heaven you'll do better .God bless you and family...

**Brigi, Jul 02 at 12:50 AM**
No, I don't believe Micheal owed anyone. Micheal owned the Beatle Collection, and all his own dats and music. He was a brillant manager, especially of his own finances. But smart enough to put it in the hands of businessmen who also had people looking over their shoulders. Micheal knew what happens when you have to use prescriptions to manage pain; watching Elvis, he knew that he too would need experts in finances to take care of his money.He owned his own dats, music and recordings, and knew what would happen if he counted on watching over all that he owned himself. The White media, especially Diane Diamond, and the two foreign reporters who he gave interviews too, who ended up betraying him, hated him for all he was and all he was able to do. Especially being named by Guiness of World Records as the worlds most charitable giver.

Can you imagine that! The most charitable person in the World, and they targeted him, and tried to ruin him. A wonderful and sensitive man.

I understand what he meant about shareing your bed, and giving up what you have for someone else, but he made the mistake of forgetting that he was grown and you have to not let what you do have the perception of wrong! In a perfect world, yes, he could have let kids have his bed, and sleep on the floor, but in this wicked system we live in, where there is a pedofile on every corner, we have to be careful, and watch what we do, especially single people, like he was. Remember, he didn't go play and rough house with boys in his neighborhood, like the average boy is able to do, he had to put together his music.

He was a genius, and will be forever missed!

**By Stephanie, Jul 02 at 01:40 AM**
i w'll be de n'xt michael jackson

**Patricia, Jul 02 at 01:59 AM**
When my youngest daughter called me on Thursday to tell me that Michael Jackson had died I was working in an office where I prepare personal income taxes. I just yelled out, "Michael Jackson is dead!!!?"

I could not believe it and immediately started to cry. All the people in the office heard me, but I did not care I went into the break room to pull myself together as I still had about an hour and a half before I was off work. Just as I was getting myself together my second to the oldest daughter called and she just bawling about Michael. I started tearing up again, and once I was off the phone with her my oldest daughter called. She said she had to leave work because she could not concentrate. I finally got myself together and a few of us at my office started discussing Michael Jackson and his family. I was supposed to go to choir practice for my church that night, but I could not go. I was glued to the television trying to find out what happened to our "little Michael."

I am at this publishing a book where I got in trouble for writing down the words to the Jackson 5 hit I WANT YOU BACK. Although I never mentioned the Jackson 5 everyone who reads the book will know exactly who I am talking about. This is so sad. My two youngest daughters were truely infactuated by him. I bought them the glove, the jackets, the dolls and all the books, magazines and other MJ stuff.

The Enchantment of Michael Jackson began when he was just a little

boy. Many of us latched on to him at that time and we never let go. MICHAEL JOSEPH JACKSON truely was one of a kind. There will never be another like him. God broke the mold after MJ was born.
I just want to say What a Loss. OMG. To the family may God bless and keep you. Keep Michael in your memories and you will see him in your dreams. Patricia

**Rebecca, Jul 02 at 03:55 AM**
Ugh, this is the first I won't be looking forward to pulling EW out of my mailbox. I never thought I'd see such a cover. Not until paper was illegal and the magazine was sent electronically straight to our brains anyway. It's too soon!! Come back, Michael!!

**Bashir, Jul 02 at 04:21 AM**
I still unbelive it, I got shock when I heard this bad news, I was on Guru Party in Bangkok and someone told me so I left that party after 10 minute. Anyway, He was gifted from god to all music lover and he was the entertainer to take over the world and we would missed him dearly. we loved his music and dance. God bless him and may he rest in peace and leave all the negative news behind him and wish to hear positive news of his career forever lots of love to his family and god bless to his 3 sons, Any three of them at least one person be come as a Michael Jackson so my three daughter can enjoy jackson music in future. I loved Michael Jackson since child hood to the death and he is the legend of music and he is real King of Pop. I am going to put one nice photo in my room as momorial.

**ennelieze, Jul 02 at 04:42 AM**
forget chuck berry fred astaire michael. jackson kickeed their arses

**posted, Jul 02 at 05:20 AM**
Dear Michael, YOU inspired the world with your songs, dance and music literary and videos. I know you inspired me to groove like you... no-one understood the pain you have endured in your childhood and your attempts to recapture your second childhood - because you could! You did't aspire to mediocrity - you non-comformist; but the world laughed in ignorance. I see, hear, and cognitively taste your sensitive soul an empathic heart of a man. Your lyrics is the revelation to your soul,

your persona...YOU will surely be missed. The media is the grim ripper, the criminal element that drew you closer to the epiphany of loneliness. The corportate suit a brother to the media made attempts to disempower you of your worth and assets... A boy raised with strong christian values was misunderstood... May angels kiss your forehead and say goodnight while you rest...

**william, and lidia, Jul 02 at 05:21 AM**
The nurse who reported on national television that Michael Jackson requested her to administer Diprovan (propofol) violated the patient/ nurse relationship and should be admonished. Any discussion between a patient and his physician or other medical personnel is privileged, and yet she chose to go on television and disclose this information. A book cannot be far behind. It would have been more proper and professional for her to have reported this information to medical personnel who performed the autopsy and even law enforcement, and yet she instead chose to go on national television. That is not to say that this request was not made of her by Michael Jackson but she clearly violated the Privacy Act by disclosing this information on national television.

**Neris, Jul 02 at 05:43 AM**
i love him for the fact that he didnt live only for himself but for others, putting smiles on faces irrespectve of race.RIP

**o.j., Jul 02 at 05:51 AM**
YOU DONT BELIEVE HE OWED ANYBODY? IS THAT WHAT JUST CAME FROM YOUR HEAD? WOULD YOU LET SOMEONE TAKE YOUR PROPERT AND SELL OFF YOUR GOODS IF YOU COULD PAY THEM? WOULD YOU?...WHO IS THIS? IS THIS YOU GEORGE W? STOP PLAYING MAN!

**Cynthia, Jul 02 at 07:05 AM**
so sad..Michael..i grew up with your music, dance n your soul..how i to forget u!! U r the greatest human in the world..gudbye Kiss to u MJ.. R.I.P MJ..You r not Alone..LuV U..

**Neeracha P, Jul 02 at 08:01 AM**
MJ the greatest singer known. from generation to generation we will miss you.

**Rita, Jul 02 at 08:11 AM**
It is so ironic seing Michael surrounded of black people when he didn't want to be black himself. He disfugured himself trying to be white.

**Nosi, Jul 02 at 09:31 AM**
i really can't get why he changed the colour of his skin but i do admire him and loved him to bits, he is trully an icon and forever will be missed. Rest In Peace MJ, you have finished your race.regards,

**E, Jul 02 at 09:34 AM**
He was actually called big-nose by his dad all the time and was called ugly and was verbally and physically abused. He also clearly has a skin disease (I know several people who were once dark like he was and is now light as he has gotten). Michael didn't have an issue with being black, he was just mentally wounded that, no matter what color he was, told that he was hideous when he was a beautiful child. The other brothers and sisters have gotten nose jobs and other things done. I believe that they wre mentally weighed on.

**spud, Jul 02 at 09:40 AM**
You know, for some of us, the passing of Michael Jackson caused no more of a blip in our lives than the passing of our mom's plumber. Not because of the allegations or controversy, but because he was just a man and entertainer, and all the things we profess to love about him were committed to tape years ago. a few weeks ago, no one (in the US, at least) was excited about future Michael Jackson music or performances. But no wthat he has died, we get all of this coverage of "What a Loss!" when most everyone, even his fans, had already written him off. So, even more coverage and tributes and special issues are a waste of time. I only hope this is considered a bonus issue, and not part of our regular subscription.

**Lynda, Jul 02 at 10:08 AM**
If you scroll through all his pictures, you can see that he was always

willing to smile, give hugs to his fans. You never saw him Spit/nudge/ hit or even go crazy like Britney Spears or any other celebrity that take physical rage against the media. He was recollected and didn't show signs of a aggression towards anybody. He was a BEAUTIFUL human being regardless of what the world may think of him. He was UNIQUE, no one can do what he did. The media will either make you or break you and what did he do, he wrote songs. He was creative, like a painter. Wrote songs to tell the world how he was feeling and what he thinking. Remember NO ONE in this world is perfect, NO ONE! So before you start writing nasty, disrespectful things about him or anyone, look at yourself first. Because the EVIL in you is quick to judge, listen to his song: CHILDHOOD and you will understand how he was feeling. He wanted love and peace. RIP Michael

**Brigi, Jul 02 at 11:45 AM**
That's not true. We will never really know what made him do what he did to his appearance, other than what he told us! He said because of his father's words about his nose, and not getting it from his side (Joseph's) of the family! He made those comments on Oprah years ago during an interview with her. Even though he changed his appearance, we could still enjoy and love his showmanship, and musicality. Think of it that way, instead of breaking him down to color and race please!!!
Or just shut up about him altogether, maybe?

**F.N, Jul 02 at 11:52 AM**
BRIGI!!!! u r so,so,so,very RIGHT!!!! BLESSING to U and the JACKSON family--to all GOOD and FAIR minded PEOPLE

**Dee, Jul 02 at 12:04 PM**
I think Michael Jackson is addicted to drugs to help him remove his pain, or to make him "feel better", whether mentally or physically. But in order for him to get those drugs that he wanted, he needed the doctor's authorised prescription. As for that Doctor Murray, I think he must have been ecstatic to be hired as Michael's personalized doctor as he would be paid handsomely. And Michael must have begged that doctor to let him have those drugs that he needed. And I guess that because Doctor Murray wanted to keep his well-paid job as his personal doctor and was afraid that he would lose this job if he didn't prescribe those drugs

to Michael, he therefore relented and gave him those drugs to prevent being sacked from his job and to keep Michael happy. My next question is, who is the one who administered those lethal drugs to Michael? Was it Michael himself or any other person/doctor?

**Claudia, Jul 02 at 02:46 PM**
Michael, You can now fly like Peter Pan! Finally! God Bless you Thank you for many years of excellant showmanship and music I will treasure forever!

**Amberly, Jul 02 at 03:03 PM**
I am a victim of sexual abuse and I don't believe Michael was a sexual abuser. Of course I don't know, but his character was not that of a violator. He may have been delusional when he was trying to recapture his youth, but he was not cocky about the subject, as molesters usually are. During that hardest time of my life ironically, he was my positive and music found me and vice ver.You people are so %at!*#ing rude,!!!rest in perfect peace Michael.
And for those who are judging just remember you are not God and your judgement day is coming so watch what you say and how you treat others because you never know when your time is up.

**1HotMama, Jul 02 at 03:08 PM**
I need to add, not that all molesters display a cocky attitude only, but they don't plea to not be judged innaccurately and claim they would NEVER hurt a child. Molesters don't care that much and they are too guilty to speak. This accusation broke Michael. He may've been traumatized himself and a bit lost, but that was the weakness the vultures honed in on. JUST like moles

**Bess, Jul 02 at 03:55 PM**
Missed his live show~~now they'll do the dead show!!! Just get it over and done!

**CRISTIAN, Jul 02 at 04:06 PM**
What a grate loss to the world... This guy is so so good in what he knows how to do best. I am from Nigeria, Wish i could get lessons from him on how to do the break dance stuff but he ain't no more. I wonna attend

the funeral but i don't have a visa. I love Michael so much, i wish this didn't happen. He is a Legend.. He is known all over the world. Maybe he should have left his normal skin... I really miss you Michael. I don't think we members of this world can ever get someone like you again. You are the BEST. RIP Michael, we love you.....

**N Larry, Jul 02 at 04:17 PM**
I grew up in Chicago at about the same period as the Jacksons. Growing up like most kids listening to the radio, buying records, 45s and later albums you had no way of knowing that a legend one day he would become. I for one felt like I lost a family member and I have lost several. His financial matters and legal problems are no different than any personality most have them

**Jane, Jul 02 at 04:35 PM**
Wouldn't Michael's family want to keep his home a private sanctuary for themselves, his children and friends? Hasn't he been exploited enough? It's time to let go & treasure all he gave us when he was alive. Turning his private home into a money making machine does not honor him in any way.

**babysmomma, Jul 02 at 06:51 PM**
Okay,so I really think that not only was Jackson the king of pop but he was a living legend. I'm only 17 years old but you give me any Jackson song and I'll sing it. But i'm not going to lie he did look like a bit of a creeper because of all of the surgerys. He should have stopped after the first nose job, he went to far with the bleached skin and everything else he did. I know he wasn't a pedo because the main reason he had the neverland ranch was because he was living the childhood that his dickhead of a father never let him have. So you people that are going to post ignorant #$!?at about him should just back off and give the man a break. R.I.P. Michael Jackson, gone but never forgotten.

**Carl, Jul 02 at 06:58 PM**
without Quincy Jones Michael Jackson his brothers sisters and father and mother they most likely never left Gary Indiana,the unimpresed kids songs they sing nobody remembers now and he be alive today looking like his brothers,normal ,hefty and full of life.

**Rita411, Jul 02 at 08:48 PM**

As for everyone who has something to say to the effect that Michael Jackson worth has declined they are a liar! Heck he's worth more dead then alive now!!!!! As for all thoes people that handle the trust of his estate! If the family knows like I know they all should be fired and start all over from the gut! Maybe that'll work in there favor

He was a great man, endowed with greatness and amazing skills, no matter what bad thing might have happened in the course of his race, the ultimate is that he lived not only for himself,but also for others putting smiles on faces irrespective and for that i will always love him. rest in peace!

**Jules, Jul 02 at 08:51 PM**

Mary, darling, it's spelled F-A-R-R-A-H. Michael Jackson was a pedophile who died of a drug overdose. His toxicology report will make Elvis' look puny in comparison. He was in rehab at least 3 times; the time he came into court in pajamas he was in withdrawal. At least he's sleeping in the ground now, and can't touch any more children (none of his children have his DNA or Debbie Rowe's DNA). Where did he get them? Yes, he was talented. So was Ted Bundy.

**Jules, Jul 02 at 08:58 PM**

Melanie: is that why Jackson settled out of court for MILLIONS to pay off two boys (now men), to avoid a court trial? Yes, he touched children. Was holding hands with his last accuser in the Martin Bashear documentary. Holding hands (which the boy seemed uncomfortable with), as he said "Sharing your bed with another person is the most loving

**Tamika, Jul 02 at 09:22 PM**

may ALLAH be with You Michael always

# JULY 3, 2009
# FRIDAY

*Fans around the world, united by Michael Jackson's extraordinary musical influence, gather in events ranging from a mass moonwalk in London and a tribute at the Walk of Fame in Los Angeles to vigils in Paris and Tokyo.*

**thegoodgood, Jul 03 at 02:44 AM**
what a losssssssssssssssssss, still cant believe it! i hear u music everyday now.. we want you back, michael

**kalpana, Jul 03 at 09:32 AM**
I wish people would have listened to what you had to say rather than exploit you the way that they did. But, you kept your head high and continued on. For that, I envy you. It's amazing what people will do for money isn't it? You will always live on in your childrens heart and mine! It cracks me up that people made fun of you for having "Peter Pan" syndrome. Most of us have it, we just can't afford to act on it. They were all jealous. I look back at the memories of me dancing around with my red MJ jacket and zipper pants trying to break dance!!! You will surely be missed! RIP MJ

**Anonymous, Jul 03 at 09:47 AM**
.Cause hes gone, you want to listen to his music,a true and real fan will be playing his music all the time, God loves us all and he needed Mike TO DO HIS THING IN HEAVEN,,,,,,MAY GOD WATCH OVER HIS KIDS AND FAMILY, WE ALL NEED TO PRAY AND LOVE EACH OTHER.RIP MICHEAL JACKSON,,,

**Joe, Jul 03 at 12:27 PM**
Goodnight, sweet Prince
I remember the first time I saw the video for Thriller, and playing the Michael Jackson video game for Sega. Goodbye my friend.

**MJ fan, Jul 03 at 12:30 PM**
The Only King of Pop
We'll miss you "Moonwalker" hope you find real peace

**Cynthia, July 03 at 12:30 PM**
♥Michael Jackson the King of Love♥
I believe the reason for such an out-pouring of love and salutations is because there has never been an artist who so deeply, and genuinely, cared about people, earth and love - Didn't matter if you were Black or White... Pink or Green. He's the type of person that knew his image was able to touch others and move us with his song, dance and love into a better world. Through his ground-breaking genius dance moves, lyrics and soft voice and soul, he was able to bring generations and races together as one...even if it were just to dance! Michael's price for fame was even a debt he could not cover...his loss of life. I'm proud of his courage to show himself to the world when the monster-media would try to abuse and accuse him of nothing but evil. Just like Joseph, they could throw their punches, but not stifle his innocence and joy of life. I'm so thrilled for him to have become a father...and be a father....and be able to give his gifts of love to his children a way a father's love can only touch them... in their heart and soul. Forever Michael will be moon-walking in my heart and spirit. I'm honored to be able to just get a mere sparkle of his stardust into my life.
Sweet dreams and peaceful eternity awaits you now.
God has his son, and we have his melody to live onward.
EYES UP!

**mat, Jul 03 at 12:30 PM**
jackson the man behind us all
pousonally i dont think it matters who you are where u come from or what u believe in i think everybody in one way or another has heard of micheal jackson.
he was the greatest artist to ever grace the music buissness he devoted

his life to his fans and the world if more people had even an ounce of the passion micheal had the world would be an amazing place he was an will always be the greatest most magical performer on earth
god bless micheal jackson the entertainer,the musician and the human being .
you will be missed forever RIP Micheal Jackson
you willNEVER be forgotten

**amelia armstrong, Jul 03 at 02:01 PM**
Dear Lou,
   Thank you for the opportunity to share with you some unique information about Michael Jackson.
   First I want to establish my credibility by stating I have a law degree (Albany Law School, 1987). I also am a writer, was a stage dancer for years, and am now a psychic. Shortly after NY Governor Eliot Spitzer was politically assassinated in 2006, I sent readings to him and his wife, Silda. In VANITY FAIR'S recent interview, his remark about "wise counsel" was a reference to me. However, this piece is about Michael Jackson, not Eliot Spitzer.
   Currently I am writing a book about Reincarnation, and other unusual spiritual topics, which will include the following excerpt:
   Knowing who Michael Jackson was in a past life sheds enormous light on this mythical and extraordinary icon's bizarre behavior, unusual character and appearance, and why the world should rejoice and feel blessed. Because it's unlikely we'll ever see anyone like him again.
   Michael Jackson was the reincarnation of the Ancient Hellenistic King, Caesarion, the controversial love-child produced by the three month affair between Julius Caesar, Rome's triumphant, uncrowned King, and Cleopatra, the famously exotic Oueen of Egypt. During his eventful side trip to Northern Africa, heralded in film, theatre and literature, the world's most powerful general took a break to travel in luxury on Cleopatra's gold-gilt barge, cruising down the Nile River with her accompanied by 400 armed Roman ships and service boats.
   Born about one year later in 46 BC, Caesarion was spurned, even loathed, by Rome's powerful rising elite, who refused to accept him as Caesar's heir apparent, and emperor, of their burgeoning, muscle-bound

new empire, following the historically famous assassination on the Ides of March in 44 BC.

Thus as a young child, pursued by sinister, untrustworthy legions, families and friends, who vehemently turned on each other in their lust for power, Caesarion and his star-crossed mother found themselves thrust onto the strife-torn shoals of the violent and bloody civil wars enflaming both Rome and Egypt at that critical juncture.

Ruthlessly persecuted for nearly fifteen years, eventually Caesarion was caught and brutally killed, probably with poison, along with his mother, Cleopatra, who fled Rome and returned to Egypt. Caesarion and his half-brother by Marc Antony, the Roman general whom Cleopatra seduced in her need for protection, were survived by their sister, Cleopatra Cilene, who quietly disappeared into the annals of history. Thus with the ignominious deaths of Cleopatra and her two young sons, three thousand years of fabulous Egyptian dynastic rule and civilization, unprecedented wealth and human history, were brought to a somber close, officially ending in 30 BC with the poignant demise of the reigning Queen Cleopatra, who was 39-years-old.

During the years Cleopatra and her royal brood were on the lam, treacherously hunted by the armed militaries of two powerful and competing Mediterranean empires, calling her "that ruinous monster," Julius Caesar's hand picked successor, Augustus Caesar, fought vigorously to deliver Rome out of the chaos and violence into which it descended after the legendary emperor's murder.

Still a child, Caesarion's premature death at the hands of the Romans, who cruelly cut him down at the tender age of 14, prevented him from enjoying childhood, or ever growing up, for that matter. One can only speculate about how difficult and frightening his foreshortened youth and stressful childhood were, Caesarion constantly demanding to know from his desperate, royal mother, a calculating and resolute woman as well:

"Why ...why do they want to kill me? My father was the king ....Now I'm the king!"

With the sting of rebuke and so much sadness stashed in his memory, harboring a lifelong fear of growing up, Michael Jackson (detect the parallel phonetics between "Michael Jackson" and "Caesarion") continued to plead his case with a similar lament upon experiencing another tough and painful childhood at the hands of his father in this lifetime, singing, "Have You Seen My Childhood?"

The trauma of his present life paralleling that of his past (new buds in springtime, we reincarnate with what were used to or familiar with and grow from there, another words, begin from where we left off) drove Michael Jackson's current love for children and celebration of childhood, as well as his paranoia about growing up. Remaining a man-child, his shyness, and haunting fear of strangers who again might want to poison him, drove him to wear surgical masks toward the end of his life, apparently finding himself surrounded again by those he couldn't trust. Building the estate he called Neverland Ranch, Jackson strove to create a safe haven and fantasy land for children who, like himself, wanted to avoid growing up for fear of what the would do to them, of which he was all too aware.

Michael's past life also helps to explain the unfortunate legal issues which arose over his curious urge to sleep with children. In his past life, as members of the royal Egyptian Ptolemie Family, the children clustered in bed together at night, for comfort and protection, as well as cultural reasons, a casual form of behavior he had grown accustomed to.

Perplexed when confronted with what to him was a normal, accepted practice, unabashed, Michael snapped, "What's wrong with sleeping with children? We're a family! It's a loving thing to do." Unfortunately, the modern world's conventional authorities and the country's moral police strongly disagreed, punishing him accordingly.

…Without delving too deeply into an explanation of Reincarnation, allow me to offer this simple metaphor for those unfamiliar with the concept:

Like snowflakes, we repeatedly precipitate or materialize out of Spirit, a realm of existence which overlays the physical one, dropping gently out of the heavens when conditions are right, such as they are for snowflakes in winter.

And like snowflakes, and here is the real miracle, each of us, one of several billion people alive on this planet, is unique. Our lives not as short lived as snowflakes, of course, nonetheless, when our allotted time is up, our bodies "melt away," our essence or spirit reabsorbed back into the Spirit world, the Creator allowing us to experience numerous lifetimes on the physical plane in order to perfect ourselves.

Michael Jackson is only one of many reincarnated Ancient Kings and Queens living and working among us today, many of whom have married their Spirit Twins. In particular, Bill Gates, Bill Clinton and Jay Leno are Ancient Kings–Hellenistic, Roman and Celtic respectively–who've returned one last time in a final effort to complete their legacies. And Princess Diana? Stunningly beautiful and regal, she was an Ancient Egyptian Queen who came back briefly to teach us about Charity.

As Caesar's only natural born son, brutally murdered by the Romans, Caesarion was denied his birth right to rule as their new king and emperor. Thus when he came back as Michael Jackson, successfully turning himself into an international icon, he finally earned the privilege, notoriety and power he knew was due him, and was his right, winning the admiration and accolades owed to someone holding the coveted title of "King."

Not a military king like his ancient father, but rather a musical one like his glamorous, artistic Egyptian mother, who was a dancer and singer as well. A celebrity regarded forever as the King of Pop, Jackson's appointed forum rightly became the international stage. But while Jackson may not fit the conventional image or stereotype of a king, as the natural born issue of his ancient royal father, Julius Caesar, he was, and continually strove to prove it, driving this crucial point home in his every presentation, up until the day he died.

And there are many similarities between Jackson and Caesar. One is that, as a gambler, Jackson constantly pushed the envelope, reflected in all of his dramatic expression–in his music–I'm Bad …Invincible … Dangerous ….Bloody–his showmanship, his appearance and his overall behavior–as he strove to take everything to the "next level."

Also like Caesar, Jackson was a benevolent, even generous man, with the unusual ability to bring people together. Exploiting this talent, Michael brought some of the most gifted artists in the music world together in a moving and memorable charity performance to help feed the starving hoards of Africa--recall the song, "We are the Children"-- arranging a similar event after 911, and another with Elizabeth Taylor to benefit AIDS victims.

Knowing who he was, and that he was a king, Michael's joie de vivre made him dance like he owned the world. Those working outside show business have no idea how much creative forethought and planning, physical preparation and labor, not to mention money, go into even a low budget production, making Michael a calculating, true showbiz genius.

And like the Ancient King Julius Caesar, Jackson's death is causing a phenomenal and powerful resurgence in his popularity, his memory, music, imagery and energy resonating around the world. And as the joyful celebration continues, there'll probably be sitings, because being a notorious prangster, Michael will hang around for a while, enjoyably watching us pay tribute to him.

But we really don't need to worry about Michael. Because in the process of claiming his right to be king, he wound up having a really great time.

\*\*\*\*\*\*\*\*\*

Copyright Armstrong 2009

Sincerely,
Amelia Armstrong., Psychic

### Margarita, Jul 03 at 02:26 PM
Michael thanks for all the wonderful memories.... You will always be alive in our hearts... Your music will live 4 always... There will never b any1 as AUTHENTIC as U!!!!!!!!! R.I.P MJ

### inkies, Jul 03 at 02:49 PM
Why don't you all just stop... I hope that you don't have to go through what this family is going through... No one knows if he really did what they say he did he was innocent as far as the jury went... He was a great singer and we should leave at that...
As for his children I think we should leave them out of it... I don't think that you would like your children in the middle of this...
Who ever gets the kids... I really do hope it is out of love and not money... Because they are going to need it without there dad...
God Bless the whole family my heart goes out to all of you...

### JC, Jul 3 at 03:12 PM
Michael you were a genius in your own right. You had a heart of pure gold a man who only wanted love and peace for the whole world. Your legacy will live on and the people who could not see what your life was

about will now look back and see you for who you were and that is a man full of humility and love. Rest in Peace my friend. You are now in a place of peace and love.

### Michale J., Jul 03 at 03:21 PM
I love michal jackson may his soul rest in peace michal is the best pop singer we always love you michal our prays are with you

### AarON J., Jul 03 at 03:39 PM
thank u MicHeal jackson for everything u have done for us u maded me think that everything would be alright when I listen'd to your music...I aaron jamison has 2 thriller jacket's..all ablums..signed albums by micheal him self..I remember when I was little and went to one of his concerts and he walked over and touched my hand...I made'd my own video to his song "who is it"...SO I'm HOpeing I can go to his veiwing to say good bye ..well really not good by cause I can just put a dvd in and see him again... well LOve U Micheal and your always in my heart

### Viv, Jul 03 at 03:44 PM
I think it is disgusting the media's still Calling Michael Jackson Jacko. The knickname was given to him as a insult he hated it. Cant you respect the dead? Even if you didn't like him you got to admit he one of the most talented performers we have seen since Elvis. Shame that some stoop this low to call him a name which is making fun of him

### bonnie, Jul 03 at 04:06 PM
I am one to believe that in life you should be respected for hell just being alive and one of God's creatures, purely respect is earned, granted, but I cannot believe that one can be so cruel and disrespectful of the passing of this great man, a man who surpassed Elvis, and for that fact "The Beatles", and trust me I loved them too. I listen to more Beatles songs than Michael Jacksons music, but collectively he out performed, out served humanity, and out lasted even the best of the best entertainment wise. You cannot deminish his talent, you cannot even come close to taking away all the good he did while alive, sure you can comment on his strange behavior but because you have not a clue as to what it is to be and Artist, a Genius, a Super Star in the midst of a den of wolves sucking your blood at every step, combine that with the sickness of Joe Jackson,

and the passive nature of Katherine Jackson, who allowed her husbands twisted influence on her children, there's no wonder why this great man-child left the earth in this fashion. Posters are getting sicker by the day, most are young and are devoid of old school mannerisms, common decent and moral standings. Note that, no matter what your beliefs are concerning Michael Jackson, his passing, his molestation "accussation", etc., you will never be able to erase who and what he was, and you will not be able to post enough negative and sick comments to change the minds of leagues of the millions of people who will always remember that little brown poor boy from Indiana, who made it to the top, stayed at the top, and would have retired at the top if he was allowed to make it through this tour. When you get the chance, look back at his life and works, look at his "Earth Song" video, look at his elastic, rubberband legs, take in his moves, and supreme artistry, then try to compare it to anyone you "think" was, or is great. You will not care to hear or see any performer sing, dance, or otherwise perform in the next few years let alone decades like you will Michael Jackson, there will be no one "ever" like him, like the Beatles, and there will be no more Kings, like Elvis, now sit your little lilly white asses down and absorb this message, suck it up, accept it and stay tuned for more coverage of MJ, more media vampiring, more lies, more disrespect etc., he will be the topic for months to come, and he will be missed......forever. How long will you be remembered after your gone, probably as long as it takes to read your posted comments!

**Cheshire, Jul 03 at 05:42 PM**
I have yet to cry about MJ's death until I read Mr.King's essay. his essay actually made me feel sorry for him

**Brenda, Jul 03 at 07:26 PM**
If the media is right, Michael supposedly owed $400 million dollars, BUT his estate is worth at least $500 million. By my calculations that would still leave $100 million dollars to the good. I could live with that.

**Julie, Jul 03 at 09:10 PM**
the king of pop also a legend that will always stay in our thoughts, RIP Micheal God bless his family.

**Earl, Jul 03 at 10:09 PM**
WELL,I BELEIVE THAT HE IS THE KING OF MUSIC AND
BETTER THAN ELVIS PRESLEY,ALSO WE MAY ALL BE SAD
NOW BUT YOU SHOULD KNOW THAT IT IS FOR THE BEST
THAT HE HAS GONE TO REST,RIP MJ.

**Jade, Jul 03 at 10:09 PM**
Give him his Props, and let him rest in peace.
Michael, did a lot ogf good things for people from his heart. But his
chilhood pain overshadowed his common-sense. He was multi-talented,
and a good human being. May God Bless him and keep him.

**Rockie11796, Jul 03 at 10:17 PM**
mj sucked balls big time and he is ugly in a gay stupid inconsiterit brat
and i hated him and so did alot of oter people and we all wished he would
go broke but we do feel bad for all the people that he owed money to and
the poor boy he raped and denied doing and got away with it poor kid
he sined alot if god wanted white he wouldnt put him on the earth black
and for raping that kid and then denieing it all then a week later it was
like no one care anymore and everyone forgot it even happened which
was a very bad thing and he did not go by the 10 emenments like "tho
shall not lie".and that is why i do not like

**Rockie11796, Jul 03 at 10:47 PM**
so my sister just posted a mean comment.shes just a big skinney meaniei
love michael jackson he wascute in the thriller video.he was a great singer
but not a good father.But i really want to know how he turned white.so i
really miss him and i know you do and if you don't you suck balls

# JULY 4, 2009
## SATURDAY

*The public outpouring of emotion in honor of Michael Jackson, of his music and ideals, continues across the globe. The world has not experienced a similar devotion since Princess Diana's death.*

**tag, Jul 04 at 06:57 AM**
EW was one of the rag mags that contributed to the "Jacko" reference and now they are going to make a fortune on his death.

**Atotha, Jul 04 at 02:34 PM**
Shame
It's such a shame that he is gone. He was so young, and was by far the best musician ever to live. Seriously how many musicians out there have had as many number 1 hits as Michael? What kills me is the fact that so many people had their go at him while he was alive, and now they have to live with that regret for the rest of their lives. I hope it eats at them for eternity.
RIP Michael, hopefully soon press and all will be out of your personal s***, and you can finally rest.

**alexandra, Jul 04 at 02:34 PM**
hero—goodbye my rose..

**alex, Jul 04 at 02:35PM**
W H Y ???

**Kemline, Jul 04 at 02:35PM**
Celebrating his life
I grew up knowing Michael as an artist, and the best artist till this day.
I loved everything he did, he had a great heart that shined through his
music. He will alwyas be remembered. To his family know that we share
in your greive, for Michael. Keep each other and God close to you in
these time of saddness he will help you through, he did it for me when
my sister passed and he will do it for you.

**fairyspring, Jul 04 at 02:39 PM**
I love you, Michael Jackson
His legend continues with the rest of the years, because he will live in our
hearts forever... He was shy, polite and so sweet. He was perfect!
I'll never forget him and his beautiful smile.
RIP my darling

**EB. Jul 04 at 02:39 PM**
it saddens me to know that the worlds greatest singer and entertainer
is no longer with us. my heart felt condolences go out to his family and
especially his children, his legacy will live on with them. He loved his
fans and we love him also. he will never be forgotten and he will always be
loved,respected and deeply deeply appreciated. there was no one kinder
than michael Jackson its a shame he went
long before his time.
'A star that burns the brightest burns for half as long'

**kristin, Jul 04 at 02:41 PM**
I'll be there.
I used to rewind my Free Willy VHS tape over and over and over again
just to watch the music video for "Will You Be There." I never got to the
movie. even in elementary school, I loved trying to dance like him. miss
you, MJ...

**Alesia, Jul 04 at 02:41 PM**
Will remember you as a great dancer, singer, like a rich personality... The
great music epoch has gone with you.. Love and respect you.

**Angie, Jul 04 at 02:42 PM**
Even though I have never met you physically, YOU were apart of my life. YOU kept me motivated with your uplifting songs. YOU kept my spirit alive with your creative dance moves. YOU kept me sane when trouble, by listening to the sweet melodies of Human Nature. YOU were apart of me

**alan, Jul 04 at 02:42 PM**
endless pain...endless tears...endless love...

**Summer, Jul 04 at 02:43 PM**
The King of Pop, Michael Jackson.
Before Michael passed away I had only 2 of his songs. Beat It and Thriller. I have ALWAYS loved those songs, especially. But since he died I have also come to love Billie Jean, Remember The Time, You Rock My World, You Are Not Alone, and a few others. He actually means a lot to me now, even though I'm only 15. Goodbye Michael Jackson... You are a LEGACY.

**Michele, Jul 04 at 02:44 PM**
RIP. I remember how I used to dance around the house at the age of 5 to The Way You Make Me Feel. I was always listening to MJ. He is the only celebrity I actually cried over. I was devastated. The world has truly lost an amazing artist. He will always be in our heart. RIP Michael. He's moonwalking up in heaven.

**mari, Jul 04 at 02:45 PM**
for loving memory to king of popo
You really mean much to me. When i was 6 i heard first time your music and there it was - i fell in love.

**Steve K, Jul 04 at 02:46 PM**
In Memories Michael Jackson..
We are the world
We are the children
We are the ones who make a brighter day
So let's start giving
There's a choice we're making

We're saving our own lives
It's true we'll make a better day
Just you and me

**Julie, Jul 04 at 02:47 PM**
For ever in my heart
When I think of my childhood, Michael was a huge part of it! When I was 5 my mom bought me the famous red leather jacket like the one he wore in "Thriller" (a fake look alike of course) I was so proud of that jacket, I had a glove to. My dad would rent his music videos and we would sit down as a family and watch them. I remember Michael as my childhood super hero. I dreamed of meeting him in person one day, I longed to be one of the kids who got to stay with him on his ranch. I love you Michael!!!!!!!!!!!!!!

**SQUIRM, Jul 04 at 02:50 PM**
To all who hurt..
Atleast your kids are safe.

**Amy, Jul 04 at 03:11 PM**
We made our own memories around his music and that's how he became part of our lives. Seemed like he insisted on making his exterior look like how he felt on the inside- broken, odd and sad. Someone who brought so much happiness didn't deserve this so I hope he now has found peace. We have lost a bright star.

# JULY 5, 2009
# SUNDAY

*Preparations for Michael Jackson's memorial service and funeral continue. There is no official announcement about the participants in the memorial service. Jackson's lifetime royalty earnings mark a milestone that will possibly never be equaled because of the fundamental changes in the music business caused by the Internet.*

**Lila, Jul 05 at 01:22 AM**
If you can find some way to spread this furtehr than your blog, please do so. if not, join me as I have been wrting to every magazine, reporter, etc.as they report extremely derogatory information regarding Michael Jackson. People that were supposed to be "friends" such as Quincy Jones have gone from crying on CNN to bashing him in DETAILS magazine. I have family that knew him and he was good. None of the garbage written was true, but often times people prefer to believe he negative because it's easier. Some reporters such as Geraldo, Nancy Grace, Diane Diamond, have raked him over the coals and he hasn't even bee buried yet!!! Please expres your discontent. All of these people have websites. The firt child from 1995 has long since said his father wanted to be a movie producer and put him up to it for money.
45 out of his 50 years were devoted to others, the very least those that really loved him can do is to never stop fighting on his behalf. He deserves it. The world took all he had, it's time something is given back.
R.I.L(Rest In Love) Michael

**Jessica D, Jul 05 at 01:44 AM**
...I am soo thankful that someone besides myself was able to go back and watch the interviews and get deep into the stuff Michael Jackson went through. I'm sitting here and i'm watching the BET Awards, and i'm thinking none of these entertainers can accomplish what MJ did. I'm crying now, because I feel that i'm to be blaamed for what he went through. I wish that someone was able to sit with him and just be there to listen to his troubles. Thats all he needed, someone to listen to him. It makes me mad, cos i think of all the happyness he brought to peoples lives, and what he got in return was sadness. I will say this, who ever hurt Michael Joseph Jackson, will definately suffer in some form for what they did to him. I was telling my mum just a little while ago of how sad I felt on his passing. And all she said to me was, sometimes people are taken away earlier than they are suppose to, and thats only because God doesnt want them to be alive to see anymore hurt or sadness. So if you think about it, he was taken for his own good...R.I.P MICHAEL JOSEPH JACKSON 1958- 2009. Gone too soon brother. We all love and miss you

**Emma, Jul 05 at 01:49 AM**
Hahaha I love the picture of him in the blue tracksuit! Hilarious. He was definitely the best looking person in his family.

**trisha, Jul 05 at 01:52 AM**
The sad thing is that he was quite good-looking in the early eighties, and masculine looking. It's too bad he had to mess with his face and make himself look so feminine. RIP Michael.

**christine, Jul 05 at 02:11 AM**
ok ACCORDING TO THESE PICS IF YOU GO OVER THEM AND OVER THEM LIKE I DID YOU CAN SEE WHEN HIS SKIN DISORDER STARTED TO APPEAR OR DEVELOPE IN THE PICTURE FROM 1978 IN OR ON A SOCCER FIELD HE IS COMPLETELY BLACK AND BLACK CAN BE AND IN 1979 HIS SKIN IS A LITTLE LIGHTER NOT TO MUCH BUT ITS LIGHTER! AS YOU GO ON THOROUGH THE REST OF THE PICS YOU CAN SEE HOW MUCH LIGHTER HIS SKIN GOT~ YEARS AGO PEAPL KEPT SAYING HES BLEACHING HIS SKIN THERES NO DISEASE THAT DOES THAT BUT 20/20

ON ABC A FEW YEARS BACK HADA SHOW ON THIS VERY DISEASE AND MICHEAL EVEN SIAD IN AN INTERVIEW THAT HE HAD IT! ITS A LONG MEDICAL TERMINOLGY WORD THAT BEGINS WIHT AN "L" THAT I CANT EVE BEGAN TO SPEL OR PRONOUCE BUT IT IS A VERY REAL THING! ITS JUST AMAZING TO LOOK THOUGH ALL THESES PICS AND SEE THE CHANGE IN HIM ITS JSUT INCREDIABLE!

**Michelle, Jul 05 at 02:30 AM**
I thought he did it back then because he paid the first accuser around $20 million. I've been reading more about Michael Jackson since his death and now I think he didn't do it. I feel bad for ever thinking that he did. Is it true that the first case was never pursued in criminal court? They just went after money?
I don't have children, but if I did and Michael Jackson, or anyone, had harmed them, it wouldn't be money I'd be after. The more I read about him, the more I think he didn't do it. It's sad that his life was filled with so much pain. It's sad that he didn't have more time.

**cindy, Jul 05 at 02:59 AM**
MJ-your music touched so many lives, there will never be another King of Pop, i grew up with you and my children adored you, I never doubted you, I only hope that you are finally pain free, I know you are moon walking with Angels now, we all miss you so very very much. RIP sweet Manchild RIP

**apple, Jul 05 at 03:20 AM**
Michael was a total hottie in the early 80's.. When he did BillieJean at Motown he was AWSOME LOOKING..He should not have gotten so much plastic.. WE all would have loved him with light skin too, just don't mess with your bueatiful face structure!! RIP MJ.

**ANN, Jul 05 at 03:52 AM**
RIP MICHAEL. I LOVE YOU, I AM MISSING YOU LIKE I LOST A BROTHER.I WISH I COULD HAVE BEEN IN YOUR LIFE JUST SO YOU COULD HAVE SOMEONE TO TALK TO, SO THAT ALL THAT YOU WERE HOLDING INSIDE YOU COULD

LET OUT. YOU WERE SUCH A VERY SPECIAL PERSON TO
HAVE TOUCH SO MANY PEOPLE ALL OVER THIS WORLD.
GOD GAVE YOU A SPECIAL GIFT, THAT ONLY HE CAN DO,
AND YOU USED IT SO VERY WELL. YOU ARE THE KING!!! I
LOVE AND MISS YOU MICHAEL YOU WILL ALWAYS BE IN
MY HEART AND YOUR MUSIC WILL PLAY FOREVER AND
YOUR SPIRIT WILL LIVE FOREVER. WACFB

**KJ, Jul 05 at 05:09 AM**
He was a goodlooking man with a great voice.Too bad they accused him
of child abuse and they ruined his career

**mjjsmooth, Jul 05 at 05:11 AM**
I wonder why the media and some of the public were so nasty to him?
now that he has escaped everyone realized how important he was. people
should really be ashamed of how they treated him. he was like a modern
mother theresea or ghandi. He was the most famous person in the world,
how would YOU behave?

**mjjsmooth, Jul 05 at 05:14 AM**
and anybody who thinks he hurt any children obviously didnt know that
much about him and certainly never met him. i hope tom sneddon goes
to his memorial so people can tear him to shreds!

**nish, Jul 05 at 05:46 AM**
you honestly don't know what you got until it's gone... so sad

**5string, Jul 05 at 08:15 AM**
Hopefully the media will let him rest in peace!

**D\*ana,** Jul 05 at 10:15 am
I have so much more to post, it has been difficult for me to gather
everything... but there was so much evidence in Michael's favor and
watching those videos of him playing with the Culkins, etc... I know
people make fun, but even last night I was out with some friends and
the subject came up... and when my friend started calling him a child
molester I proceeded to spend the rest of the night telling her... no. His
life was about extremes... extreme talent, extreme heart, extreme pain,

and I just attribute the plastic surgery to all of that…. and he wasn't very good at selecting the best doctors, that is all coming out now as well… Anyway, what Quincy is doing is sick…

KARMA IS A BITCH MARTIN BASHIR!!

To Michael's family, may god grant you peace on this not so great time.

**lady sue, Jul 05 at 10:40 AM**

You are not alone. Your soul and spirit will always be with us. Our dearest RIP MJ, we miss you. May Allah bless you. InsyaAllah see you in heaven.

**Charla, Jul 05 at 10:47 AM**

Generations from all over the world are coming together to say goodbye to Michael. " Michael, In life, we weren't always there for you… In death, our spirits are united in saying: "YOU ARE NOT ALONE"…

Your inspiration and passion through music and dance will live in our minds and hearts forever…We love you.

**Twosugarbabies05, Jul 05 at 11:13 AM**

Will there also be a Holiday for him too? I mean We only will come across a Historical Musican like this 1 time, and He is now gone from mistakes from Doctors and So called Friends-Those are who I blame. If You can't hold back or say No then you shouldn't be serving in the Celebrity World, as they are not Gods -They are more like Spoiled Children. And once given into You might as well Kiss YOUR A** goodbye. This all happened for the Wrong reasons and I am still upset over such a lose to the World- Michael Jackson had so much more to give to EVERYONE and was unfairly taken by Selfish People who couldn't just give him an answer of No or a placebo -easy as that. Who will be next? Rest Your Soul ,Dear Michael-You will never be forgotten and Your True Friends-Liz Taylor and Your Family will carry your Legacy on FOREVER.As You are Not Alone.

**Bimley1, Jul 05 at 11:31 AM**

NO WONDER HE WAS SO PITIFUL….A BLACK MAN TRYING TO BE A WHITE WOMAN….WONDER WHAT HIS CHILDHOOD WAS LIKE….PROBABLY IF KNOWN, THERE

## WOULD BE A LOT MORE SYMPATHY FOR HIM....SORRY WHEN ANYONE DIES........

**Binieltrahan, Jul 05 at 11:39 AM**
good riddance. one more dead pedophile. And he was not the greatest musician. His music sucked. The Beatles were 100 times better.

**Rathcrest, Jul 05 at 11:39 AM**
Michael Jackson created his own world and he and he alone has to accept the responsibility of his own actions. Many played a part in it but in the end the responsibility of his actions is Michael's alone.

**Nrthdude1, Jul 05 at 11:45 AM**
Frankly, I was more saddened by Farrah Fawcett's death to cancer. Her battle was epic as was her suffering. She was brave and courageous and I am surprised that the media, after hounding her in life, showed very her little TV coverage in death, and instead focused on poor Michael. It just isn't right.

**corv36hotmama, Jul 05 at 12:10 PM**
i also lost a daughter with drugs an i feel the dr should have to be held so what respondful but they also have a choice an i am sick of hearing about michael, he made his choice he must not have cared alot about the kids or he would have been a better dad why have we not heared anything from the brothers an sister

**By.OneLess, Jul 5 at 12:12 PM**
One less high profile pedophle, on the streets this ones for you Macualay.

**cindy, Jul 05 at 12:14 PM**
Goodbye; Do you remember the time ? too much memories shared with you beautiful music. thanks for giving us lot of fun and lot of memories. you will never die in our hearts, with love Cindy

**Jonar, Jul 05 at 12:14 PM**
When i saw you ! The first time I saw you, Michael, was the only thing I could say wow. After that it was only Michael Jackson in force. I listened

to your music all the time. I tried to dance like you, I pretended that I was on the scene and were you. My grandmother sewed the same clothes as yours. My aunt bought your discs for me. Then when I became older, so I started listening to hip hop. But now when you died, I have taken the star you were, and has again begun to listen to you. And still can not believe you have gone away I can not get it in the head. According to me, you have been a hero who can not die. I love you Michael, rest in peace.

## Pathetic, Jul 05 at 12:16 PM

It's sad when this man can recieve this much national attention and a soldier dies in Iraq and nobody gives a hoot. Shame on you all.

## Nanna, Jul 05 at 12:23 PM

Thanksgiving King!
Dear Micheal,
I wanted to thank you for everything you gave us
and learnt us to give
How could we not love you
Rest in peace, though I feel you're still with us
May God bless you
Love and bliss. Nanna

## Nanditha, Jul 05 at 12:23 PM

he's an angel
o god i don't know what to say..the fact he's no more on earth makes me awfully sad..i just can't say how sad i am.. i've been skipping meals the past few couple of days..because i'm too sad to do anything..i've cried so much that tears won't fill me eyes anymore..i've been praying for his soul every night n' then i would cry my self to sleep..there were times i even considered suicide!!cuz this feeling is awful!! i wanna be with him.. he wasn't only a great entertainer but an amazing human being as well.. he's heavenly..n' my only intention is to go to heaven n' see him..i've been praying to God to make him speak to me..i can't bear this anymore.. i love you michael,from the bottom of my heart!!!!!!

## Lina , Jul 05 at 12:23 PM

one in a billion

No one cared about people and the future of the children as much as you did. No one had as big a heart as you did.
the press made up horrible lies.

**COSTA, Jul 05 at 12:25 PM**
The King will live 4ever..this world was not for him...

**Drago, Jul 05 at 12:25 PM**
I pity you
The professional life is only one aspect of a person life.

**Amy, Jul 05 at 12:25 PM**
End of Tragedy
Dear Michael - the King of Pop, hope u will have freedom and LEAVE U ALONE with the End of Tragedy...
Miss u... Love u...
The MAN IN THE MIRROR... U R NOT ALONE...

**Isaac, Jul 05 at 12:28 PM**
Thanks for expanding my vision of what life can be.
Thank you, Michael, for being true to your passion and heart. Thank you for allowing the grandest splendor of your being to unfold. Thank you for allowing the Creator to express love through you. I am a child of the 70's. I came of age then and you and your brother's music was my soundtrack. I imitated your songs with some neighborhood children. Of course, I was Michael Jackson. I still am.

**Ruth, Jul 05 at 12:28 PM**
A part of my soul...Your songs, your dance, your life- I feel we grew up together, same age...I loved you since the days of Jackson's 5, following you with admiration...RIP,
As long as I live you wil be living in me

**Nit, Jul 05 at 12:29 PM**
God bless you Michael.

**Heather, Jul 05 at 12:29 PM**
The soundtrack of my life

I cannot remember a time in my life that I did not have a Michael Jackson song on my mixed tape, mixed cd, or on my ipod. His music has been in my life for as long as I remember. I had the Jacket with the zippers and the glove, I remember crying the first time I saw the short film for Thriller. I know that sounds weird but his sensual face and sweet smile melted my heart and I was in love from that day forward. Your generosity, talent, passion, and love cannot be matched. You will always be on my play list. Rest in Peace Michael, tell my grandpa hi. God Bless.

### Michael, Jul 05 at 12:29 PM
I'm not dead! Nevermind guys.. I'm not dead yet! I'm alive!! Don't go kill yourself anymore.

### Jack, Jul 05 at 12:29 PM
My Icon and Inspiration
Since i was a child i would always listen to your music when i was feeling sad, feeling happy, or felt in the mood for dancing. your songs and words helped me through so many difficult times and made me the person i am today. It has been an honour to have known of you and to have been on this earth at the same time as yourself. it is something i feel very priveliged to be able to say and very proud. Michael Joseph Jackson, you will forever be in my heart and soul, forever helping me to make decisions in my life and i look forward to the day when i can teach the next generation of children about such an amazing man and show them how music and dancing began, Michael, Thankyou, I Will Always Love You x

### Nadia, Jul 05 at 12:30 PM
MISS YOU MICHAEL
What can I say? Michael you are the greatest entertainer of all time. Your awesome, your great, your wonderful, your a magician, your a superhero and more. Losing you to this world to me felt like I lost a close family member, because when I heard it it hit so hard to my soul and spirit that it was something I couldn't fathom. But, I know right now that you are in a place with no pain and no negativity. You are in a place that is pure wonderment and amazement that you have shared with this world and will continue to share with the world through your music until the end of time. I will truly miss you and your wonderful smile. You will forever be Peter Pan in our hearts and a beautiful soul and spirit to all that have

been blessed to hear your music and/or have seen you perform. I love you Michael and know that you will continue to be loved forever by me and by all.

**deps, Jul 05 at 12:32 PM**
you're irreplacable for sure—your music, your voice, your style , your dance , your so fantastic in every way,

**darren, Jul 05 at 12:34 PM**
i was a young child when i first heard your song, "beat it" back in the 90's when cassette tapes were around, i ran that tape till it could not run it anymore, just listening to that song..the world loves you MJ, R.I.P

**Betsy, Jul 05 at 12:34 PM**
His legacy
I have always liked Michael Jackson's music but I admit that until now, I didn't fully appreciate him. Probably like many, I am being introduced to his full repertoire only now that he is gone. He was a true genius in so many ways, and he will live on in the hearts and minds of millions. I'm sorry I never got to see him in concert, but thankfully we have all his music videos and albums.

**wish, Jul 05 at 12:37 PM**
Wish people would have treated him better in life Whoever helped you made the decision on your facial surgeries, whoever tries to take you fun personal time away by accuse you on child abuse should be punished.

**Dolly, Jul 05 at 12:37 PM**
His Mission—Micheal seemed to have been handed a Mission in his life. His was to make us understand and to know that "It Doesn't Matter if You are Black or White!" He spear headed the "Heal the World" campain. He seemed to be all about love and acceptance of your fellow human being. He was a GREAT MAN, A FANTASTIC SINGER AND A DANCER OF UNBELIEVABLE EASE! I miss him so much. RIP Michael

**Axel, Jul 05 at 12:39 PM**
Dream—Last night i had a dream, and it was with you..i was talking to you and i was bagging you to quit those treatments and all those pills.

i was telling you that you are going to die..and i was crying so badly...i didn`t know what to say to you Michael, because you didn`t listenet to me so much.. like you belived me but you didn`t had any other choice.. i`m extremely sorry that our gone..my dream will never become a fact. but your dream is a fact ! Yes Michael, You changed the world! You changed the whole world into a better one. I will NEVER forget you and i promise that neither my unborn kids will. Forever Love you!

### Michael, Jul 05 at 12:40 PM
Sexy memories—I remember when Micheal Was Doing the moon walk and I had the biggest crush on him in my entire life,he was my hero in my mind and I always wished I was that sexy man, my mum always told me that she called me after him with made me the happiest boy on earth,I then started drawing Jacko naked which made me really horny,I LOVE THAT SEXY MAN AND I WISH I COULD RIDE THAT SEXY THING ! But after I realized he only dated women I was demolished but hung onto the believe that he would convert for me! I was turned off by his new plastic surgery look so I continued drawing him but the way he looked before. I never came together with him, and, actually, I am now married, happily, to a beautiful woman and have two kids with her: Michael and Jackson. I still admire Jacko but not in a romantic sense anymore, all I want of him now is his fabulous music.

### Zé, Jul 05 at 12:42 PM
Rest in Peace Michael...
I grow up listening MJ in the early 80's... 30 years had passed, and more then ever i still listen his music, i feel privileged to born in 1979! I remember the 1st time i saw thriller!! i was 5 years old and realy scared cause of the warewolf... God bless the best entertainer of all times in this world we live.. a world that we made very wrong... and Michael was just trying to change what he could.. was not a fair fight for him, so i beleive that those who tried to put him down were the responsible for his sudden death... yes we are humans, but sometimes we have no humanity, not even animals act like we do sometimes... strange race we are!!! Michael, forgive those who made you suffer, the good thing is that humans can forgive... and can also regret. Thank you Michael!! You will never die in our hearts, in our minds you are alive!!! FOREVER!!
Peace...

**Deirdre, Jul 05 at 12:42 PM**
Staten Island NY
for me my regret is I never saw you in concert. For you I am so sad for
the difficulties you had in your life. Why, because I believe that you were
truly a good person with a good soul and misunderstood. Sadly, you
didn't see your true outer and true inner beauty. You were ALWAYS a
beautiful boy, teen, and man. I pray for you children. I am so sad you are
gone. I am very sad. I wake up every day and say...oh God, MJ is dead.
Rest in Peace

**priyanka, Jul 05 at 12:43 PM**
why did u have 2 go???n leave my world so cold...
i wish i was the 1 who had left in your place...because den d sorrow
wouldn't have been so enormous..there wouldn't be millions suffering
behind you..i wish i can still bargain with god..v terribly want u back..!!just
wanna say that you will be cherished for the person u were..in addition
2 d soulful music n your inimitable moves..feel like crying forever n
have truly never felt this aching loneliness in my life before..miss u..love
u..RIP MJ!

**inky, Jul 05 at 12:43 PM**
There are no words to describe what you mean to me, my generation and
society at large. Your impact is indellible, your talent unmatched and
your spirit beautiful. You were a star that shone a light on a dark world.
Your music healed our souls. Your humanitarian accomplishments
healed many not just here in the U.S. but in the world. There will
NEVER, EVER, be another. My deepest sympathies to your entire
family, especially MAMA Katherine. MAY YOU FINALLY HAVE
SOME PEACE! We loved you through it all....then, now eternally.
Who's BAD....undeniably MICHAEL JACKSON!

**Agnieszka, Jul 05 at 12:43 PM**
Thank you Michael
I remember your songs since I was a child. Thank you for being such a
great star... Rest in peace

**John, Jul 05 at 12:44 PM**
the greatest—MJ was the greatest "chester" alive if he had to choose a

little boy or pam anderson he would go ape s*** on little billy. it didnt help he was black but he got that taken care of.

**abdallh, Jul 05 at 12:44 PM**
woooooooooooooooooooow
the beast of the beast

**Taryn, Jul 05 at 12:47 PM**
DEEPLY HURTING—GONE TOO SOON!!!! You have touched this world in a very special way. We won't ever be the same without you. You cared. I can't stop crying. My heart hurts so bad, I wish that you were here to see all of the love this love. You were the music to my life for 42 years. you were in my life musically since I was 7, I saw you at the Uptown and I was hooked. You will be a part of me forever. I loved you more than I ever knew. I will always miss you, forever.All my prayers and Blessings to the Jackson Family May GOD hold you and keep you in this time and always.

**NETTE, Jul 05 at 12:48 PM**
REMEMBER THE TIME
I love you for this song and all of for hits. They make dancing a real joy.
AGAIN THANK YOU

**gaivz, Jul 05 at 12:53 PM**
michael is the best
he dead at 50. his music is dead aT x000. he is in my heart. 4 ever. i pray 2 god to let him reincarnate

**Rajni, Jul 05 at 12:54 PM**
Black & White
I love all this old music has good meaning and i have live my life by many of this music. The best music is Black & White which really tell us colour doesn't matter

**La, Jul 05 at 12:54 PM**
It still hurts
Even though it has been a little over a week since you left this Earth, it still hurts. Your music has touched my heart even though I never got the

chance to meet you or see you in concert. Your kind-hearted spirit will forever be missed. As I try to cope with the fact that you will no longer be on this Earth, I hope that you are with God, happy and at peace because you deserve it. Your music will live on...I love you Michael...

**Gabriel, Jul 05 at 12:54 PM**
A fan you never turned his back
As a small child my mother said she knew you would be a big influence on my life. Watching me dance and sing all over the place. Michael I would like to thank you for the memories and happinies you brought me. A man with a great career and great heart will always be with us. You will be loved and missed.

**Manny, Jul 5 at 12:54 PM**
I dont understand why the world is full of hate. Im pretty sure if it was one of your relatives that passed away, you wouldnt want people making fun of them. God bless us all....

**Abijah G, Jul 05 at 12:54 PM**
He was a legendary performer...I wont comment on his human side coz first of all i never met him, secondly, i hv no right to judge him! But as an avid music listener and fan, I mourn his death...a big loss not only to the music but also to the performing arts! Hats off MJ! R.I.P

**Rana, Jul 05 at 12:57 PM**
You will live forever!! You will rule the hearts of many men, women and children in up coming generations Michael, God bless ya!!!

**S, Jul 05 at 12:57 PM**
You're music is absolutely amazing. Thank you for the wonderful music. You shall NEVER be forgotten. May you rest in peace. Love you always x

**nicole, Jul 05 at 12:58 PM**
You are an angel—You have touched my heart in many different ways threw your music. Thank you you are a angel and yo will live on in all of our hearts.

**SELENA, Jul 05 at 12:58 PM**

WISH I COULD HAVE MET YOU! I GREW UP LSTENING TO YOUR MUSIC AND I FELL DEEPLY IN LOVE WITH YOU. I'VE ALWAYS WANTED TO MEET YOU BUT I KNEW THAT IT WAS IMPOSSIBLE. BEING POOR AND LIVING IN A HICK TOWN IN SOUTH CAROLINA. I ADMIRE YOUR WORK AND I LOOK AT YOU AS A POSITIVE INFLUENCE IN MY LIFE. I NEVER GOT A CHANCE TO TELL YOU THAT I CRIED WHEN YOU GOT BURNT FROM THAT PEPSI COMMERCIAL. I WAS HORRIFIED BECAUSE I THOUGHT THAT WE WERE GOING TO LOSE YOU. I HAVE SO MANY FOND MEMORIES OF YOU DOING THE MOONWALK, DANCING AND SINGING. I CANT EVEN BEGIN TO UNDERSTAND THE PAIN THAT HAS CAUSED SUCH STRESS IN YOUR LIFE. JUST REMEMBER THAT YOU DONT HAVE TO GET REVENGE ON THOSE THAT TOOK ADVANTAGE OF YOUR LOVE AND KINDNESS AND ESPECIALLY YOUR GENEROSITY. GOD WILL HAVE THAT LAST VENGENCE ON THEM AND JUSTICE WILL PREVAIL. I MAY NOT HAVE THE CHANCE TO MEET YOU IN PERSON BUT IM LOOKING FORWARD TO MEETING YOU IN SPIRIT. GOD LOVES YOU AND SO DO I.

**miss, Jul 05 at 01:01 PM**

greedy people took advantage of you and caused you so much pain in your life…should be punish. You are such a sweet COOL boy who deserve a better personal life.

**Twiggi, Jul 05 at 01:01 PM**

Our love to you will never die.
I Miss U Michael Jackson, a part of my heart is gone, and always will be. I remember the first time I heard one song from you, it was black and white. I was a child, a little girl around 6 years old. But it was about when I was 12 years old I really started to listening to you music. Now I am 20 years old, And I can never let your music go away. Your songs, Your love, Your dance, Have change every bodys life. Your are the LOVE. And you are my true king. I hope you find peace

**Loza, Jul 05 at 01:02 PM**
R.I.P King of Pop
Michael Jackson was a true legend. I am shocked at this news.I can't stop dancing when I hear a Michael Jackson record.

**Daniel, Jul 05 at 01:02 PM**
Love
It is hard for me to express words how great Michael Jackson was. He was truly a kind and gentle soul. RIP.

**aida, Jul 05 at 01:02 PM**
you will live on in our hearts
i can't stop crying, it hurts so much...i just can't describe the pain! my heart is broken.nobody can and will replace you NEVER!!
you live on in our hearts & your music will never die.
r.i.p. my legend and thank you for your music.
in lovin'memory of MJ ---I LOVE U---

**WELL, Jul 05 at 01:03 PM**
Nobody did it better—Years will pass before the world comes across with another musician and human being as Michael. I can see Jesus embracing him and giving his love like no one did in this world.

**Julia, Jul 05 at 01:04 PM**
You Will Be In Our Hearts Forever...
Michael Jackson,he was an amazing singer,he was and will be an inspiration for many people and the memory of him will live on and on.

**Claire, Jul 05 at 01:04 PM**
We will always remeber you..A new star in the sky..We will never forget you and your music..Wish you had a happier life..and a real childhood.. RIP in heaven.. we love you..

**Janessa, Jul 05 at 01:04 PM**
Billie Jean
I was too young to experience the hype that surrounded Michael Jackson of the 1980s but I believe that anybody who saw him perform at

Madison Sq Gardens in 2001 will agree that we got a taste of it. The best performance of the evening was by far 'Billie Jean' because he played it up so well and the crowd got really hyped. When he slapped his suitcase down on the stool and piece by piece assembled his iconic outfit for the song the place was alive and buzzing with excitement. There's nothing quite like it, and seeing him dance is one of the greatest experiences anyone will ever have.

**Dorothy, Jul 05 at 01:17 PM**
my handcaped son misses you alot was a big fun of you and the photo he has of you in his room to pray for you before he sleeps

**Ryan, Jul 05 at 01:32 PM**
I think that was very nice of Madonna. I don't understand why people would bash her for paying tribute to a deceased fellow musician.

**j3161usa, Jul 05 at 01:38 PM**
The attention may be a little much since most of you are only "Thriller" fans of MJ. Many of us however are MJ5 fans from as far back as the early 70s. Most of us know the B-side to most of the jackson 5 singles. Most of us were "moonwalking" long before "Thriller" We are fans because we grew up with them and their music. Most of the hatefull comments come from people who did not like his music and were not fans--at all. I understand, many of us were not Elvis fans and didn't listen to his music (some of us even hated him). So I really don't listen to the critics or the hateful "who cares" comments cause I know if it were one of their "favorites" they would be just like us. MJ the dark, large-afo little boy who sang "maria", "rockin robin", "I'll be there", "Sugar daddy", "ABC", "going back to indiana", omg, to those of us who knew and loved his family's music will miss him very, very, much.

**Buffy F., Jul 05 at 01:56 PM**
atSkyla...the difference is that people aren't going to funerals of dead soldiers or policemen or firefighters while they're willing to enter a lottery to be a part of this sideshow. Most of these people will have to take at least a day off from work. How many of these folks would take a day off from work to attend funerals of the others I mentioned or just to spend

some quality time with their own children? I'm willing to bet none. Some really sad priorities some people have.

### mj fan, Jul 05 at 02:01 PM

don't pay attn. to the haters. they're hypocrites, they hate someone but gotta waste their time reading and watching all about that person. and i agree, michael was a person. why the hate? he never did anything to anyone expect help them. and he's still treated like trash? thank you madonna!! it's nice to see another 80s icon pay tribute to the king of pop.

### Silent Hill Fire, Jul 05 at 02:18 PM

Mike fatigue is beginning to set in. They need to bury his bones and thee storys too. I can't for the life of me understand what people are full of praise about. He fed kids wine, slept in the same bed as little boys, dangled his own infant out of a 5 story window and He was a known addict and a compulisve spender. Yeah he was very accomplished in the music /entertainment biz. If not for fame and fortune he'd have been in jail.

### Jeffrey G., Jul 05 at 02:41 PM

MJ who was devoted to children throughout the world, how come in his last will he did not leave anything to the starving children in Dafur-the Sudan-Africa? J.Gazal

### Nickthehood, Jul 05 at 02:44 PM

Wacko Jacko One less sicko. That's what happens when have no respect for the things and people around you. Good riddance!!

### Penny, Jul 05 at 02:44 PM

Please let the man/boy rest. How much more can we stand.Much greater one's have passed without all this fanfare.

### Rose, Jul 05 at 02:47 PM

Michael You will always be in my prayers and in my heart. I hope the best for your family. Rest in peace and one day I will see you in heaven. Love you.

**antonella, Jul 05 at 02:49 PM**
Hi Michael, Seeing the photos and the videos about you and your children makes my heart happier. They are simply beautiful and it's obvious that they were loved by their father. I will write you forever like you were still alive, because for me it's so.. you're alive! For now it's enough. Bye MJ.

**MomPom321. Jul 05 at 02:49 PM**
I just heard on the news that Debbie Rowe will fight for her kids. Duckthis will be a battle!

**julisa, Jul 05 at 02:53 PM**
i love michael Jackson—hi michael is the best he can dance,sing and he was the best father to his three kids.he was also kind to let children sleep in his bed and he would sleep on the floor.michael jackson is the best.

**Mirella, Jul 05 at 02:55 PM**
Missing You
You were the most mesmerizing and fixating performers of all times. I taught many a child to sing my favourite childhood song..Rockin' Robin.
I just had to hear the first three notes of Thriller to get me on the the dance floor.
Thank you for sharing yourself with the world. I will miss your superb talent.. and good or bad, I will miss the man Michael Jackson.
RIP

**sofia, Jul 05 at 02:55 PM**
until we meet again
that amazing charismatic man one of the most brilliant minds that have ever waiked on earth that lived among us and gifted us with his music and passion for art for dance for joy for goodness but above all the will to live to love and to forgive cannot be dead .... in this world you are what you are born .. and you michael jackson you are ONE OF A KIND no doubt abou it .. you will always live in our hearts ..... on a time like that on the time of your loss as inappropriate as it is i will say this "" the same people that have killed the idol over and over and over that made his suffer and brought a great deal of pain to this angelic artist are the same ones that now are finally taking a bow in front of your greatness and

finally realise you really have been "" .. i`m so proud that you have been a fellow citizen among us on the same crazy world that we all live in .. the same world that is trully empty from your absense .. you are finally free and i hope that you will finally be happy away from every kind of evil that hurted you for the last 50 years .. we love you .... until we meet again ..

**Larry, Jul 05 at 02:58 PM**
How and why blacks can embrace Michael Jackson is a mystery. He so clearly wanted to be white. His talent was and is overshadowed by his peculiarity. His fans can only be portrayed as brainwashed.

**Mahmoud, Jul 05 at 02:59 PM**
Good Bye Michael
I never forget you my best singer . (you will be there)....in my heart .(All i want to say is that they do not really care) if you are (Black or White) so (I want you back)to (remember the time)and to be sure (You are not alone) and you are a part of (History) and we never forget your (Smile). i think you live your life as (Stranger in Moscow)but you are always (Unbreakable).Do not (Cry) we will (Heal the world)to save (Little Suzie) . We will (Come together) to say (You are my life)............Good bye my (lost children)

**luke, Jul 05 at 03:02 PM**
i saw him live in london at his bad, dangerous and history tours. the memories and emotions i had will live with me forever and i feel priveledged to have witnessed such a musical icon in all his greatness. i know he had his fair share of bad press and no one will truely understand the enigma that was michael jackson but no one can take away te fact that he made great music over five different decades. no other artist will ever compare to the king of pop and he will live on in his music and my memories forever.

**wamuyu, Jul 05 at 03:03 PM**
What a genius! I was a busy hard working teenager in the '80s. But Michael was everywhere. I have only just watched Michael's videos and they are unbelievable.

**Yilin, Jul 05 at 03:04 PM**
1993 I was 11, and ur concert was AMAZING
I just want to tell you, watching u from the cheapest ticket, and being at the stadium where u performed, watching u LIVE.. and your Dangerous Tour being the first concert I had ever attended was the most exciting day of my life! You brought me great joy as a child and even now. Thank you for being brilliant at what you do.

**roberto, Jul 05 at 03:04 PM**
...my soul kid..
you are my soul kid..you are my peter pan..i l love you.......

**Emily, Jul 05 at 03:11 PM**
my memories of michael jackson
the first time i saw mj perform was on the movie free willy when i was a toddler i remember that day like it was yesterday i instantly fell in love with him and his music and would talk bout it with my grandma all the time. it was a bond we had and his music will always remind me of those day i spent and made memories with my grandma and i want to thank Michael soooo much for making an impact on my life just by singing

**ursula, Jul 05 at 03:13 PM**
Friend—It was a pleaseure knowing Michael. The wonderful times taking him to dancing lessons and coming over to our house, spending time with the brothers. They were very special times. Michael was amazing with my children and was so kind to them. Thank you! Michael, you will be missed beyond words. I know that now you will be at peace. God Bless!

# JULY 6, 2009
# MONDAY

*Michael Jackson's family announces who will participate in Tuesday's memorial service. People from all over the world continue arriving in Los Angeles with the hope to say goodbye to their beloved musical icon.*

**Haha, Jul 06 at 03:22 PM**
The opposite of bravery is talking shit about the dead.

**harlequin, Jul 06 at 03:22 PM**
There was a clause in the settlement which states that Jackson in no way acknowledges any wrongdoing by signing the settlement. And another clause which specifically states that a settlement in the civil case in no way affects the recipients' right to testify in a criminal case. Moreover, it was a CIVIL case that was settled in 1993, not a criminal case (they just wanted damages -MONEY!). It was in the 2003 criminal case wherein Michael Jackson was TRIED and ACQUITTED on all counts. As a congressman one would think you would have at the very least done some research as to the facts of the case before spouting off to the media.

**Kathryn, Jul 06 at 03:22 PM**
Michael was not convicted because there was not enough evidence, and therefore it is presumed that he is innocent. I think that Mr. King's comments are rude, inflammatory, and wholly unnecessary.

**harlequin, Jul 06 at 03:26 PM**
Yes, MJ's fans, who have at least read up on the facts of the case, looked

at the documents of settlement (leaked to the public, look it up in the smokinggun website) are crazy. While those who haven't read anything except perhaps sensational headlines are not. Crazy too are the 12 impartial people on the jury who acquitted the man. Yeah that sounds about right.

**Paulson, Jul 06 at 03:29 PM**
I may be wrong, but let's talk about pedophile priests,Mr.King. Long Island is a cesspool of bigoted morons.

**surforia, Jul 06 at 03:31 PM**
i am an attorney, and although it's not my speciality, his remarks aren't slander because Michael Jackson is considered a "public figure." People have a Constitutional right to free speech under the 1st Amendment, but sometimes such speech is considered slander. If he had called you or me a "child molester," then it would probably be slander (unless, of course, it was true!).
Because MJ is a public figure, though, the Supreme Court decided in a famous case against Larry Flint (who had published a political cartoon where a celebrity preacher was shown banging his mother in an outhouse), that people have a right to comment about public figures b/c such commentary is a "matter of public concern." Therefore, his comments aren't slander - and it doesn't matter if he's dead or not.

**Sara, Jul 06 at 03:34 PM**
I totally believe in ghosts. But I'm also rational enough to believe there's probably an earthly explanation.

**JP, Jul 06 at 03:34 PM**
We need to elect this guy President. Finally, some public figure put this clusterfatck of celebrity worship into the proper perspective. Come on! Would we be as fanatical about Michael Jackson if he was still alive. Look at the sales numbers and all the snide comments made about his messed up life. No, we won't. Anybody has the right to complain about hypocrisy, it's this guy and others like him who see this as the bullsh!t that it is.

**Martha, Jul 06 at 03:34 PM**
The civil case is the one that was settled, i.e., the parents of these children looking for money. The criminal case is the one in which Michael Jackson was found INNOCENT. Say what you will about his life, he was never convicted of any criminal wrongdoing.

**leigh, Jul 06 at 03:36 PM**
do you know mj personally to say those things against him? are you trying to steal the fame from mj by saying those things? screws you peter king! how about you?

**omg, Jul 06 at 03:37 PM**
here u c what the media has done 2 mike and got reminded what kind of ill people r out there..

**Michael Jackson, Jul 06 at 03:38 PM**
Wasnt he the African who bleached his skin to become a white person? whacko jacko they showed what he would have looked liked if he never changed his features Big african fat nose and dark. dont try to be something your not mr jackson.

**Bjork'sSwanDress, Jul 06 at 03:42 PM**
If you look at this video closely and in slow motion, there is absolutely NO OTHER explanation other than it must be the ghost of Michael Jackson. This makes perfect sense. If you notice the way the apparition moves along that far way, it is just the way Michael used to walk. It would make sense that Michael's spirit would want to settle there at Neverland, no? The ghost in this video seems so comfortable there, knows its way around, etc. I can only hope that whoever takes over that place treats the ghost with the respect it deserves. Ghosts are friendly most times, and if they become unfriendly, all you have to do is ask them to leave the room and they must do so. I think it's wonderful that they've captured this raw footage of MJ's ghost. The world entire should view it, and reflect on it. It is a message, a sign, a wish for a better future. It's not a shadow, I'll tell you that. There's no way it's a shadow.

**Anonymous, Jul 06 at 03:45 PM**
I'm not really a Michael Jackson fan. Michael Jackson was never convicted

of anything, and was found innocent in a court of law. So these comments are total slander. And it's extremely disrespectful to Michael Jackson's family and fans, who are still in a period of mourning. Like I said, I was not particularly a fan of Michael Jackson's music, but I won't deny the fact that MJ touched a nerve with a lot of people, who hold him in high regard.

I think Peter King should have kept his opinion to himself.

**Kevin, Jul 06 at 03:45 PM**
I'm sorry to burst anyone's bubble but, that looked more like someone's reflection coming into the room from outside that room's window.

**Danielle, Jul 06 at 03:46 PM**
I can't wait for the "Ghost Adventures: Neverland Ranch" episode where the dude w/ the hair (I don't know their names) starts taunting Michael Jackson "If you don't like me, come here and moonwalk across my foot!"

**MIKE, Jul 06 at 03:48 PM**
I HAPPEN TO AGREE WITH KING IF WE KNEW THE FACTS THAT WERE WITHHELD FROM THE PUBLIC. WE WOULD LOOK AT IT AS ANOTHER PEDOFILE OFF THE STREETS. SPEAKING FROM A FATHER OF 4...

**Levente, Jul 06 at 03:48 PM**
If anyone would refuse to leave earth and haunt their home it would totally be MJ!! Hahaha. I believe. :) Ghosthunters episode forthcoming, I hope.

**stereotypes, Jul 06 at 03:50 PM**
He's a politician, he should be careful not to damage whatever remnants of credibility he may have. Unfortunately he proves that they never really do depart from stereotype. Nice contribution to the world muppet

**ben, Jul 06 at 03:50 PM**
For a congressman to disdain from the justice system for a more seditious media influenced one fuelled by sadism.....says a lot about their character. I do not hold contempt for this man, just sympathy

**Chris, Jul 06 at 03:50 PM**
Rationality and ghosts don't co-exist.

**Chris, Jul 06 at 03:52 PM**
Really? This couldn't just be a crew member walking behind the camera, casting a shadow down the hall? People want to believe whatever they want to believe.

**Candice, Jul 06 at 03:53 PM**
Oh, please. I will say that I do not believe in ghosts one bit but this is just plain ridiculous. As if Larry and Jermaine were the only people in that house during the interview. I'm sure there were no less than 20 people (production staff, cameramen, etc) milling around that house, if not more. People need to get a little common sense about this.

**A concerned PARENT, Jul 06 at 03:53 PM**
I agree with most people on here but the ones who are using the 20 million as an excuse to say that Michael was guilty, I would hope to God you are not parents. If anyone ever touched my child this is no way on God's green earth that any amount of money would make that ok. No caring parent would ever not go after his butt legally and get him put behind bars. Not only for what he did to my child but also the future harm he would do to other children. I can see however and have see where people pay money to have things go away even if they didn't do it to save the horror of a trial. You have to think about this is a parent and I can say without any doubt that if he did it there would have bene no amount of money that made that ok. I would also leave my child with michael jackson faster than I would leave her with some hate spewing man who feels its ok to belittle dead people who achieved so much in the lifetime.

**The crotch grabber, Jul 06 at 03:59 PM**
He was a 100% Solid Wierdo freak who played with little children in his Never Never land mansion. Its not normal for a grown man to do these things. He also admitted to playing in the bedrooms with he little children that is STRANGE and BONE TINGLING WIERD for a Grown man to act this way and dress this way and not to mention look like a plastic maniquin.

**Bjork'sSwanDress, Jul 06 at 04:00 PM**
It's a shame that there are so many cynics.Why can't you all just let us believe, that MJ has returned to his favorite place on Earth as his final resting place? Like I said in my previous post, there is absolutely no other explanation other than this must be his ghost. I heard from a source within the compound that that room we saw the ghost in was OFF LIMITS to all television crew people, etc. Can't we just let this man rest in peace? Seriously. Also, for all you cynics, I'd like to see the proof that DISCREDITS the claim that this is MJ's ghost. There isn't any! So that proves it.

**Josie, Jul 06 at 04:02 PM**
HA! that made me laugh out loud! Now I'll be seeing crazy moon walking ghosts everywhere, I'll let you know if any of them start emitting falsetto ghost wails!

**luvwknd, Jul 06 at 04:03 PM**
I hope the Michael Jackson ghost doesn't molest little boys like the real freak did! Rest in hell Michael, rest in hell!

**LITTLE BOY BLUE, Jul 06 at 04:04 PM**
This is a shadow of a person walking either outside of a window or inside the room where we cannot see to the left.

**Fred, Jul 06 at 04:08 PM**
That is crazy!! There is no way it's his ghost. He isn't dead. You guys are falling for the classic Jackson tricks. If you read his wikipedia history you will see that almost all of the "strange" things he was accused of he actually leaked out himself. This was a brilliant plan. It increased public interest. So a few months ago he said he is have "a come back". And now he is dead? Kinda fishy. HE FAKED HIS DEATH!! He did for real, what people have joked Elvis did. Then he will come back in a year or two and be more popular than ever.

**preston, Jul 06 at 04:08 PM**
lol, I just found some guy on eBay selling soil from the spot where Michael died...this is too good!
Haha you have to see it. It contains MJ's ghost!

**Snarf, Jul 06 at 04:13 PM**
Shadows point of origin seems to be from two sources of light behind the walls, making it look like a shadow passes in front of a doorway with nothing creating it. Either that or they caught a ghost on film.

**JL, Jul 06 at 04:15 PM**
Since when can a shadow reflect itself through walls? It's walking and is reflected on the wall and the floor through a wall from the outside???

**MJ Admirer, Jul 06 at 04:20 PM**
No. If you know Michael Jackson's religious beliefs while living on the state of the dead, i.e. that the dead sleep and do not know anything, then you know how ridiculous he would think this. Jehovah's Witness use the Biblical texts of Ecclesiastes 9:5, 6, 10 and Psalms 146:4. He sought advice from other spiritual leaders but the Jehovah's Witness belief was ingrained in him. This belief on the state of the dead is the reason he made the disclaimer at the beginning of the Thriller video regarding the occult. If there was a ghost presence he would tell that it was a demon, not Michael.

**Fred, Jul 06 at 04:21 PM**
im with sherry, Mike didn't do the "child stuff" he was accused of. People took advantage. But I still think he is alive. He's been setting this up for years. You don't think he has enough loyal fans or billionaire friends to pull this off? Please!

**C.D., Jul 06 at 04:24 PM**
I applaud Mr. King for standing up and speaking the truth. The fact that Congress held a moment of silence for Michael Jackson, a drug addict and child molester, is beyond me. There are so many other people in this world doing great things for humanity that should be honored way before Michael Jackson. His death was tragic, but more than likely Michael Jackson killed himself with drugs, so B-O-O H-O-O. The real tragedy is the important issues that are being pushed aside to cover this ridiculous circus of circumstances surrounding his death.

**Swingline, Jul 06 at 04:24 PM**
Who elects pig-headed trash like this? Say what you want about the

OPINIONS you may have about MJ's case(s), but coming out with a statement that stupid just shows how unqualified elected officials have to be in this country.

Truth be told, I don't want to hear my local congressman talking about MJ, unless it's a brief word, and then moving on to the business at hand. And in generalizing Michael's life so much (he sang, he danced, big whoop), he's got a big set of balls to act like he doesn't mingle with unethical perverts that generate government paychecks on a daily basis. The notion of another congressman getting into an adulterous affair and ruining the lives of everyone around them has been played over so many times that it doesn't even matter anymore. And if this guy spent even a day looking real people in the eye, it'd be easy to see Michael's life and music affected people more than most ever will. You don't have to agree with everything the man did to accept that, but there is little doubt to the influence of MJ's work.

### cc, Jul 06 at 04:25 PM
BTW- we also have hear ton of disgusting news everyday about our fellow politicians like you, who have extra marital affairs and then they apologize to the public for deceived them to get votes. Shame on such people. Before you accuse someone, look at what you do to people just to stay in power.

### MJ Admirer, Jul 06 at 04:25 PM
Michael would not be dishonest and fake his death. If he did, he would not be the Michael that we have all come to love. Think about it. He would not cause doctors to be accused of something they did not do. He was too loving to do this. If you accuse him of faking his death, you are discounting everything he stood for and believed.

### 5TH STREETFRED, Jul 06 at 04:25 PM
WOULDN'T THE GHOST MOONWALKED AND GRABBED ITS CROTCH IF IT WERE MICHAEL?

### DRUGS!!!!!!!!!!!!!!!!!!!!, Jul 06 at 04:26 PM
Michael Jackon was an abuser of drugs! Enough said! well maybe also he played with little children and looked like scary!! Jason from Friday the 13th lol

**Layla, Jul 06 at 04:29 PM**

Indeed, could be a shadow and not a ghost... after all, Peter Pan lost his and had to fly from the stars to get it back! Why not Michael? ^-^ (btw... "innocent 'til proven guilty", so nice if you saved your personal "judgments") ~Rest In Peace, Jacko~

**rose, Jul 06 at 04:31 PM**

Oh please don't start the "fake his own death" rumors thats just what went on when Elvis died.

**Christine, Jul 06 at 04:33 PM**

This is something which if you believe is true is just that, we all are here by the grace of God and sometimes he takes people too early, maybe he wanted his music up there. I hope it is his Ghost but I also hope he is not dead. No need for any people not MJ fans to join in this, if you didn't like him - go somewhere else. MJ best signer and entertainer of our time the world IS a sadder place without him, sadly missed.

**MOI, Jul 06 at 04:35 PM**

The media were always made up JUNK about him when he never did anything wrong. he was FRAMED ppl, bcos some poverty stricken sickos wanted to be millionaires, (why dont you haters google michael jackson framed and see, look at the Chandlers background and see, the father once took out all of his patients teeth bcos he was so psycho and he said, "And if I go through with this, I win big-time. There's no way I lose. I've checked that inside out. I will get everything I want, and they will be destroyed forever. June will lose [custody of the son]…and Michael's career will be over." Surely if there was ANY truth in the case it would be about justice and not what you want ($) it was all because of money and who ever doesnt believe that is on the side of the twisted media who have ruined nearly every celebrities life(for example princess diana and who can forget Britney)- they say fame comes with a price and they're right. Its about time ppl spoke out for MJ, today's media makes me sick. oh ye i forgot us congressmen are perfect, they know everything about everything dont they? NOT

**Diosa, Jul 06 at 04:36 PM**

You know I cannot belive that all of those that are decrying the media coverage Michael Jackson is getting was not dancing to at least one of his songs in their lives! I also cannot believe that someone who was elected to serve in our legislative branch would be such a jackass as to totally ignore the fact that 'presumed innocent until proven guilty' is something to just brush under the rug. He settled out of court? Well wouldn't you if you had the money to do so and was under an exhaustive media attack? Wouldn't you again, if you had the money, and was constantly being threatened to be sued unless you 'paid up' and last but not least, last I checked the man is DEAD, now isn't it truly very easy to throw dirt on him now when he is unable to defend himself? SHAME ON YOU and SHAME on the fact that you're one of the lawmakers in this country! You sound like a narrow-minded, witch hunter, who even though a person was found 'not guilty' by a jury of their peers, it's not enough for you. So climb aboard your horse and ride off like a 'good ole boy' shoud do!

**Deepak, Jul 06 at 04:41 PM**
I'm not much of a Ghost believer. There were a few things that intrigued me when I watched the video closely. One thing I noticed is that not only there is a shadow, but a reflection of the shadow on the shiny floor. This clearly can't happen if its some camera crew's shadow, because then you won't get its reflection on floor. More over the shadow does not look bent on the edges of wall (like a normal shadow of a person would). Lastly shadow of a living person should change height as it moves (assuming light source is fixed and not moving at the exact speed as the person walking). whatever appeared in the video didn't seemed to change height, as it moved. Spooky!

**Tim, Jul 06 at 04:42 PM**
Wow - not even a good fake. Amazing what you can do with tech these days but they should have made a better attempt.

**Shirley, Jul 06 at 05:06 PM**
Mj did not touch Jordan Chandler. Chandler admitted that he lied for his father.

**The Silent Majority, Jul 06 at 05:08 PM**
The Silent Majority knows the truth about the molestation, just like we know about O.J. Simpson. Similar outcomes.

**Buffy, Jul 06 at 05:12 PM**
The good thing about Michael Jackson's death is that we normal, rational-thinking people are able to weed out all the mentally ill people in our midst. Besides if this was Michael's ghost wouldn't he be moonwalking or carrying around the ghost of a little boy?

**Mrock, Jul 06 at 05:18 PM**
Even if that wasn't real it was still scary!

**candi, Jul 06 at 05:19 PM**
If it was his ghost then here are two things u would do well to remember:
1). Michael Jackson did NOT move from place to place by just monnwalking. he used to WALK normally too, or did you forget. Also, grabbing his crotch, well yea he used to do it alot but not all the time. So why should his ghost be obligated to do any of these things? Next you might be asking him to sing Thriller for you and be all like "well if it WERE Mike, he would be singing" I think u expect too much from him. he's HUMAN. leave him alone for once in your lives.
2). If it was his ghost and not just just some miracle that it was something else, then ask yourself this, what better place for him to haunt than neverland? I think that when u LEAVE NEVERLAND ALONE and let it rest in peace, then maybe, just maybe, he will too.

**JB, Jul 06 at 05:21 PM**
This 3 ring circus is going to be in town a loooong time. How has society sunk so low as to make this creep into a super hero? To get more press coverage than a dead President is disgusting. What's next? Micheal the victim movie? Thank God for Netflix.

**DC, Jul 06 at 05:25 PM**
I sort of agree. No, we can't say he was a child molester, he was acquitted of that. But we have to admit that for the last 15+ years, MJ did nothing but ruin the legacy that he'd built. He WAS inappropiate with children, he DID physically turn himself into an alien, he WAS a financial disaster (including accepting money for deals that he never concluded), and he WAS a socially unstable human being. The very fact that everyone suddenly ignores all of that, just because he's dead (yes, I'm making little

of the fact that he's dead) is appalling. Shame on all of you for your idol worship.

**ann, Jul 06 at 05:33 PM**
i lived in a haunted apt in brooklyn new york, so i know spirits exist. i saw the film and got chills. if he has not passed over to the other side as yet, his spirit will remain

**Thomas, Jul 06 at 05:34 PM**
if i was michael (and i am not by a long shot) i would make myself known that i am around also, and i would have the phone mysteriously dial in pizza delivery for the crew! :P

**Trey, Jul 06 at 05:35 PM**
Pathetic!!!... I hate this old Pro-war people... people like him make the problems in this world...
1. Michael Jackson was innocent wich the accusor admitted himself!
2. No other singer has impacted so many lives in such a good way, of course the world is mourning. It's a huge loss.
3. Sure a soldier is a loss, but a soldier is expected to be lost, and respect to them for protecting the innocent. Maybe if nobody enlisted into the army WORLDWIDE, we could have peace. It's not the government, it's us!
I wish nobody gave this guy attention so when he passes, he will go without a tear from a single person...

**Trey, Jul 06 at 05:41 PM**
Martha... you say paying someone 20 (22 million) if you are innocent doesn't ring true... to counter that... if you're child is molested in such a way described in the case, what kind of parents would accept 22 million instead of punishing the accused... they knew what they were aiming for. Michael Jackson didn't touch a child in any sexual way. Michael Jackson wanted to be a child since he never had a chance to be one. He wanted to do what kids do and many kids sleep in the same bed during sleepovers and such. He was fulfulling what he didn't have as a child. Chances are, you've had an uncle come closer to mollesting you than Michael Jackson did to that Jordy Chandler character...

**Queenie, Jul 06 at 05:42 PM**
Finally - someone with the balls to speak the truth. We've become so damned politically correct that we've become a spineless nation. King makes some valid points and I respect the fact he has some balls. Any moron can see that Michael Jackson was a liar - he stated in one interview that his white skin and re-sculpted face was the result of normal growing. Please!!! Go ahead and love your heroes but don't deceive yourself - delusion is a dangerous game.

**dancer, Jul 06 at 05:43 PM**
The media should disappear

**kk, Jul 06 at 05:45 PM**
ok king for the comments u did on jackson were very wrong.i think u have to shut ur mouth.u have no right to talk like that about such a great person.

**thia, Jul 06 at 05:50 PM**
Michael Jackson was a tremendous influence on the music industry. He had a huge talent and he was great in his prime. In the past few years he's been nothing but weird. He has been acquitted of child molestation. But he will always have the stigma of being a molester. As far as the media attention - you ain't seen nothin yet!! Remember when Anna Nicole Smith died suddenly?? Michael Jackson is far more of a celebrity and we had to listen to all the speculation surrounding her death and who dat baby daddy?? And blah blah blah ad nauseum. And we still have to celebrate little Danni Lynns birthday and Christmas. So all you haters are gonna have to change the channel. People will pick apart every single thread of Michael Jackson's life and times. RIP Michael and Anna Nicole and Elvis and Jimi and so on and so on

**Who are you to judge, Jul 06 at 05:50 PM**
Mj Did a lot more then congressman they held a moment for him because in his time mj dontaed a lot of money to proverty stricken countrys, also donated to aids research which a lot more then what are goverment does and the irony is that is mad about press well instead of feeding fuel to the fire you should stick to what you know troops and teachers oh no wait you rather slander someone what ever happen to proven innocent,

153

didnt chandler come out and said he was force to lie about what happen everyone that has sued was after money and I am a victom of child molestation if it were me I would want to prosucte instead of getting money I would rather see my abuser rot in jail then take any amount of money, they all wanted money not to send mj to jail if he really did do this the truth would of been out the moment he died I dont belive he did this and for people and pete to slander someone who is dead and proven innocent is disgusting. This just proves my dislike for republicans point the finger but when they do something they try to hide it and apologize to the public, so you wanted your 15min of fame pete here there are go do your job instead of spouting at the mouth go talk about rush limbaugh and other dirty goverment officals you racist prick

**Josh, Jul 06 at 05:50 PM**
Michael Jackson was a child molester people, he was a very disturbed man and people who defend him have no morals what so ever! If you all are this blind I would hate to be your child! Michael Jackson paid millions in settlements to children he molested. His house was raid and plenty of proof was found, the only reason he got off the 1st time around was because he paid that kid 20 million dollars to settle! I used to like his music, no one doubts the man had talent but he was a pedophile and YOU all know it.
All of you need to get some brains, if you can not see the truth about him then something is really bad wrong with you, do you think God will reward you for idolizing a devil?
Man no wonder this world is going to hell in a hand basket, everyone is supporting the work of the devil.
Its discusting...

**k, Jul 06 at 05:55 PM**
Shame on people who think it is idol worship. It is a question of giving some respect to the greatest singer and an amazing human being who was not just a good singer but a good human being. Who is perfect in this world? He just became victim by people, who were jealous of his fame and wanted to extort money. He was mistreated when alive, at least show some humanity not to do that when he is dead. He will still be alive in people's hearts for the longest time to come.

**Kara, Jul 06 at 05:55 PM**
Great. Now the poor kids who MJ molested and abused have to worry about his ghost? Come on now. MJ is not a saint. He screwed up his career, abused children (don't give me that "he was found not guilty" garbage. Jurors admitted ignoring the evidence and let him go because of who he was). He has not had a decent cd released in over a decade. I save my sympathy for people who are not self absorbed child abusers.

**ohYesIdid, Jul 06 at 05:56 PM**
Why is everyone such a disbeliever in life after death? Why can't ghosts exist? I think everyone is just scared to admit in something they can't touch or control. Everyone automatically dismiss this as a shadow or something else. Who are you to say? Were you there? How does a shadow get cast with no body around? I'm not saying this is Michael Jackson, or a ghost, but I just hate when people laugh it off and say it's a shadow without any research or discussion. If somebody were to actually stop and take footage like this seriously, we might be able to learn something.

**Maloney, Jul 06 at 05:56 PM**
to sum up the dumb comments people will make...
1 .Jordan Chandler confessed he lied for his father and that Michael Jackson didn't molest him. (22 Million was the value of that lie.) Michael Jackson was NOT a pedophile. Proven!
2. Michael Jackson did NOT bleach his skin for no reason. Read about Vitiligo. It's a skin disease and i'm sure you've seen people with it. You lose pigment in bloches. It's either, be covered in white bloches. He bleached using a medical procedure so he wasn't filled with spots. This was the start of the infamous glove. For most people, the disease starts at the hands. So go ask a family who had there child molested... would they accept $22 million instead of servicing the bastard that touched them and they will agree that Jackson was innocent. (aside from the fact that Jordy confessed recently). You don't like how much converage this news is getting, don't watch... go do something productive.

**Dave, Jul 06 at 05:58 PM**
Ahh, the wonders of editing with low opacity. Fooling the idiots of earth since 1845

**Hal, Jul 06 at 06:02 PM**

And so the marketing begins...

**Gerald, Jul 06 at 06:02 PM**

People how stupid you are, YES the freak did not molest the last kid who sued him, it was true it was a set up, BUT... Michael Jackson did molest a lot of kidsd prior to this and HE settled OUT of court millions ands millions of dollars, and YES they had plenty of proof to convict him when he was 1st accused, but sadly CA law saved him since at the TIME the kid who was molested had to testify so Jackson paid them off, the laws were changed because of this. He was a pervert child molester, the facts are clear like OJ he had the money to get out of it.

People need to stop defending people who are guilty just because of race or superstardom, it does not take a smart person to know Jackson was disturbed and hell people most of you are defending him because he was a black man in the 1st place what does that say for us as a community? That we don't know right from wrong for one. And the man clearly rather be with white people anyways than his own race, all his so called women where white.

We need to start making our decisions about people based on what and who they are not what color they are, you just don't defend a guy like this because he is the same color as us and everyone I know is only defending him because he was an black man we all know he was nasty old pervert!

**I, Jul 06 at 06:03 PM**

1. Soldiers died on the 4th of July in Afghanistan serving our country. They barely were mentioned because of coverage. It's Anna Nicole Smith all over again. Mother Theresa who gave her life and gave up her fortune to help the less fortunate in a third world country dies and she gets a blurb. ANS, who is only famous for being a dumb blonde bimbo that marries a man two sneezes from death... passes away from drugs, and there's weeks upon weeks of coverage. This is our society.

2. After the police raid of neverland during the second molestation hearing, unless the molestation charges were true and he can't find rest so he's doomed to wander the halls where the crime happened.

**Arthur, Jul 06 at 06:04 PM**

I have reviewed the clip at least 60 times. It should be completely obvious to even the most fickle critic.

The visage passes from the left of the hallway passing partially through the Arch, turning slighlty in the direction of the camera as it passes into the hallway before turning and passing through the doorway in front of the apparition

**APRIL, Jul 06 at 06:11 PM**

JOSH MARTHA AND REP KING I WILL PRAY FOR YOU TO GROW A HEART THIS WAS A BEAUTIFUL SOUL THAT IS WHY JESUS TOOK HIM HOME TO PROTECT HIM FROM IGNORANCE FROM PEOPLE LIKE YOU.

**Davidfromupnorth, Jul 06 at 06:13 PM**

I believe it to be the ghost of a Chumash Indian, probably a member of the tribe that lived on the land long before Neverland was built. They weren't happy to lose their land. The hauntings by Native Americans often goes by the wayside in the news. If you got tossed off your homeland by European conquerors you aren't important like a dancer. But just looking at the image I can't tell if its Michael Jackson or a Chumash Indian, can you?

**M, Jul 06 at 06:50 PM**

They say that "ghosts" occur when the person's "soul" or spirit is not at rest due to a sudden or tragic unexpected death. Michael's death certainly fills that requirement. In many cultures around the world and in many faiths there are confirmable stories with ghosts of people who have met a sudden and unexpected death. They will not "transition" onward after death due to their worry. Michael could likely be worried about his children, family and fans. I hope he will be able to find peace soon. I dont know if the shadow is Michael. But I wouldnt be surprised if his spirit is not at rest yet due to the circumstances of his death. When his children's future is secure and his family is doing better, then perhaps he will move on. Or he may continue to stay nearby for his children until a later date. I hope you can find peace Michael, may the angels hold you in their gentle embrace.

**Pipian, Jul 06 at 06:54 PM**
This whole Michael Jackson scene is really grotesque. Since when, has a California celebrity without a brain become news?

**Denise, Jul 06 at 06:59 PM**
He was a Jehovah's Witness and they believe that only 144,000 will be allowed in Heaven. Guess they ran out of room for poor Michael. LOL

**K2, Jul 06 at 07:02 PM**
Well, there is a belief in Asian culture that when a person dies, their spirit remains on Earth for a period of time before heading to judgement. There's also the concept of a Hungry or Angry ghost.

**Joni38, Jul 06 at 07:11 PM**
I've been a paranormal investigator for many years. I have debunked many pics/videos. But I can't debunk this one. That was a shadow apparition and it's a fantastic catch!

**Mildred, Jul 06 at 07:16 PM**
I really do not know where to start, but I do not believe that he faked his own death for one minute. The jackson family are good people and I do not believe that they would for one minute get caught up in a lie like that. For the people that are finding Michael guilty of a crime that a jury of his peers found him not guilty of, you need to fall on your knees and pray to ask God for forgiveness. Who are you to judge anybody you just do not have that power. Keep playing and making jokes on Micheal jackson while his family is greaving at this difficult time and you may find that the joke could be on you.

**CF, Jul 06 at 07:18 PM**
Bjork'sSwanDress...please don't procreate.

**Rob, Jul 06 at 07:28 PM**
There's no such thing as "ghosts".If anything that was a demon or it could have been satan the devil himself.READ Revelation 12:9.

**Obsessed Fan, Jul 06 at 07:32 PM**
I think when MJ died, he saw the light and went to Heaven. So why would

he want to come back to this horrible world where he never found peace? He saw the light and found peace. That "shadow" was probably a crew members reflection. There are alot of explantions for a silly shadow.

**chen, Jul 06 at 07:44 PM**
If that is MJ, I will run to him, hug him, kiss him and tell him how much I love him

**rainbowridge, Jul 06 at 07:52 PM**
I have seen this type of phonomena before.Time means nothing in the spiritual realm. You "sense" the presence of spirits if you're gifted that way. From the film it looks like he is lost, wandering back and forth, and what you are seeing is the "shell" of a person who needs guidance that we cannot give. If you pray for him, whatever your beliefs, that he find peace and be able to move on, sending love and comforting thoughts will reach him. Reach out spiritully, forget the material, the house, the courts, the money, and think only of his soul, which exists apart from these things. It's over. Send love. He will be guided but it's not for us to know why,how,where and when.

**Debbie, Jul 06 at 08:13 PM**
Maria Michae Jackson Please put down the crack pipe and no, there is no tooth fairly and elves do not live in trees grown by Keeblers.

**christi, Jul 06 at 09:45 PM**
For those who like to be the judge and jury for whether Michael hurt children or not, we will never know exactly what happened..it is only your speculation. Since when can we judge? Michael could have just paid the settlement to just get on with his life; sometimes you have to just give up the fight to get on with your own life, as opposed to be wrapped up in a long court battle. Plus, when you see someone else accusing Michael of child abuse, why would another parent allow their kid to spend a lot of time with him after witnessing the accusations? Why in the world would a parent allow a kid to have a sleepover with a grown man, who is certainly not family? To me, this is more about others' opportunistic greed, and not considering how stange that could for their child, whether Michael did what he was accused or not. I would be more concerned about the parents that would allow their children to have sleepovers with an adult man..who had no kids at the time.

# JULY 7, 2009
# TUESDAY

*A memorial service for Michael Jackson, preceded by a private family service, is held at the Staples Center in Los Angeles, California. Family members, friends, celebrities and 17,500 winners of the internet lottery (out of a 1,200,000 internet applicants in a 24 hour period), celebrate and honor his legacy. Michael Jackson's Memorial Service, is broadcast worldwide and watched by a billion people.*

**sweetgirl, Jul 07 at 12:39 AM**
Like always...when a celebrity or someone important dies; there is always controversy of all kinds...Michael used to be a Jehovah's witness but died as a Muslim; but whatever that was on this video...we will always miss him...No one else like him as an entertainer! Rest in peace!

**smelly, Jul 07 at 12:42 AM**
..to the person that quoted everything that a trashy tabloid would write,.. the naked book was books sent to him by fans, of simple children. If you have no naked pictures of babies in your photo albums, then the rest of the world must be nuts too. He did not sleep in the same bed, he slept on the floor, though he tried to get the point across of why it's not wrong with sleeping with children in the same bed, if you never slept in the same bed with your parents, or had kids jump in your bed that wanted to sleep there and be close to you, then the rest of us are crazy. Michael was about pure innocence, not what the rest of the world is thinking about, where you might find real pedos on Dateline MSNBC shows. Your own

Doctor or Lawyer, or best friend is probably the guilty one, not Michael Jackson. People see in others, what they Hate in them self!

**sheena, Jul 07 at 12:43 AM**
People who always use bible verses as a answer to everything seem to forget about the things that are most important. like not training or beating your kid to what you want. or judging or verbal abuse. The only verse I read is the UniVERSE.

**Suzai, Jul 07 at 01:16 AM**
I want to address a Wayne... that bloodclot, battyhole needs to remember MJ is passed and however one may have felt, the rest of us loved him for who he is. I hope that Wayne is a perfect man. To the Jackson family pls excuse my anger and accept my condolences, to all his loving fans remember the times. Bless

**christina, Jul 07 at 02:00 AM**
i think MJ was the true peter pan in all aspects. he was the greatest artest that ever lived and his music will live forever. i loved you MJ and i feel that you are truely happy now that you are with God. my prayers to your family. i just wish the media would let you be.

**Mancy, Jul 07 at 03:26 AM**
So soft spoken, sweet and kind soul. I can not believe that you aren;t here with us. I am watching "heal the world" on tv now, and Im just heartbroken, There will never be antoher person like you! You gave us so much joy, and you where so compassionate and sweet too all people. Your dream was too heal the world and make it a better place. It really was when you where here with us Michael. Nobody will ever live up too your kindness and no other star will ever be as colour blind and humble as you. PRINCE OF PEACE AND KING OF MUSIC. God wanted you back because you where too good and pure for this world.

**Angel, Jul 07 at 07:45 AM**
Seriously, Michael Jackson was a fabulous performer and singer. Give your respect but its like putting on a circus having everything which is being displayed. Give the proper respect ! A ghost ? Custody of the children ? The Estate ? Gezzz Ain't even laid him the rest and already

going to court over all this stuff? My momma when she passed being a regular person her house was in probate for a long time !!!! The Jackson family and friends of the family need to all work together and know those children come first. Just think what they are going through and listening to when they hear everyone talk about their father ???? Think before you ACT because in the future it could seriously affect these children's hearts.

**Tyrone, Jul 07 at 08:25 PM**
Attorney at Law
I grew up with you and will always miss you. Enjoy heaven!

**Zully, Jul 07 at 08:25 PM**
"You Will Live In Our Hearts For Ever"
Thank You for such great music and for caring for the world.. you are in a better place with the lord. You will be in our hearts for ever...

**monica, Jul 07 at 08:25 PM**
the best singer ever
i just want to say i love michael jackson and there in the heaven nobody can hurt him again cause so many people believe him and support always

**Diew, Jul 07 at 08:25 PM**
NL-Breda
For ever in our hearts, greatest artist with the most amezing dance moves ever...!

**Renee Seya, Jul 07 at 08:25 PM**
Forever!!
We are not promised tomorrow. We are only promised eternity. It is only the "now" that counts. It is only when we see the dawn of a new day, then we must be thankful. Michael was a treasure, a treasure that will be sorely missed. Michael, the music that you made will live on forever in our hearts. You gave us so much joy, so much love, and so much happiness with your music. Even now you are still giving. It was Michael's God given awe inspiring talent that touched so many of us. His talent only came from God, and it will never be seen again in our generation. In everything there is a purpose and a reason. In time God will reveal it.

Thank you Michael for sharing your life with us. You taught us how to love more, give more, and how to heal. It is your turn now; it is your turn to be truly happy. No more sadness and no more pain. Your turn to smile that beautiful smile of yours. We miss you and we love you Michael. This time you will be smiling forever!!!!

### Doriana, Jul 07 at 08:26 PM
Rest in peace MIchael...you are not alone!!!
I remember when I was young...i was listening to "heal the world" and I was just a young girl in front of the power of music...you Michael are the music, and the music will live forever!!! I love you, we love you.

### Fede, Jul 07 at 08:27 PM
In our memories.
I want to write for the family of MIchael Jackson.
First of all, I want his children to know, that your father was your father, and nothing that was said is going to be true for you, you must be very proud because of the father you had, and up your head and keep on walking through the life. Everybody knows, that in this days you are deep in sadness, but you must be power, and get out of there.
My thoughts and praies for you and for your father. He is going to be in our memories for the rest of our life.
Rest In Peace Micheal!.

### Dee, Jul 07 at 08:27 PM
you will be greatly missed, thank you for everything
Michael jackson, at time I still cannot believe that you are gone. I am sorry that you were taken for franted while you were on earth. Sometimes people do not realize what they have until it gone.

### Kennisha, Jul 07 at 08:27 PM
RIP MJ
My first concert was a Jackson Five concert. I remember being excited on the drive to Dodger Stadium. I was excited to see MJ on stage. I wouldn't leave without buying the photo book. I'll never forget the impact his music had on the world. He'll truly be missed. My heart goes out to the family. I hope that they're able to search their hearts and find peace. My God be with the Jackson family always. Thanks for teaching me how to

be a humanitarian MJ. I love you and I'll miss you, but I'll see you again one day. I'll be praying for the family.

### Doesn't Matter what my name is, Jul 07 at 08:27 PM

I just want you to know....

I don't know that anyone will read this. But I hope someone does. He was the first person I ever thought to be "cool" in my entire life. And it's sad to say I forgot just how "cool" he was until he was gone. Long live the king.

### Michael, Jul 07 at 08:27 PM

I love you, angel

I am so sad yet so hopeful that you will finally rest in peace with no agony or pain... I love you with all my heart is truly an understatement... You were an angel on this earth, yes I believe it... how can I not? I love your pure heart and I love your children... I love anyone you loved, and I love everyone who loves you... you are greatly missed, but never ever be forgotten... Farewell MJ, and hopefully we will see you in heaven later... I love you, you king!

### Tina, Jul 07 at 08:27 PM

Fan

Michael you have touched people in ways you will never know, we all mourn for you MJ. I feel you were one of god's special children. You were an amazing one of a kind artist and entertainer. Your music moved people along with your dancing. Michael Jackson you shined bright as the stars in the sky when you took the stage. It was sad to have heard that you passed away. God had better plans for you in his glorified kingdom. Even though you were our king while you lived on earth, your name will always remain a legend to all. Michael you will be trully missed in this world because, you made a difference to us all. You {MJ} inspired the world. Rest in peace now Michael Joe Jackson. Thank you for everything. Trully Honored, Tina

### Megan, Jul 07 at 08:28 PM

R.I.P Michael Jackson

Michael Jackson is a icon. I'm not going to say "was" because he still is a icon. He will forever live & my prayers goes out to his family. God Bless his family. Michael I never got to meet you & now I wished I did. I always loved your music but I really appreciate it more ever since you died. I heard most of your music but never really paid that much attention to your music until your death. Now I see why people loved you. You are a sweet, caring person & you will be remember for that. R.I.P Michael Jackson!!! You will forever live!

**Sandy, Jul 07 at 08:28 PM**
For Paris
You're an amazing young lady. It took a lot of courage to get up there and speak from your heart. Your dad must be so proud. Just remember, You are, and always will be his "Little Girl" and don't let anyone tell you different. My heart goes out to you all.

**Jasmine, Jul 07 at 08:28 PM**
Teaching God to moonwalk
I'm a really young fan of yours, so I never really got to experience the biggest part of your career, but that didn't stop me from reliving the old days by listening and being touched by your hits that came out before I was born. I was only two when HIStory came out, so the only CD I really remember coming out was Invincible, and boy, did I love that CD. When I first heard You Rock My World, I couldn't get enough. I played it over and over and over again memorizing every word while trying to dance the way your gracious and fluent body carried you. I will never ever get enough of you, Michael. You will always have a place in my heart.

**Erik, Jul 07 at 08:28 PM**
The Prayer: Dear,Michael Jackson & The Jackson Family & Kids. i Prayed and cryied today *Paris* you did a Great job in the loving memory of you father. my heart goes out to The Family we will miss him dearly. Michael you changed the world of human anti race FOREVER. you Music,Spirit & Soul will be on our cold world today. I LOVE YOU Michael & The Jackson family and friends.

**Lori, Jul 07 at 08:28 PM**
Michael is and will always be a living memory. The world lost Michael but we will never lose his music or his love for all the world. Jesus knew what he was doing when he created Michael in his image because Michael

brought hope, love, happiness, and healing to all of us through music. Let us remember him and honor each word he sang to change the world and make a difference. Thank You Michael. The Jackson family is in my prayers.

I love You!

**Michael, Jul 07 at 08:29 PM**

Mantra for Daily awakening—Man In the Mirror

**Anette, Jul 07 at 08:29 PM**

The Memorial was so great and a tribute for MIcheal Jackson...thanks, A great Memorial, great singers und speechers..but the best was coming through, Michael Jackson as the person he was...a man, who wrote songs like "Man in the mirror" and "They dont care about us"(reflecting) and all those billions dollars, he gave to others. Not a moment, I could believe, that he could have abused a child or anybody else. There was a realy cut with his death...and now the world is watching, who is really gone....a person, who can never be replaced of another. He is now everywhere around us...and I don't have to say...God bless you ...he is in the sky and already blessed. We will see you soon.

**mjfan4evr, Jul 07 at 08:29 PM**

Michael Jackson,an amazing man,will live forever! He was a genius,a wonderful father & a very nice man. All the years we have wasted criticizing the king....is that how we should have acted...as people of God??? I would never ever like to be treated like that. They treated him bad so bad that they lost him,this lover of life,of us.So long live the KING OF POP.....Praise him,Honor him,Respect him,Love him.Sing his songs,watch his videos,learn the moonwalk,wear the glove!Love life as he did and always,always keep a place for him in your hearts.

**kerrie, Jul 07 at 08:30 PM**

Love ya Michael. You were an inspiration to me my whole life growing up. I have never met you but i feel i know you so well as well as all of your other fans out there. you touched so many lives. We would all like to thank you for the great things you have brought upon us all. You will always be in my heart and never forgotten.

**Bridgot, Jul 07 at 08:30 PM**
Fondest memory—My fondest memory was when the thriller video first came out. My dad rented the video and took me and my brother to a friends place to watch it. It was amazing and still is today. I watch it every time it plays and will never get tired of watching. I love all MJ's songs, everyone was a hit. I cannot pick only one as a favourite. I will keep his music alive forever.

**Liz, Jul 07 at 08:31 PM**
Thank you. I am ashamed to say by the end of last week I was feeling enough already he has passed away young yes but maybe because of drugs, still its sad but enough. Well by my own choice I watched the entire day of his funeral and through this entire ordeal, I had forgotten that there are children who have lost their father, the only parent that they have ever known, a mother who has lost her baby son, brothers & sisters who have lost their brother, friends that have lost a good friend, and entire nation who has lost a voice. A voice that has helped raise money, fought for the truth, gave us thousands of songs that somehow in our lives we can relate to, or wanted to be like. He lost more than most people because of his fame, and had to go to great lengths make parts of his live private. Did we understand no, instead we judged him. Shame on us for that. Thank you for all you gave up for us, thank you for what you have done for the world, thank you for making the world a more beautiful place with your music. May you find peace for once in your life. May you walk in our fathers home without being afraid.

**Michell, Jul 07 at 08:31 PM**
There as I grew up
I remember my first dance class experience. Our Drill team used songs from The Wiz to dance to. So too did my jazz classes later on. My mom had your albums, and every night I went rollerskating with friends the rink would play the Thriller video and dim the lights while we rolled around. As my world grew and changed, there was always his music old and new somewhere in the background.

**Patrick, Jul 07 at 08:31 PM**
The spirit never dies.
After having made such an incredible impact on virtually the entire

world he has gone nowhere. Though he is unable to give us any more of himself via his physical body, he still speaks to us through not only music but countless other outlets in our society. He lives in the hearts of anyone whose life he ever touched.

### Alexandra, Jul 07 at 08:31 PM

We Love You More I cried so very hard today watching your memorial. Even as I willed myself to control my emotions, tears cascaded effortlessly down my cheeks. It is too difficult to smile right now. Your children are beautiful, and your daughter spoke with a love so deep for her papa. I hope they live the same innocence, honor, and dignity that you carried throughout your life. We love you, Michael.

### Kathlene, Jul 07 at 08:31 PM

His Memory will Live Forever. A Man of Honor, Courage and Strength— May the Good Lord be with his Family and especially his Children. He Lived and Loved Life with them and the memories made and shared can never never be replaced. God Bless you Michael Jackson

### Segun, Jul 07 at 08:31 PM

The King of Pop

As the tears role down the side of my face, my eyes heavy and hurting, I remember that night curled up in front of the TV awaiting my birth to your work at 8 PM December 2, 1983 and doing the same again in September 1987 and on November 14 1991 eagerly awaiting your Bad and Black or White videos. On Saturday mornings I watched your videos on LWT and imagined the glow of square chucks of street beneath my feet as I walked along. In an age when it was all about Fame and break dancing you brought me the moonwalk. I even attempted your anti-gravity lean four years later. Despite the twenty one year gap I grew up with you like a super fast aging brother. Your words made me cry as you sang of Ben. I felt your frustration as you and sister Janet let off a load Scream after those lies printed about you in 1993. I stayed up till the early hours to listen to you share your world with Oprah and as I sit here recording a tribute show in your honour, I smile as I think of is the joy you've brought to my life, the roller coaster of emotions finding tickets to your "This is it!" tour which sadly was never to be. R.I.P.

**Danny, Jul 07 at 08:32 PM**
Just had to say
All I want to say is that MJ you really were and are part of my life and in a funny way your original influence on me has a direct link to where I am today. Now 42, I am still a DJ with a passion for music - and yours is amongst the music I love the most. Your music is part of the soundtrack of my life and so Michael - thank you for the music. Danny

**Robert, Jul 07 at 08:32 PM**
They won't go when I go
Stevie did a wonderful tribute. Some powerful people tried to diminish the light Michael shined all over the world. He dedicated his life to breaking down the barriers of race, religion and region by bringing people of all backgrounds together in the love for his music and his message of love.
Even in death they are still trying to diminish his accomplishment but we wont let them take away what Michael instilled within us. His message of love and world unity is too strong to be doused by their message of hatred and division. We can continue to honor his legacy by embracing with passion and remembrance the love we have for each other as the miraculous human beings we truly are. We must never again let our corrupt and heartless leaders make us to fight and hate one another. Michael was able to united more people of varying backgrounds than anyone before or after him and that is why he was dangerous to the vampires that feed off of war, famine fueled by our hate and fear of one another. Never again do we let them manipulate us into unjust war. For Michael.

**Greg, Jul 07 at 08:32 PM**
Still in shock! I grew up listening to Michael. My second album I ever owned was Thriller. I have always been a huge fan and have enjoyed all of the Jackson's music. It really broke my heart when all the negativity started. I never believed a word of it and never will. Michael is truly the king of pop and nobody will ever come close. His memory will live on forever in his music. My heart goes out to the Jackson family during such a sad time in their lives. Don't stop til you get enough!!!!!!!!

**Tanya, Jul 07 at 08:32 PM**
RIP Michael Jackson! I remember wearing the red jacket and glove and holding a Michael Jackson doll. Singing and dancing like him. I am 31 years old and I will cherish his music and when my kids are older enough to hear his music they will listen to it and know him as i have through his music!

**Renee, Jul 07 at 08:32 PM**
Forever!!—We are not promised tomorrow. We are only promised eternity. It is only the "now" that counts. It is only when we see the dawn of a new day, then we must be thankful. Michael was a treasure, a treasure that will be sorely missed. Michael, the music that you made will live on forever in our hearts. You gave us so much joy, so much love, and so much happiness with your music. Even now you are still giving. It was Michael's God given awe inspiring talent that touched so many of us. His talent only came from God, and it will never be seen again in our generation. In everything there is a purpose and a reason. In time God will reveal it. Thank you Michael for sharing your life with us. You taught us how to love more, give more, and how to heal. It is your turn now; it is your turn to be truly happy. No more sadness and no more pain. Your turn to smile that beautiful smile of yours. This time you will be smiling forever!!!!

**a fan within a fan, Jul 07 at 08:33 PM**
My memory of Michael was on my birthday Sept. 2001 when he and his brothers performed at MSG in NYC! Before going I told everyone... "Im not gonna cry...no no not me" Then he stood up and waived at the crowd... I Cried my butt off!!! His aura was like no other... I felt his presence... and so did everyone in the arena... grown men were crying... but not tears like your average concert tears of seeing someone GREAT!!! My condolnences go out to his family... I LOVE YOU!!! (N we LOVE YOU TOO MIKE)

**Michael, Jul 07 at 08:33 PM**
Again and again in history, some special people wake up. They have no ground in the crowd. They move to broader laws. They carry strange customs and demand room for bold and audacious actions. The future speaks ruthlessly through them and they change the world. Michael was

truly a special person whose music celebrated life and touched our souls. What a wonderful time to be alive.

### Christopher , Jul 07 at 08:34 PM

Take a look at yourself and make the change. Man in the Mirror has and always will be the most inspirational song i have ever heard. If only everyone could listen to this in unison. Thank you Michael for all the great music. You have entertained millions and will never be forgotten.

### Jessica, Jul 07 at 08:34 PM

In my heart always and forever..
I feel like my childhood was torn away from me. Like a strip of my heart and soul has been removed. I have such great memories of Michael Jackson growing up. I'm 23, so I've grown with his music from birth. I'm praying for paris, prince and prince II. I hope that they never forget their father because he loved them with all of his heart. He'd give up everything for them in a heartbeat. He was a great humanitarian and just a great person. He may have not been understood by most, but I think the select few that new him felt blessed. I didn't know him, nor have I ever met him, but I feel blessed to be alive at the same time as him. Rest In Peace Michael. The world loves you!! You've given one heck of a show right down to the end.

### DJF, Jul 07 at 08:34 PM

MY MEMORY OF MICHAEL JACKSON!—The king of pop will never die in our hearts and minds! He will live forever! To make a long story short, when I was around 4 or 5, that is when I knew who Michael Jackson was. My older brother and sister would always listen to his music. My sister had some of his album collections, that I enjoyed listening to. we bought the Thriller/Making of Thriller on VHS once it came out. I got jealous of my older brother and uncle, and Willie, because they all had the black and red Thriller jackets, and I didn't. I have been around music since I was born. The two most heart breaking music artist, to me, that we have lost are Selena and Michael Jackson! As a DJ I always play a Michael hit, and I always will! Just like most of the world, Michael Jackson is our musical Father, Brother, Uncle, Best Friend, we are not alone person! Thank you Michael for all of your Love for us. We will miss you forever! God bless you, and may everyone in Heaven enjoy your talents for all eternity!

**anita, Jul 07 at 08:34 PM**
missing you—dear michael you are a beatiful soul we as people didnt know that you would leave us so soon i pray that you are giving god that some talent that you shared with us .i pray that know you can rest your werry head and dance and sang in heaven !thank you so much for sharing your dreams and talent with us , wheather white , black , asian, or even hisspanic you loved all our racest god bless and rest in peace

**Andrés, Jul 07 at 08:35 PM**
Portrait of a master—Michael Jackson taught to the musicians and artists from all over the world anything to play with magic, heart and inspiration. He will be remembered as a genius who divided history with his music, and the live performance will never be the same without him. We Lost a master, a pioneer and a very special human being who preached the love to each other. Michael Jackson will need more than a single human race to dissappear...

**Annette, Jul 07 at 09:20 PM**
WHO SHOULD PAY FOR THE POLICE? ALL THIS TALK ABOUT WHO SHOULD PAY FOR THE POLICE FOR TODAY, WELL DONT YOU THINK MICHAEL JACKSON HAS PAID FO ENOUGH? WHAT ABOUT THE POLICE RAIDS, AND THE EMBARRASSMENT HE WENT THROUGH ON THE FAULSE SEXUAL CASE? I FEEL LIKE HE PAID WITH HIS LIFE. ALL OF THE STRESS. YOU POLICE OFFICERS SHOULD FEEL PRIVILEGED TO ESCORT THE KING! THOSE BOYS WHO LIE SHOULD BE ASHAMED AND SO SHOULD THEIR FAMILIES. ABOUT HIS DRUG USE STOP BLAMING THE FAMILY THEY TRIED, START BLAMING THE DOCTORS FOR GIVING THE DRUGS TO HIM. MAKE AN EXAMPLE OUT OF THESE DOCTORS BECAUSE JUST ABOUT EVERY DOCTOR IN AMERICA IS GUILTY OF THIS. TO MICHAEL AND HIS FAMILY I LOVE YALL AND MY PRAYERS ARE WITH YALL YALL DID EVERYTHING YOU COULD! SOME LOVE FROM TEXAS

**Snowie, Jul 07 at 10:30 PM**
Michael Jackson was NOT a child molester. He was a caring, loving man who also loved children. Was Jesus a child molester? He hung out with children too. Shame on all of you for tainting Michael's good name.
I hope, Michael, that IS your ghost in Neverland!

**Jennifer, Jul 07 at 10:30 PM**
Wow...I can't believe...you're gone. I appreciate the memories that I will pass onto my children. I know what it feels like to be on trial all the time (with family, friends, and the public). Throughout it all... you just smiled. You did what you had to do and took it like a man. You were not strange. You had a huge heart that you just shared with everyone. For the children, you should be honored to have such a great father, an icon... someone that will always be remembered. Stay strong. We love you from California.

# INTERNATIONAL POSTINGS

**Dinolla, NEW GUINEA**
We love you MJ....RIP....our thoughts and prayers with your family and friends.....YOU WERE THE BEST....from Papua New Guinea!!!

**Hamid, IRAN**
unbelievable.RIP MJ. you are with no doubt the most popular foreign artist in Iran and you always will be in our hearts.

**Kathy, CANADA**
Im from Canada New Brunswick.Its sad too lose such a great singer.I grew dancing and sining too all his music.Hes at peace now and will always be sadly missed.

**Yorlady, COLOMBIA**
This is a sad loss, as a human being, man, artist! always to Michael, here you will remember forever!

**s_p_teal, PHILIPPINES**
PHILIPPINES IS THE NUMBER ONE FAN OF MICHAEL JACKSON, THIS IS SAD LOSS AND YOU WILL ALWAYS REMEMBER.

**hassan, PAKISTAN**
GOOD BLESS HIM IN A HEAVEN.
HASSAN FROM PAKISTAN

**Anujkrsharma**
World has lost a great soul. They say he died of cardiac arrest. It was

only natural that something of eventually happened, but his death was hastened by those in the media & others who took great joy in filing false criminal complaints which only ended up in acquittals & reported widely & made fun of. Its a fact that those celebrities who today give out condolence messages with great panache were the same people who avoided him during his end days because of him being controversial & financially weak.

**Mahdi,**
I am an Arab Man, and what am i going to say that, no one can take jackson's place, he is the legend and he is the true dancer, Rest IN peace Micheal, we will always remember you.

**Alyssa, ITALY**
michael died and that is what u say?? god should forgive u ****!poor michael...and poor anyone who dies so young...you are just a piece of **** for saying that.. good job..hate your ass hole

**george, GEORGIA**
we love too michael. Tbilisi

**NETHERLANDS**
i think that m.j an angel on earth was, now he`s in the heaven, the world will missed him for all the good things he has done for young and old people. michael my friend rest in peace the world dont forget you

**Rene, COLOMBIA**
Que Triste me siento i feel so sad.

**JJ, CANADA**
WHAT AN EXTRAORDINARY TALENTED SPIRIT. I WATCHED HIM IN CANADA AT HIS FIRST FAMILY PERFORMANCE AND KNEW HE WAS SPECIAL. HIS SONGS TRIED TO HEAL THE RACE MADNESS, BLACK OR WHITE AND TOOK ON OUR PREJUDICE BY ASKING US TO SEE THE PERSON IN THE MIRROR, THE CHANGE MUST START WITHIN US. MICHAEL HAS GIVEN ME MANY HAPPY MOMENTS AND MEMORIES. MAY THE GOD OF LOVE,OF

LIGHT, OF FORGIVENESS, OF PLURALITY, BE THERE TO MEET YOU. FAREWELL SON OF MAN.

## kjerim, MACEDONIA
I regret that I do not know to write well in English but I want to say that no birth mother to Michael Jackson ... this was our first and last of this planete...

## Cathins, RUSSIA
Stranger in Moscow. Its a beautiful, sad song/video. Perfect for the sad feelings of the day.:

## DevilOnTheRun, BURMA
Burma is like other world from all the countries. But Michael, you've reached there...You're without a doubt one kind and almost everyone in the wolrd know "Michael Jackson" and your moonwallk.

## Glaucia Martins, BRAZIL
The music lost its greatest pop idol of all time Michael Jackson, here in Brazil and he is very dear, God bless him always, and protection to their dear children, which later

## Cristina, CHINA
China is crying for you.

## Judith, BOLIVIA
I so very sad, because you leave usI
yes, I´m very sad, because you leave us, But, I save the hope that see you again, in the new world, a new world of God Jehova, where isn´t dead and pain, See you again, I´m sure, I love you my dear Michael. Judith T.

## Mj forever, PALESTINE
michael your music help in much situation... RIP from palestine

## edouard, FRANCE
RIP MICHAEL. MICHAEL, THE FRANCE YOU LOVE (L)

## beli, BELGIUM
from belgium
good bye…you was a star I have many memories whith your songs thanks
good luck to your children.

## Sveta, UKRAINE
Michael, you God of dance, you are our idol…we love…but you always
live in my heart…R.I.P. from Ukraine

## beata, POLAND
you're king of pop forever.
we love you forever! R.I.P. from Poland. ;(( I miss you

## Mads, ROMANIA
Hope the angels will take good care of him
I wasn't such a big fan of Michael…I mean,I have to admit it…some of his
fans have a lot of his posters,photos…they were all fainting when they
saw him…maybe even on TV…spent all of their money on buying some
tickets just to see That Big Star singing…I can't compare to you guys…you
deserve to be his No1 fan…I…I had 1 year when he came in Romania in
'96…I couldn't remember his face even if I was at his concert then,but I
just wish he would have come in our country again so I can see him -_-…I
admit I didn't wish that when he was still alive,because 1He was going to
have a concert in London…2He was 50…I thought,man he still has years
to live…but,guess I was wrong-_-ok…now I'll be short from now…I think
he was still inside a child…he loved Peter Pan…&he created Neverland…
But now that big star is shining up up in the sky…we just need to look at
it…now he sees us from above-_-But just think…he was a star…now he is
a star shining up high and he will remain a star!

## GREECE
I honestly cannot believe he's gone. It wasnt until the news came on in
england to say he's dead that i suddenly realised how much he meant and
how much i didnt know about this man or his songs. I've been looking up
stuff on youtube and listening to them and they are truely amazing. There
will never be another michael jackson, certainly never in my lifetime. I've
never cried over a celebrity death but the more I've found out about him
the more I have. I have to say he was certainly VERY good looking up

to the point of the late 1990's. I miss you and wish I had taken time out to meet you and not to "judge a book by its cover" and i cannot express how sorry i am for that. You were an angel given to us in disguise. just wish more people saw. Your music will live on forever. Please look over your family now and show them a way to go on. Im sure Allah leant us you so we could see how rigid we all are, and im so greatful, RIP Michael Jackson. I love you.

**ERINA, JAPAN**
R.I.P You loved all fans. Therefore I love you. I do not forget the miracle that you showed us. Thanks Michael heartily. "ARIGATO,SAYONARA" from Tokyo Japan

**Katrysia, UKRAINE**
R.I.P.from Ukraine. I love you Michael… I cry,cry………

**A. Jylland,**
Smile, even though your heart is breaking
Smile, even though your heart is aching
Smile, even though your heart is breaking
Michael Joseph Jackson. You didn't get that old. To be honest, I actually don't think you lived as long as you should have. You were a great, great man. A great man that it didn't seem that the World really saw for who you are, but for what the media made you. But you are a man filled with love. A man filled with compasion. A man filled with caring. A man filled with peace. You are the King Of Pop, but your heart is so much bigger than that. Your heart is what made you never give up. You are an inspiration. You are one of the first artists I listened to when I was little. I remember the first time I saw the Thriller-video. I didn't dare to blink. I was so amazed, I felt so humble, I absolutely adored you. I thought that it was the most brilliant thing I had ever seen, ever experienced. You were a part of the foundation of why I love music. Why I believe in Peace. Why I believe in Love. How can I keep up my believes without you here to tell me to keep on fighting? Michael. You told me to raise my voice, and so I did. And I haven't lowered it since.I promise you, that I will keep fighting. Fighting for the World. Fighting for Peace. Fighting for Love. Fighting for you. Michael, I love you.

**Ivana, CZECH REPUBLIC**
Dear Michael, Michael, we love you. Forever...

**Agata, POLAND**
...From Poland...I'll Never Say You Goodbye

**Anastasia, RUSSIA**
FROM Moscow! KING OF POP!!!!!! Michael Jackson! ...The PERSON WHO ALWAYS SMILED, And HIS EYES were CHILDREN'S And SAD!!!!
I SINCERELY BELIEVE, THAT MICHAEL JACKSON HAS NOT DIED..... THAT IT HAS SIMPLY LEFT SOMEWHERE FAR AWAY FROM ALL THIS VANITY AND SEVERE, SILLY PEOPLE AND WILL LIVE THE QUIET LIFE...... I LOVE YOU MICHAEL, NS FOR EVER WILL REMAIN IN MY HEART AND YOU ALWAYS WILL BE THE KING WITH WHOM ANYBODY NEVER WILL REPLACE!!!!!!!!! ...

**D. Agudo,**
"Heal the World" Aside from poking my baby sister through her playpen while singing and dancing to "Bad" in the late 80s, my most vivid MJ memory was when I was asked to participate in a rendition of "Heal the World" in front of my entire elementary school while in 1st grade. A few other 1st graders and I dressed up like children of the world and sang along to MJ's track. Now every time I hear it, I get teary-eyed. I love ya MJ!

**Diane, KAZAKHSTAN**
He will live forever in our hearts. R.I.P. I LOVE U

**mario, CROATIA**
WE MEET AGAIN—I cant remember what i want to say!!!but when i die I want to see you in PARADISE WILL YOU BE THERE???i think KING that we met in BETTER place for YOU and for me!!!i am from croatia...and KING you always be in my heart!!!RIP FROM CROATIA

**meise, GERMANY**
i miss you Michael...R.I.P FROM GERMANY-COLOGNE

**Zamira,**
Love for M.J.—Sad to see an inspirational icon go, he will live forever, but why does it matter if he is in debt? why does it matter if you used drugs or not? For once in a life time can America live up to their ideal democracy and realize that he was no different from everyone else, if anything we should beg him and thank him for all the times he has forgiven us, for he never acted wrong, he just wanted to sing and entertain, may he rest and peace always and forever, America needs to live up to their true democracy by appreciating the joy,love, and acceptance he brought to us in a world like this. R.I.P Michael Jackson

**kaveh, IRAN**
Iran—He will live forever in our hearts.

**Asaad, MOROCCO**
love from morocco R.I.P

**Christine Iversen**
He thrilled me!
I was maybe 7 years old when Thriller came out. We couldn't afford the record but a neighbor kid had it. I'd go to his house and he'd play it for me. Every time the song Thriller ended and Vincent's laugh filled the air I'd run and hide in the corner, half with freight and half with delight. Then I'd get up and ask him to play it again! I can't believe he's gone, I took him and his music for granted, he created the soundtrack of my youth. It was a beautiful memorial, I cried a bit. He will always be my number one pick on the dance floor, he was a giant that nobody can topple. Long live the King!

**BORISOV, UKRAINE**
Jackson THE BEST....I don't understand english good, but he was the best. i liven Ukraine,KIEV. kIEV LOVED HIM.

**Ilaria, ITALY**
Remember when i was little girl that I loved Michael for your songs,

remember when I was crazy for your dance, it's very very beautiful, fantastic. I'm a italian fan, and i'll never forget this beautiful man, I hope that in heaven above will find the peace that false hypocritical world has found nothing. So we observe Michael, and I know that your eyes are your songs, I will follow my path in the near, as always happened so far.

**Jose, CUBA**
Michael you are the one—I'm Cuban and always dream to see you in person, in a concert. Now I know I never do it. Rest in peace whereever you are. Friend.My Idole.

**Ashley, CHINA**
RIP from Hong Kong—RIP Michael Jackson, the one and only King of Pop
HIS MUSIC WILL LIVE FOREVER. Yea. That's Right.

**arpit, INDIA**
king is no more...he will always be the king of pop...wot he gave the world is next to nothin...being in india we were not exposed to much of english songs earlier...but i always used to hear him.....since i was 3 or 4.....i was always a bigtime fan of him

**parande, FRANCE**
from paris...i grew up with you music! My children will never know you. But they will listen your music by me! You will never be out in our heart and life. We love you, we love your music, you are still the king of music and god of pop. we love you

**Ingalill, SWEDEN**
we will miss you here in Sweden—Your music will live forever...Rest in peace

**Maria**
You're truly a legend. I grew up listening to your Dangerous album around 1993-1994 and I heard you visited our country during that time. I attribute to you my inclination to music and dance; it is through you that I became passionate in this field. It still feels surreal that you are no longer physically present, but your legacy will be remembered forever.

**Karthik, INDIA**

Michael Jackson - I love you. Right from the day I was born ppl around me use to say "Man u have to see MJ's dance", he is the best break dancer on earth. But i've never seen any of his videos til then, every one right from a kid to a old man seem to be overwhelmed by him, inspite of the fact that here in India we don't listen to english music much.... But one day I listened to one song on radio and i fell in love with that song "The way you make me feel".. I came back home and downloaded that video and saw it over & over again... Then i saw more videos of MJ & then i started reading about him & that's when i realized that this man is the most famous, loved person to have walked this planet... I can't believe his is no more... I was so much looking forward to see him perform on his come back tour, but not to be.. Still Love you Michael...

dedication and love will be remembered forever. My condolences to the family Jackson, From Chile; Roberto.

MJ :-) The living god—Michael we here in denmark are destruet too see you go, bot now i know that an angel singin will be you, and now GOD has the greatest singer by his side. In the sky stars will be your support, and the sky will be your now neverland. your voice fill our hearts with peace..

**Vera, SWEDEN**

Man in the Mirror—It's a grey and rainy day in Stockholm, Sweden. A day where I have to face to make farewell to my idol, Michael Jackson.

**Esqandar, MALAYSIA**

For Michael—Michael I Cried Day And Night For Your Loss.Nearly 24 Hour A Day I Listen To All The Music You Left For Us. You'll Be In Our Heart Forever...From Malaysia(Melaka)

**Tyago, PORTUGAL**

God Bless you MJ—Hi my name is Tiago from portugal, i'm trying to somehow tell some words to discribe what you mean to me, but its so hard for people who grew up listening to your songs and for all of us who knew the wonderful human being you was, to express in a couple of words!! Being a dj i'll never forget those times i played your songs (still playing today and will play forever), those days when i was young playing them on my walkman whille going to school..you inspired many people in the world, and i'm not an exception...I cant stop crying when i'm listening your songs and live performances, when i see the public going crazy when you sing and dance at your best...i just done a playlist of like 30 songs of you to play on my car when i'm happy, when i'm sad, anytime!! You may now rest in peace, god wanted you next to him, you're now in a better place for sure! I LOVE YOU MICHAEL JACKSON!!! From your eternal fan and soul brother: Tyago

**Nicklas, DENMARK**
The one and only true king
Michael we here in denmark are destruet too see you go, bot now i know that an angel singin will be you, and now GOD has the greatest singer by his side. In the sky stars will be your support, and the sky will be your now neverland. your voice fill our hearts with peace..

**Alf, NORWAY**
Rest in Peace Michael--Words fail to describe the impact you've had on our world.You've made it a better place for us all. You've maybe left our world, but you'll always be here with us through your music. I want to dedicate a song sung by another undying legend, Freddie Mercury and Queen: Queen - No one but you (Only the good die young)Rest in Peace Michael. Deepest love from Norway.

**George, GREECE**
From Athens: goodbye...i cried so hard for you as watching your memorial today. i will miss you. you took a piece of my youth with you forever. say hi to my mother, Michael. and sing a song to her up there with the angels...love you. Goodbye.

**Jörgen Rosenback, SWEDEN**
I really can't explain with words how much i appreciate your work. Your songs, your moves, but most of all, your message. They say that one man can make a difference, with the difference you made, you're more like a god. I don't really have any great memories or good stories to tell. But the biggest memory is within all of us and the biggest difference you made was in all of us too. It's sad now that you're gone, but maybe it's best so that you can finaly rest in peace. Even though we should've done it sooner, i really hope that people all over the world will really open up

their eyes and look at each other with respect and with equality, just as you wished we should. I must admit that before you passed away, i just admired and liked your songs, and now when it's too late i realize how much you REALLY mean to me,not only me but millions of others too. You are truly an angel amongs angels, Kings amongs kings, but most important of all, you were a human being that really saw our broken world and wanted to make a change. I hope your message and legacy will live on and make a change in all of us. Michael,
Thank you for your time here with us, eternal blessings is not enough for you! You've Healed my world!

**Georg D.**
Thank you Michael, saving my nephew—I have nephew Ivan(son of my Brother).He was born in 1980.Around 1982-83, he was struggling with depression because of drug addiction of his mother ,with parents divorced ,with bed scores in school, he wanted and did try to kill himself. He did not wanted to talk to any body and you can see he was fading away. My sister had to sent her son from the capital to be his friend(They were cousins and friends the same age to be in the same class and watch him and help him to overcome the depression and isolation he was feeling ).And then come Michael Jackson and Billy Jean and the moonwalk My nephew IVAN, start practicing like creasy, listen the music and practicing till become "perfect moonwalker" and discover that he is very good dancer. All the kids from the school start loving him for his performance and In 9-10 grade he overcome the depression, overcome his shines ,perform his act in front anybody and become the most famose kid in the school and he loved it. Thank you, Michael, for saving lives for saving my nephew.

**XeraN, POLAND**
You were, You are, You'll be... I know You can't read this, but...In my life there has always been a music...In my life there has always been YOUR music, so You were a piece of me...I'll never forget these unforgettable parties, events, common walking down the street with headphones... You were one of these people who really could be loved...Not only for Your songs, but for Your character! If I wanted to write Your virtues down, I would write an essay...You showed people that a star has NOT to be conceited, capricious and unsettled-down...I'm only 22 now, but I know

there will never be such a GREAT singer as You in the future! REST IN PEACE JACKO! POLAND WILL NEVER FORGET YOU!

**Silvia, BRAZIL**
Miss you—day 25 of June of 2009, the sky with certainty was different, as nobody never had seen before,
therefore the star most shining came back toward it... Michael Jackson... only existed one and just he will exist!
Love we you very, we wait that he has much peace and joy where you stay now...KING forever! a brazilian fan;

**Tze Yi Koh, SINGAPORE**
MJ, R.I.P. You are a true legend and will be greatly missed. Your work on Earth is a masterpiece and will be treasured forever. The World celebrates your life today.

**g. rancho mirage,**
the best are always the first to go. i try to cry but have not help me, i have try sleep but i can't, i try everything but nothing make any sense any more! is like i'm in a big nightmare and i can't wake up! but you cd and video give some peace! the lyrics of your songs and every single step is printed on my mind your soul will be forever with us!
i know you love us and this sick planet, you did much more of all president of all countries around the world!
and you will be in the hearts of everybody without discrimination with love for you your kids and your family

**Michael M., GERMANY**
The greatest popstar ...I'm from germany but I've heard all the songs of him! Every song was a great song for me. I loved the music and the way he moved. Thank you for all beautyfull times with your music you gave me...! I hope you'll find a better place! Now you are a legend for all your fans.

**Ahmed N, EGYPT**
Rest in peace.
There will be only one king of pop, thats Michael Jackson , Rest in peace and thanks for helping me improve my English , my view of the world

and simply thank you for doing that much good in your life. RIP From Egypt.

## Vinnie

Long Live the King... Like Elvis is the king of Rock and Roll, Michael is the King of Pop and he shall live on like all those preformers whom we have known to love an cheer throgh out time. Michael's music has insipred some of the most prominant voices in music today and will continue to inspire many more for years to come. I remember when i first heard "will You be there" and how empowered i felt then. i was 8 years old and i was watching "Free Willy". here i am at 17 and now i feel just as empowered as i did then if not more. Thank you Michael for all that you have done for the world. now it's time for the world to do somthing for you. Rest in Peace. Long Live the King!

## Georgia Sa, GREECE

Love you for ever
I grew up in Greece listening to Michael Jackson's music. I am now 35 living in San Clemente, California and still love his music.Nobody sang or moved like Michael. The music radiated through his body and through his every move. I am crushed by his sudden death. I was so looking forward to his comeback. I never seen him on a tour and I guess I never will. The world lost a musical genius and a great humanitarian. I will always remember YOU!

## Mr. F. Marlinghaus, GERMANY

I'm German and I moved to Miami 4 years ago. I and lot's of other people in Europe grew up with his music and inspiration. Remember this great man and performer as a gift to everybody! I and my family won't forget you and you'll be missed forever! Thanks for being a part of your life !!

## pissocher g, FRANCE

thank forever et very much emotion for staple center
thanks for all to do it, i'm French i was born with Micheal's generation and i live with michael, now who you leave for the sky, you music will be missing, you dancing will be missing too.i wish to tell in your family all my consideration and respect with a person who was michael jackson if

in the sky do singing and dancing all people died thank you very much and good luck for yours new life bye michael

### Eduardo Guimarães, BRAZIL
I fell like I've lost a family member... I'll miss you, Michael, even that I didnt knew you personally. I love your songs, and the way youre dancing. I pray for you soul. May god give to you peace. Someday, we will met. Everybody in Brazil is sad. Here in Brazil we have a song, "Canção da América:" Friend is a thing to keep in the left size of the chest. Inside the heart. This is what tell the song that i've heard in America. But who sang this song cried, when he saw his friend leaving. But who stayed, keep the memory, the rememberingfor tother that leave. And no matter what, someday, i will see you again. Someday, i will see you again, brother.

### J Barragan, COLUMBIA
an angel go back to heaven, jackson family i want to ask you for something. Michael jackson was an angel in earth a great guy, a child in memory, an awsome guy. im just a kid, im only 15th years old, i started to listen him about five years ago, and i really fell the pain about his dead, RIP Michael Jackson.
Jackson family, im yust a kid, im an actor, an i am writing a pay about him, i dont know if you really care about this, but I want to have your permission to present my play just in my school, no more. im from colombia. sorry about my bad english if i have it. thanks

### Daniele, BRAZIL
The best... !!!
{♥} The Brazil love you forever... !!!
{♥} King of pop.. !!!
{♥} Best star... !!!

### J.R., INDIA
he was the thru it all!---the joy! Laughter !t ears!-u are an angel! Micheal was a angel sent on this earth to show us what it meant to be a true human being,i am from india now canadian but yet continent so far away still embarassed Michael,from the slums to the richest....but i grew up all my life from a baby to now with him,it felt like he was family..like blood!like loosing d best thing this world ever had!he brought every one

together...i remember every Christmas i listen to the Jackson 5 cassette Christmas edition too&reading they're comics and then came "off the wall"...he was with me in all my life..even thou i was never lucky enuf to see him in reality...he was a man that gave more than he received and yea he was childlike at heart...and that was a blessing in disguise..coz no1 cud think like Micheal and its sad that he isnt here to to watch his children grow and to love them&teach them his ways and share his knowledge like he planned to...life without Michael is never gonna be the same..to know that we wont have the honor to see him in life never again brings an aching pain in one's heart...i know we will celebrate his life and legacy.. but i cant help but feel sad..wish he never left..the good ones god always calls first...i miss u Micheal..i feel more remorse for his kids who he was mam and dad to..they lost not one but 2 parents when he left..god be with them and i know he will too..he died working and doing what he did best for his kids and the world.

Even in his times of turmoil..he never tot about himself..he did everything we are expected to do as humans..as time goes i know people will see who he truly was..and regret why we never gave this man what he wanted which was to be loved and understood...i know i will save all his collections so when i have children i will let him live on in my life forever...i miss u Micheal..the world would not be the same if you never came along and now that ur gone it wont be the same without u there to set a example for us..u are genius..but most of all you are my hero..my inspiration...A BLESSING !

### Jonathan M., CANADA

the pain in my heart—When I heard MJ died I was in total denial. Saying no their lying its just a media frenzy. But when I watched the news, My Family and I started praying and weeping at the same time. I will always listen to his songs. And he actually made a difference with songs. He was a Entertainer and Humanitarian. MJ your Awesome and will always be the King of Pop, no matter what.

### Nathan, JJ, FRANCE

Gone too soon—My name is Nathan I'm 20 and i'm from paris. When MJ left i was really in a sad mood and i asked myself "why am i so sad about this i didn't even known him he's not part of my family?" so i thought about this and i understood.here is my answer. How could i not be upset about the death of someone who has always made me happy with his songs and dances into the best and the worst moments of my life listening to billie jean remember the time bad man in the mirror workin'day and night she's out of my life you rock my world black or white rock with you earth song and so so much other songs , someone who deeply believed in the peace on earth and fought for it. So for all the support and the joyful moments he gave to me by his talent i want to thank him. There is no day without thinking of him. THANK YOU MICHAEL I WILL ALWAYS REMEMBER YOU MAY YOU REST IN PEACE YOU'LL ALWAYS BE THE GREATEST.

## BOB, ENGLAND
## TO THE EDUCATOR OF WISDOM IN AN IGNORANT WORLD

I Don't know exactly where to begin my comment and in which would be the best way to express the emotions....

Farewell to a legend that came to this earth to express gods love through music, dance and lyrics.

MJ you are beyond what words can describe.

Every soul on this earth has objectives that need fulfilling and you have done everything that no-other artist or person has done before.

Now there is no-one left to express words of wisdom that did it like you in its most unique and unimaginative form.

I recall my retro 80's childhood waiting up late at night to watch your world music video premieres of 'Thriller' and 'Bad' with my family in the United Kingdom and watching you in the hilliarous 'Wiz' movie. I collected your Trade cards with free Bubble gum swapping these with my friends at Primary school.

I bought the Moonwalker storybook and Off the Wall magazines, orignal released Bad album cassette all which I have still kept. My wish was to see you in person or watch you perfom live at a concert before I died,.... not the other way round by you leaving us... your fans ...it doesnt seem fair but,

I strongly believe this and am sure that your family and fans support me for saying this, That we are all born on this earth for a purpose, and until we dont complete our objectives we will never leave....

God kept an close eye on you and had seen that you have done so so much for humanity and set trends and educated others and your words will continue to be passed onto generations just as messiahs, prophets, pundits, priests and gurus have shared there words of wisdom and teachings of love and equality.

I only pray that we dont become our own worst enemies and that we live life to its max..love and laughter just as you taught us.

I was looking forward to seeing you at the O2 Arena this year, but somethings are beyond the control of us and in the hands of the big man above us all God.

Rest In Peace.

Lots of love to the whole Jackson family and fans world-wide.

RESPECT LOVE PEACE

BOB :-

## Nici, GERMANY

Dear Michael,

I will never forget you. If i think that you has gone too early i must fight with the tears. You were really the king of pop and everything what you have done was great. I hope you find enclose. And I hope you has find a better place in heaven and your wishes come true. I always miss you and you are every day in my mind. I can't stop crying.

You my inspiration, for music and for everything! I love you..for ever and ever. God bless your family.

## Amar, NETHERLANDS

R.I.P Micheal Jackson.

Rip the king of pop i might just be 16 years old and live in the Netherlanths but your music influencend my live ever since iv been a child i tried to moonwalk and i apprieciate your music and have alot of love and respect for you RIP.

## Samii

When a King becomes an Angel—we love you michael, we will never forget you. I hope that I can one day make some of your wishes come true. you were an unbelievable and unforgetable person...rest in peace an may god keeps you in a peacefull place. I LOVE YOU

## Aneta, POLAND

Idol—I remember first time seeing michael on tv. i was about 7 maybe. i live in Poland then, and i remember watching black or white. and that song ever since i heard it made me happy. i fell in love with michael... literly. i grew up dancing to him. i'd close my bedroom doors and just dance. he was a true legend i love and will miss forever. there will be no other like him. i love you mj rip.

## D.B.Ri.Moreira, CHILE

R.I.P, LOVING YOU FROM CHILE...I cried watching this damn afternoon the funeral of Michael Jackson, is that I love him more than anything in this world! .. His voice, his dancing, his screams, his long high quality videos made by great directors of cinema, uff.. a lot of stuff that made his music a masterpiece of high quality .. nobody will be the king of pop, no one take his place, is unique and unmatched! anyone can put him out of his. God bless you Michael!

## Darwin, N.T., AUSTRALIA

GOD BLESS YOU MICHAEL
F Rest in peace xxx Forever and always will your love, joy and kindness live on in our hearts

## V. Armario

I miss you—Michael, we all miss you so much...I always said that I was going to meet you someday, before I die. But life has been unfair for you, your family, your friends and fans. I learnt what music was with yours, I learnt English thanks to you and your lyrics, and that's really important in my life, because since then I've always wanted to be an English teacher...You ARE an inspiration, and you didn't leave us, I know you're still here and will be here forever. Your music, your passion, your kind heart won't leave us...I love you.

## Mike, HAWAII

Live in Sky—even though "the king of pop" is dead, he lives on forever. I live in Hawaii, my mother had countless records, casstette tapes so grew up listening to his music. Even though he had his legal problems we're not perfect. But putting that all aside he was and is the greatest performer to live nobody can match his creativity his energy or love for music R.I.P. Mike

### Dewei Kong, CHINA

Forever Michael, Fovever His Songs......I'm from China,he is the most famous singer in our country.We can't forget you,Michael, you are the king of pop. Please remember: Michael You Are Not Alone!!!! You will heal the world!!!

### Mme, GERMANY

my youth my life—"Bad" was my first album I bought. I'll never forget this moment. My little pocket money... all for this album and just to have it. I didn't knew his moment when I bought it. But since this I loved him and his music. So many times I heared f.e. "heal the World" and "We are the childrens" I started to cry. The memorial ceremony was great, in my opinion. It showed who Micheal is. It was Michael. I it was great to see how many people shared this heavily way for his family, his friends, his childrens, his fans - all people who loved him ever. He did so much and affected so much more. Thank you Michael.We will miss you. I will miss you. And I hope that all the other with there bad opinion will get a sign to check out who really he was. I wish you all much of love all times - life is to short to forget to live it. many greetings

### The Garcia Family,

I grew up with you, even though, I never new you personally. Michael, I feel like I lost a brother, even though I didn't know you in person, I knew you by your works, I knew you by your kindness, I remember when you were the first person to visit our community after the Cleveland School Shooting! I feel like you were family. I remember when my son was growing up, he fell in love with your music, and tried to emulate your dance moves! I remember, when I was bout 7 and would get up on Saturday morning's and watch the Jackson Five programs! I remember the night Thriller debuted, it was like going to a gangbuster movie! I remember when! You are now and forever will be special in my life, and watching your memorial today, made me understand, your really gone in body, but your soul will live on in me, and all of us forever more. We love you Michael, and thank you for giving us all your life.

## Tim Rocks, RUSSIA
Forever in My Heart. For MJJ.........From Russia with Love.

## Jeannie, PHILIPPINES
Thank you Mj—I am a Filipina from the Philippines...God Bless you Mj..You will be sorely missed by the people who loves you..by the people whom you have inspired....Thank you for your gift to the world. thank you for your music, thank you for your dance, thank you for your heart, thank you for showing that you care..that you really really care....Thank you.... We will miss your presence..but in our hearts, you live forever.... forever..... And we will pass on your legacy of greatness to the future generation...

## chela,
hello my name is chela and i am 13! i have loved all of michael jacksons music since the very first time i heard his music!! he is soooo talented!!!!! my little brother who is 10 years old is very good at dancing and he loves to try be michael!!!! its sooo funny !! but he is very good at dancing like michael!!!!!!! michael jackson was such a beautiful adorable boy! although it is a real shame he got all that plasic on his face! :( i think it looked good when he just changed the shade of his skin a bit whiter and his nose but then he just went way over the top! :( but i really wished to meet him one day and tell him al about how much i love his music and tell him about my brother so he can laugh about it! lol...anyways put it down to 3 words?
MICHAEL JACKSONS AWSOME!!!!!!!!

## Neasha, TRINIDAD
Heaven Sent—He was a heaven sent who had a special gift from god to bring together people of all races, cultures and ethnicities. He saw equality among everyone and i am truly sorry and regret that only now that he is gone, that i have stopped and really took the time out to see that... i really wish that somehow he will know how much he is missed by the world. I live in Caribbean island of Trinidad and in my country i believe Michael has only performed once, and that was so long ago, back in the days of Jackson 5... god didn't even send me into this world as yet. i remember when i use to live with my grandparents, there were only three local television channels, and one of them, once in a while showed

the black or white video, i loved that video so much, i really don't know how to explain how much i loved it, i think it was all the different people on the video doing all the different dance and stuff. i have never had the opportunity to meet Micheal Jackson, to see him in person either far or close up and have never went to any of his concerts... but yet still i am proud and privileged to live in the same era as the great Michael Jackson. i know it is always best to be a leader and not a follower, and Michael was a true leader, i too will like to lead one day, but for now i will like to follow M.J.'s footsteps and legacy and be one to unite and bring together this broken world. My heart goes out to his family and all of his other fans across the world and i will like to let his family know that no matter what his memory will live on in this generation and the many more to come. i plan to get married some day and i also plan to have kids, and when I'm teaching them about all the different people who made a difference in this world there will be Ghandi, Martin Luther king, Nelson Mandela, Rosa Park, Arther Cipriani, and so much more, but most of all Michael Jackson would be in that list. My heart goes out to his family once more and i would like to say to them how deeply sorry i am for realizing Michael's achievements after he is gone. he will live on in my heart and in the heart of so many. Michael... we love you.

**Luca, ITALY**
From Millano: Lion Heart—Michael - your music, your love moved mountains. Your memory will move us to be better. I watched you live at RFK Stafium long time ago, The Victory Tour. I came all the way here from Europe for that. I wonder - what can I do to perpetuate your memory of a unique Human Being...Your Heart, a Lion Heart, stop beating at the time God wanted. For God also wanted you.
Your was an example of Victory thru pain.

**AAlvaradoV, COSTA RICA**
thanks for your inspiration—thanks a lot for your inspiration, you were my first artist idol, all days i put the triller LP in my radio to listen your music, i will never forget you, thanks to give me a greath moments in my life with your music

**K (21yo), FRANCE**
A new star among the sky...Michael Jackson, this name won't be forgotten.

He was the one, the only one able to make people dancing & crying of joy like he did. When I heard the news, I was really devastated...it was unbelievable ! So Michael, if you can read this, I won't forget you, your music, your genius, your moonwalk...you gave to the world something that no governments may give...Rest in peace.

**Omar A,**
Michael or Mikaeel. It Doesnt Matter—Michael, you are a true legend. A lotta people tried to imitate U but it was impossible for them. Whether black or white, whether muslim or christian. You will always be the King of Pop
LONG LIVE THE KING
the letter that says I won the tickets. I have framed

**Sherryann, BARBADOS**
Love you more!!—I remember when Michael Jackson's Thriller came out, I was 13..My best friend and I saved up enough money to buy the record, when we got home we played it over and over the entire day until we had every word for every song written down, so that we would be able to sing along to all the songs...After that I had a jacket, posters and more records when they came out.. I always felt so close to Michael, as we are both Virgos and seem to be very similar...As I grew into a woman, I always followed Michael and always loved him. I never once thought he was guilty during his trials because I knew he was not what the media was making him out to be...I have been very sad over the past few days but today was the day that I shed tears while watching the memorial service...I will miss seeing you Michael, I wish you the peace and eternal happiness in heaven that you did not seem to find while you were among us.. I currently work with children, so I feel especially sad for your children and I pray they will continue to have the love and support of the one person who loved and supported you, your Mom!So Michael, as you would say to your brother Marlon and which I always say to my family...I LOVE YOU MORE

**genagen, RUSSIA**
Michail did not want to live........ anymore... And now he has peace in the haven.But people <ichail will remember you long ,long years.because

you are KING and we all adore you and your songs.Thank you for your humanityand goodness,which emanated trough you.RIP

## zaliha

MJ u r always in our heart...
U are KING POP to music lovers...
U are soft hearted & loving person to your childrens...
U are lovely person to your families...
U are unique to yourself...and...
U are everything to me that will live forever in my heart
love u always..MJ

## Kulshona, MALAYSIA

Micheal, I'm gonna miss you deeply....Dearest Michael, i have known you since the 70s' and will never forget you ever. My mother always says, God calls the person who he loves the most and i know that you are with god, watching us down here. Michael, you are not here physically anymore, but your soul is here with us forever, i'm sure of that. Rest in peace, dear friend. Kul and family

## Mitchell gosling, FRANCE

R.I.P Michael Jackson we shall never forget the perfect enternainer. the memorial was perfect, touching and the best tribute. you still are the king and always will be. Paris was amazing she made me brake down. Love to your family & children. and thank you for every single song that you done who did change the world
never forget the king of pop

## GRN,

Heal the world—Dearest, dearest michael..Tonight there is a special magic over the fullmoon. You are there with us- We are not alone,Michael and its like when I call out your name YOU ARE THERE I can feel from above your loving happy smile spreed over the earth- healing it.. Thank you for a beautiful sermony you and your family shared with us - the howle world- nothing could have been stronger..
we all cried together.. the howle world.. The gifts and messages you have been given us for so many years have finaly given a wakeup call to this

needing earth Everything you have been trying to tell us through your music becomes even clearer and stronger to me now-

You have been my inspiration and gidedance since I was young, and will always continue to be...You have given me a new strengh to help the children of the world- and I will do..-I will be true to my hart...As I was waching the fullmoon tonight I thought: If we could all pray together from every corner of the world,like we did today, at every fullmoon to come, for love for our planet- in the spirit of you ,Michael- we could start to HEAL THE WORLD TOGETHER..I will think of you every fullmoon, thank you for EVERYTHING. God bless you and your family. With love and light from me

# LOVE, APPRECIATION AND CONTRIBUTION

**Kevin**

There was a time when Michael Jackson was hugely popular and widely admired, and the music he made during those years cannot be dismissed. However, I think his influence on music has generally been overstated. As an active musical artist, Michael Jackson ceased to be relevant years ago. I don't know anybody who likes his music who owns copies of anything he made after Bad, for example. And let us not forget that the "King of Pop" label was something he (or his managers) invented, not something that the press spontaneously started calling him. Michael Jackson's true legacy is more apparent in music videos. I don't recall seeing groups of people dancing in videos before "Beat It", but we've definitely been seeing them in videos ever since. And "Thriller" was pretty much the first video of its kind to receive significant notice. His other contribution to music is the use of rock musicians in R&B. Before Eddie Van Halen's solo in "Beat It", such collaborations were almost unheard of.

**DJV05**

What a talented man- he provided many years of entertainment to the world, both musically and as a subject of speculation for the gossip magazines. You either loved him or hated him, but you could not ignore him.I am sad that he passed away before what could have been a great "comeback" with his British Tour. Michael Jackson has made an indelible mark in the music world, many of us will have fond memories of his landmark and standout performances.I don't know what was happening in his different world, but I always sensed that he was a gentle and generous soul. And a musical genius.Like so many other legends, he is gone too soon.His family should be assured that he will never be forgotten, and that he was loved by many.His detractors will move on to someone else...

## Adrian Duggan

R.I.P Michael. Your music influenced a generation so much it scared a government.Ever since he became political with his songs about racial equality and saving the planet the American Govt tried through whatever means possible to silence him...slurs and accusations,especially those to do with Children, are a common tactic to destroy some one with so much influence on the common man,especially a black man with more recognition and cross over around the planet, than had ever been before!!

His music inspired not only the masses,but also the musicians,artists and creative generations that followed.

I will miss his music as will millions of others.

## Tina

Music genius and innovator who changed videos, dance, TV, music,....

## Ms.Lisa,

Hi my name is Lisa and I would just like to say that it is just so unbelievable that you are gone but I would just like to say to you Michael how much of an impact you had such an impact in my family's life. You bring me back to my childhood such an innocent time in my life a place wish I could go back to. To the Jackson family I would just like to say I feel your pain, I too recently lost a brother it is so hard for me at times because I had such a close relationship with him he is so special to me, and to you Janet you could not have said it any better when you said to his fans he was an icon but to you and your family he was the heart of your family. That's what my brother is, he is my heart, he is my family's. Please do me a favor Michael and tell my brother hi for me and that I love and miss him very much. I love you Michael.

## Jelena,

Dear Michael I still cannot stop the tears and I still do not want to believe!!! U live and U will always live for me and for us all!!! I love You, the greatest man, the greatest person of us all!!! Now U are gonne, now that your honest and misunderstood heart is gonne, I can pray for someone like you to be born again or this world will soon go to its end without the heart like yours and the love U had for the whole world... Forever

**Sasphia**
an incredible star has fallen...i was born 32yrs after this legend & there was no generation gap between us because everything that he sang about was deep and it appealed to the nature of the dying world,which he tried to save through his songs...he's gone but he will always live on in my heart and home. micheal's music will contiune to live past him into a time when we have also past. when i hear his music,it actually heals some little place in my heart and i hope it does the same for you too.

**10901**
Michael is a great talent: a chreographer, a composer, a great dancer, a musician. A genius. A real artist. Only jealous/ ignorant people make fun of him...

**SweetestSin xOh**
you rockk my world should be on the top 10! RIP Michael Jackson you will never be forgottenn.

**WINDGATED**
When I was 10, no one could have told me that I was not going to marry Michael Jackson! I have been listening to and enjoying his music all morning. To the Master - rest in Peace! No more stress, no more ridicule, no more ugky gossip and stories. You will be here for ever.

**Leilani**
Michael you have brought so much joy to so many people through your precision of music and dance. Rest Michael, there is no more stress to please others anymore. I don't think the world really know how much you loved them. I only hope they can see it now. I'd believed in you through all the controversy, so sad so many others didn't. We could have enjoyed more of your amazing talent. You will be missed. Blessings go out to your children and family. Finally rest your broken heart Michael. I luv U!

## CogJm4

To Michael Jacksons' family, We all lost a great humanitarian, song writer and singer. There was alot of talk about certain areas in his life, but to each their own. LEAVE HIM BE!!!!! HE'S GONE NOW AND LET THE REST OF US REMEMBER MICHAEL IN OUR OWN WAYS. REST IN PEACE MY DEAR FRIEND. Lots of LOVE, Jeannine

## Randi S,

The King of Pop has left the building—Michael Jackson was my first love. I got my first Michael Jackson doll for Christmas when I was about 4 years old wore out many a Michael Jackson cassette tape. I danced to his songs in my bedroom, my living room, my front yard, at school dances, and anywhere else I could possibly dance. Michael spoke to me and I fell in love with him. I will always believe in my heart that he was one of the greatest artists to ever walk this Earth. He was an amazing talent that few can possibly compare to. He was cursed with fame but blessed with a gentle spirit and imagination that most would envy. It was a sad day when the world lost Michael. He will forever be alive in our hearts and in his art. I will always love you, Michael, till I join you

## Andrea

No words could ever express the great loss this world has suffered with the passing of Michael Jackson. Michael Jackson was a man who for the most part was very misunderstood. True fans of his music had the opportunity to get to know of him through his wonderful music, electrifying performances, and the out pouring of love from his fans and peers. He will be sorely missed by all that knew and loved him and by millions of adoring fans. Let's not forget the great loss his family has suffered. May God continue to bless his family and give them the enormous strength and courage they will need ove the days to come. I thank God, his heavenly father as well as his Mother Katherine and Father Joe for their wonderful gift to the world. "MICHEAL JOSEPH JACKSON". GOD BLESS YOU! R.I.P.

## guardthedew

I think this will just get sadder as the days go on. I mean, he's Michael Jackson. Grandmothers in Peru have heard of Michael Jackson. I've been very cynical towards his career. I dig some stuff. And I keep that to myself. I mean, I am a rocker after all. And although I don't own one album, now that he's gone I realize how much his music was a part of my life. How much I enjoy hearing "Rock With You" when it's plays on the muzak at work. Being young and seeing Thriller for the first time on Mtv, And witness it turn the music and video world on it's ear.

I think I became a fan yesterday. He deserves it. And although I've joked and judged in the past several years, I choose to remember him, and miss him, as a fan.

## Mary E A

To me he was the ???vision maker??? ??? his music videos were so incredibly entertaining that it raised the bar so high that I do not think anyone can ever reach it. I grew up with his music; his lyrics and his dance accepted his ups and downs and still loved him. He was a kind, gentle human who sent such powerful messages through his song ??? ???Black or White??? & ???Man in the mirror??? . I can never say goodbye to Michael Jackson the one and only King of Pop. Truly like your song ???Gone to soon??? Now RIP

## Dolores

Michael Jackson was and will always be the KING of POP, and a very GREAT outstanding INDIVIDUAL from the very start of the Jackson5. You may have left us, but YOUR MUSIC is gonna keep on PLAYING through out the WHOLE UNIVERSE!!! Love YOU Michael You are happy now, and no more sorrows etc,.

## MHEJ4

Michael Jackson death has hit the entire globe, you see pepole around the world crying as if it has happen to someone in their family. And for the most part you can understand why, when you grow up with someone so famous and well known you cannot but feel for him and his family for there lost. He was a entertainer but most of all a icon and he well be miss. I know that God well give the family striaght......Michael may you rest in peace and God be with you in the HEAVEN

## Patrice

The year I was born 1969 Born and raised in G.I,I grew up on the

Jackson5.My eldest syblings went to school with a few of the Jackson5 syblings Roosevelt High,I also attended in my freshman year,my older syblings raised me on the singing group I 've followed them to the end.I remember when I fisrt saw them on SoulTrain,every since then i grew with them before and after the group went seperated ways,right now today Latoya,Jermaine,Rebe I've enjoyed.Michael will always have a special plac in heart

Janet I'm a fan of your music also thank u all for inspiring me with your beautiful talents. I would like to send special prayers out to the Jackson clan from myself and family, God Bless you all and stay strong.

**ac**

Michael Jackson the king of pop loved us enough to share his lollipop boy was it delicious now the taste is bittersweet like the tears i cry cus god has taken away a saint to escort an angel to comfort a genius in heaven he was persecuted for being overly affectionate dead now resurrected in our hearts and minds closed eyes cant see but when opened see love gods greatest love of all a child will teach them the ways of all aspects of entertainment by his stripes we are healed by gods greatest love

**Jelena,**

Dear Michael

I still cannot stop the tears and I still do not want to believe!!! U live and U will always live for me and for us all!!! I love You, the greatest man, the greatest person of us all!!!Now U are gonne, now that your honest and misunderstood heart is gonne, I can pray for someone like you to be born again or this world will soon go to its end without the heart like yours and the love U had for the whole world...Forever

**Mika,**

Love you, Michael—Thriller was the first album I ever bought. As a teenager, he was one of the highlights in music. I was saddened to see what happened to him in later years, and I wish that I had spoken up more at the time he was accused. I'm sad to say that part of me wondered. But I don't any longer. "...You'll see the sun come shining through for you." Sleep well, Michael. I hope those who knew better than us greeted you with open arms, and that you are happy now, and at peace.

**Anna,**
I grew up with MJ—Ever since I can remember I have loved Michael Jackson. His music and dancing exhale so much energy, and his will to help the less fortunate set an example for all the world. Now my daughter is 3 and she already loved MJ. She just pointed to the drawing on this page and said "Look Mamma, Michael Jessess"... RIP MJ. Enoug

**Jesse "JayManzz",**
Why did you have to go
You only notice how much someone means to you when they leave. Your the one that taught me to belive and achieve. You taught us that we are the world, and there is no difference between us, boy or girl. Now your gone, high into the sky, and if I look high, Im sure you will say hi. Let us not mourn, but rejoice, for the music you created will be born, again with the sound of your voice. MJ 4 EVA R AS your MUSIC WILL LIVE for ever ALONGSIDE YOU

**Laura,**
I will never foget--I've loved your music and videos always.
Never believed what was said about you. I know in my heart you were always a true humanitarian that loved children. It is up to us now, to share your music with future generation and tell your story. God bless and finally rest in peace among the angels.

**Bridgette R McCul.A,**
Good night My King
I cannot count a day, or remember a moment of my life when Michael Jackson's songs and music was not a major component. His music brought me through my childhood, allowing me to dare to dream and be whatever I wanted to be; His music cradle me through the deaths of my beloved Grandfather and Grandmother; His music walked with me through my own challenges in life and made be believe that anything was and is possible. Michael Jackson for me was/is truly a genius, one that comes along in a blue moon. Michael Jackson for me is a messenger, a voice for the voiceless, a heart for those whose heart is broken. Michael Jackson for me as an African American is my inspiration. I may have not known him personally, but for some people to live during their moment here on

earth, is all that I need. Rest in Peace My King. May G-d continue to cradle you. Peace and Love to You and Your Family,

**LORI E.B.,**
You will live forever in my heart. Thanks for being a part of my life and sharing yourself with us(your fans). Your children are beautiful and will ALWAYS feel your love. Love you Michael!

**Aditi,**
What A Wonderful Human Being.
I just wanted to say that not only will Michael Jackson's music live on, his humanity & love for others will stay in our hearts and minds forever. He was as talented as he was kind, and he never let his troubles show to his fans. He was just a great person to everyone. In his short time on earth, he did his best to make the world a better place through music. He healed the world, even while being misrepresented by the media. So rest in peace, King of Pop. We love you so much.

**Monica,**
dear michael jackson nobody can hurt u you are in the heaven now ,thanks for everything you teach
we miss you a lot and we love u i will never gonna forget u

**Kelvin Casey Chin,**
i will always remember you for ever....
thank you for being a part of my life. You changed my life from the first moment I heard your music when I was just a small child. I still can't believe you're gone, I love you Michael.Thank you for the gift of love,now you're sharing it up above.You had many things to say. All in a caring way. You always saw good in everyone,No matter what they've done. You were always the one we could all lean on.Even though it must have felt like a ton.Now we must let you rest calmly. I know you will always be in our hearts and mind. 'You are not alone' you have inspired many people with your spirit and generosity..

**Jones,**
I look to heaven to fulfill its prophecy...Set me free. Listen to the lyrics of "They don't really care about us"

Image what he felt.. Michael Jackson wasn't only the king of pop. He was the creator of pop. He set the trends throughout the world. It's hard for one, not to mention little, guy to do that. Us fans took away his childhood. And he let us. Now who would let anyone take away their own childhood. I know its been the past years of my life. He Preformed from a little tot to an olden, Just to entertain people. People don't understand how remarkable this guy really was. I remember the first time watching him was on Alvin and the chipmunks. I was a little one then. Still to this day and many days to come his music will live on. And it has sure set the bar very high.

## lynda

michael was an awesome human being. he was brutalized by his father which made him want to stay a child forever when he was older because he had the money to do so. he also was never proven as a molester, i don't believe he was. i think his sleep overs were genuinely innocent in his quest to stay and act like a child because he didn't get to be a child in his childhood he had to grow up too fast and if he didn't act like an adult his dad would brutally beat him. i feel his parents should be in jail for child neglect and abuse. but now they will cash in on his death. they couldn't treat him respectfully when he was here. so everyone please leave michael's memory alone he was tormented for years because of malicious rumors. let him rest in peace with dignity. he deserved that after all the wonderful music, concerts and videos he gave us. he really really made a difference for all of us

## Tia

Michael Jackson lead a life of great stress and turmoil from the time of like kingergarten. The man never really had a life to call his own, he had to share it with the world. He wanted to be a star, sing, and dance, have a family, and do all the things that normal everyday people do to. But instead of giving the man some time and peace people awlays bobarded him with pictures, rumors, allegations, autographs, screaming and yelling, taking advantage of him so they could say they are a "friend" to him. The media built him up so high, and when he had a human moment -as all of us do; they publisize it because as long as the media is pointing the finger at someone they don't have to stop and check themselves. Instead of printing nice stories and reminding america that he is a great caring person, they destroy him little by little, showing no mercy for someone who is just as human as we are. The man was on more charity boards and involved in more foundations for child hunger, education, safety, and so many more things. He had Never Land Ranch with so many kid and family friendly habitats because he just simply cared about people. He cared about the humanity of people, and yet so many people wrote him off the first chance that they got.The fact of the matter is that he was a great man that many of us knew nothing about personally. He was a son, brother, father, friend, musician, dancer, humanitarian, and so much more that the general public just does not know about. He has been loved around the world for decades because he simply cared in so many ways about the world we live in and those in it. He did so many things not taking into account for himself and his well being. He wanted to heal the world. Micheal Jackson is and always will be known as the king of pop. But he should also be remembered for all the great things he has done throughout his life.

**Valmir A**
michael's sudden demise is such a tragic news for the world. we lost the greatest entertainer, a genius, a lover of nature and mankind, a truly remarkable individual. his legacy will remain forever... instead of being sad, let us now rejoice for he is eternally in peace with God...

**Penny**
You are someone so special Michael that touched hearts and minds throughout the world. Your physical presence will be very missed..But your energy will surround our souls forever. Thank you for sharing your gift for so long...though still...You are gone too soon. LOVE YOU MJ

**Daniele**
Michael, I miss you SOOOOO much. You were my favorite artists' favorite artist and a most beautiful person inside and out. Your vision will live on, and the good works you've done will never be undone. I'm coming soon for dance lessons. Until then, RIP my Love.

**eliana**
Boy, it's amazing how much one can suffer the loss of someone who didn't even know that I even existed. I grew up on his music and there

was never a time where he wasn't a part of my life. The love gift that he showed the world through his music is a sign that could only have come from the Father in heaven. I know his legacy will live on forever and in performances will now take place in Heaven, at no charge. RIP Michael and God Bless.

**What An Actress**
The grief in our hearts is a testimony of the love we have for Michael Jackson. To love life, means to hate death. Michael Jackson was a legend, not to be forgotten. But even more, an loving, genuine, innocent man who wanted nothing more than to share his love with his fans, with you. His songs testified this; his life testified this. Michael, like many others, are viewed by media and worldly people who have "facts" that may give him a good or bad review. Only God can judge. It's not about what we did. It's about love that covers a multitude of sin. He showed this love, not by being a great musician, but through the trials and tribulations from a child to the end, he didn't stop believing in generously sharing his love. He never gave up. He wanted to come back bigger than before. :) He already has. You never died Michael. No matter what the media says. No matter what the grave says. You are here, in our hearts. :') May you truly Rest In Peace. I pray for his family and fans. I pray ...

**Alex**
I will never forget you my beloved icon; Thank you for your time on earth and survive and thrive; Thank you for your passion on making other happy and satisfied; Thank you for NOT making me feel alone in this world; Thank you for raising my thoughts through your delight voice Thank you for make me a believer Thank you for making me believe in myself. Thank you for making me believe that the impossible is possible 1000000000000000 thank you for everything that make me happy every time I hear you voice. RIP THE KING of love, compassion, respect, and all that make MJ the best.

**Serbay F,**
R.I.P KING—You're really Magnificent , You're the Modern Marvel of our century I have a huge respect to you , You will always stay our hearts and minds. I hope ALLAH be with you

**Camila Assi,**

MJ - King of Pop; I was thinking...what about an exceptional person like this? I found the right words to describe MJ, but I would say since I know his work, always enjoyed your wonderful music, its unique and original way of dancing, in short, an incredible human being! For the little that I know, I know that MJ was the very needy people, especially this dication by children. All this criticism that the press did it is just bulls*** to me. At the bottom of my heart I believe him and know he was a boy who never grew up ... my eternal Peter Pan! When I heard of his death, did not want to believe. How someone so dear could have gone so soon and so suddenly? It was a shock...I think that nobody wanted. Still had hope that everything is just a misunderstanding...Unfortunately Michael has left us orphans! Honey, thank you for doing all these beautiful things, and God bless you and your family well for this long way to go. His passage here on earth was short but very valuable ...Thank you for being part of my life, my story; Thanks for making the world a better place to live; Thanks for the wonderful music and choreography; Thanks for everything...You are not alone, rest in peace Michael. We miss you...We love you forever!

**Quint PMina,**

THANK YOU! Thank you Michael for showing everyone on this planet your light, your smile and your wisdom. Thank you for sharing your story with the world. Thank you for letting us in. We love you. I love you. Thank you.

**A Alvarad J,**

thank you michael.. Michael.. you have been an influenced my life from as early as I can remember. I have been so emotional that its taken me so long to gain the strength to post this now. I have so much I want to say, but in all honesty there are not enough words to express my feelings. I know so many of you out there feel this way. I will just say this... Thank you Michael, for everything you have ever done. You have touched so many people's hearts from each corner of the world. You will live on in my heart, as well as the hearts every other person on this planet. I love you Michael Jackson.. We'll see you again some day.. Rest in peace..

**Vanessa,**

I LOVE YOU—oh how my family loved you. you will forever be in hour hearts. my aunt tammy was your biggest fan, she passed in 91. her day has finall come that she gets to meet you. rip my idol

**Christy,**

Never forget...All of my youth is tied to Michael Jackson. My first record was Thriller. I had the glove, posters, magazine clippings... I had a pillow on my bed of him standing in front of the American flag...I remember sitting in my friends' bedroom listening to Off The Wall and Thriller all night long...dancing our little hearts out and yakking about how cute he was...and of course, we all knew how to do moon walk. I also remember taking a walk to the local 7-11 with my Aunt...and seeing a poster for the Victory Tour in the window... It stands out in memory as if only yesterday. Around the time I moved from one state to another, We Are The World had just been released. I endlessly begged a family member to buy the record for me when we were at a mall one day. She finally relented and bought it but I never got to listen to it! We moved the next day and somehow it broke during our trip. I was heartbroken of course... It wasn't until years later I was able to finally download it! How times have changed! But his immense talent and originally never did. Michael Jackson... thank you for being such a huge part of my best memories... You have been a part of my life since I was born...I can't imagine that you are no longer a part of our world... but your voice will live on forever...

**Ed,**

To Michael...

Thank you for the music. Thank you for the smiles.

Thank you for the dance. Thank you for the dreams.

Thank you for the passion. You are now, putting on your best concert yet.

The scores of angels are your back up vocals. I wish we could see it.

**m. anthony**

Thanks—When i was young i used to study Michael movements how he dance how he was like a god in mortal form. My mom told me when i was young i dance like Michael i learned the entire Thriller song dance, i learned how to dance because of him. No matter what any one says i loved Michael Jackson, my dream was to one day meet him and learned from him and carrier on his legacy but i well just have to do it on my own and become jus

**k.villado,**
growing how can i forget practicing infront of the tv the famous moves and steps to thriller. hey but i never got the steps nailed..I grew with his music! with his moves and passion! He open the doors for many! my mom introduced me to his music! and im so glad she did...and being impacted and being part of a legacy of his music! i will never forget him! we will never forget Him! he is the best entertainer ever existed and no one will get up to his level! under his memory "lets change the world lets heel the world" love our brothers and sisters!! he made history!

**Si. Sharma**
The man in the mirror—You were many things to many people but in the end when you looked in the mirror I hope you saw how remarkable a being you truly were. You gave and gave and although you were kicked and pushed you rose and rose. I hope your children the best and I wish you many happy jam sessions in that astral plane you're in where the greatest of the greatest belong(Marley, Lennon, Hendrix...) RIP

**abdullah h. z.**
hay michael i have always loved you and always listening to your music. what you did in this world was two thumbs up. and now what u have to do is serve the creature of the solar system, whatever you name, allah, jesus, guru, or whatever youknow. i think this call was one of the easiest way to get you out of the life problems. those busterds and blood suckers that put all the blames on you, they will never be happy niether in this world nor in the next world, i promess this with you. you know why, because they were gelious of you and they couldn't keep up with you. come on man, i will be missing you, you will be in my mind and you will be in my prayers. God be with you.

**Kenetha P**
The Best Ever!!!!!! I just wanted to show some love to the biggest and best love giver the WORLD!!! M.J you really taught my generation to love Music, Life and Ourselves. You taught me it's okay to be different, cause they will love you anyway especially when you have a beautiful soul, like

YOU. I am so thankful for your family sharing your home going with the world and it was truly a beautiful celebration for a beautiful person that really deserves it! God Bless the Jackson family- especially M.J's beautiful children. Thank you Michael for making the "World A Better Place" Gone But Never Forgotten, You live in my Heart Forever!!!!!

**wahabmirza**
Michael - Nice moves u had. Micheal, I, and many others in this world, admire you for all the charitable work you have done to help the poors and the needy....May Allah have mercy on you. To Allah we belong and to whom shall we return.

**cheryl charles**
God must have needed him far more—in the words of Stevie Wonder... This is a moment that I wish that I didn't live to see come. But as much as I can say that and mean it, I do know that God is good and I do know that as much as we may feel - and we do - that we need Michael here with us, God must have needed him far more. - Michael you have truly earned your wings spread them now and fly fly fly freedom and happiness is your - your master has called you home so be happy and at peace in his loving embrace

**D.R. Shoo**
I love him so much
I was born when the Bad album came out. Michael Jackson was my very first idol. When I was about thirteen, I had to perform the part of the pharo in "Joseph and the technicolour coat." It was originally supposed to be an elvis-like performance, but I insisted that it would be in the style of the greatest, MJ. I moonwalkedee, kicked, sung my heart out. The audience cheered. It was then when i went into what i call an MJ-craze. Before re-discovering his music, I was comfortable enough to finish school, get a normal job and settle down. But he had an effect on me that no other performer has ever had, he taught me that the sky was the limit. We are placed on this earth for a reason. As far back as I can rememeber, Michael Jackson's music has been a part of my life. I somehow felt like I knew him personally. One of my goals was to see him in concert, in person, it didn't matter.I just wanted to see the man that I had listened to my whole life. But just as he was brought here to serve the wolrd with

his talent, it seems like it was already time to serve his creator. Whilst a part of me has dies with his passing, I have accepted that his music will live forever. Michael, although we never got the chance to meet, you will always have a special place in my heart. I know that since your in a better place, your closer to me than ever. I love you so much.
Rest in Peace.

## Mr.rmaltase

I'm 40 years old and still have my J5 records. I've always been and will always be a Michael Jackson fan. My wife and daughter are fans too. I saw MJ at his last US concert Jan 27th, 1989 in LA, and it was awesome. Like millions, I've been getting the MJ email updates and always looked forward to Michael's next work of art. I feel like a member of my family has passed on. I will miss you Michael. -Ron Maltase. I spent my day looking back at clips from shows like Carol Bernett, Cher, and other early performances. I would have been 7 or 8 years old then, but I remember watching them like it was yesterday. It's how I choose to remember Michael, because to me, that's when he seemed the happiest.Thank you

## E.jo.R. Fonseca

Tu eres mi inspiracion—I remember when i was just a little kid and my dad use to play Michael's songs and use to tell me how great he was. I really didn't understand it that well, but as i grew up i began to understand what my dad was talking about. I use try to dance and sing like him and a couple times I got it down pretty good. Now that i am old enough to make my own decisions i just wish that you were still here Mike, my dream was to meet you or at least even see you in concert. All i can ask for now is for god to give me a prosperous and succesful life, because just like Michael i wanna give to people ever since i was little. Michael you always put a smile on my face and made me feel good about what my plans for this are. I love you Michael Joseph Jackson and i hope to finally meet you when my time comes. Long live the KING and samaritan TE AMO

## Shaniece

Long live the king of pop—I won't lie I didn't really listen to Michael as much. but because my family did, his music was all i could listen to. Michael really should be an inspiration to every little kid out there. Even though the world tried to break him to his feet, he still tried to help everyone. Michael Jackson is one of a kind. He is a gift from God. He's nothing like what people say he is. I'll always keep Michael and his family in MY prayers. And I'm sure he will continue to watch over the people he has helped because that's just the kind of person he is. HIS KIDS ARE BEAUTIFUL AND I WANT THEM TO KNOW THAT. SO LET THEM KNOW THEY DON'T HAVE TO HIDE THEIR FACE IN THIS WORLD. THEIR FATHER WILL ALWAYS BE WITH THEM. AND I'M SURE THEY ALREADY KNOW THAT. REALLY READ THIS LETTER BECAUSE THIS IS COMING STRAIGHT FROM MY HEART. I never had an inspiration before, until I found out what Michael Jackson was going through. Long live the king of pop and I'll always remember him!!

**Marc,**
Thank you
Thank you for those great moments I had and i will have.
For the little that I know, I know that MJ was the very needy people, especially their dedication by children. All this criticism that the press did it is just bulls*** to me. At the bottom of my heart I believe him and know he was a boy who never grew up ... my eternal Peter Pan! When I heard of his death, did not want to believe. How someone so dear could have gone so soon and so suddenly?It was a shock ... I had not gone, I think that nobody wanted. Still had hope that everything is just a misunderstanding ...
... Unfortunately Michael has left us orphans! Honey, thank you for doing all these beautiful things, and God bless you and your family well for this long way to go.
His passage here on earth was short but very valuable ...
Thank you for being part of my life, my story;
Thanks for making the world a better place to live;
Thanks for the wonderful music and choreography;
Thanks for everything ...
You are not alone, rest in peace Michael ...
We miss you ... We love you forever!

**Rhonda S**
Lessons learned... Michael, Thank you for being you. You will never be

forgotten and will forever live on through the music you left behind, your trademark dance moves that will forever be performed by others around the world, and being a true example of what a humanitarian is by helping others and bringing a smile to the sick and dying. When you left us, I cried because I thought that w no longer have a person to follow, to give us guidance and reassurance that it is ok to be yourself, lend a helping hand to those you see in need, and to face criticism in the eyes knowing they it will never pull you down because you are better than that. I was scared when you left, but then a faint voice in the back of my mind told me that this was the reason you were placed here on this earth in the first place; to be that example so when you are no longer here we can look within ourselves and tread down the path you paved, and do good for others as you look on from above.

You were a good teacher as well as an entertainer and I thank you for all you have given us over the years. You were placed on this earth for a reason; to be a higher powers' hand until you were asked to come home.

:::I love you Michael and you will live forever in my heart:::

# SOME NEGATIVE, UGLY AND HATEFUL COMMENTS

**One Bad Apple**
Convicted or not, it's clear the man physically abused children, arguably the worst crime possible in the eyes of man and God; and you are willing to ignore this fact simply because he sang a few songs that you liked? What kind of upside-down priorities are those? Superficial talent and popularity do not cancel out crimes against nature. All people should and will be judged, ultimately, by the entirety of their life, good and bad. Oh, and my favorite song of his was Billie Jean.

**What are people thinking?!?**
The man abused children! The world is a better place without him! I don't care who he is or was - he ABUSED CHILDREN! He got away with it because he had money and that was all. Just like most celebrities get away with things that would put the rest of us behind bars.
At least now, hundreds of little boys can sleep safely, secure in the knowledge that a predator has left this earth and gone to hell where hopefully he will endure the pain and torture he inflicted on his victims!

**NickC**
We know how he died, the puke took a overdose and we got people like Wofl Blizter crying over this dip shit. The guy was queer as a three dollar bill, he tried all his like to become white rpt white. The guy will make the unemployment jump a whoe per cent by all the nager ons around this jerk.

**Mac171169**
Chester the Molester is dead??? Tell me it ain't so!

**Freakymofo87**
I HAVE NEVER SEEN SUCH A LARGE AMOUNT OF HYPOCRITES IN ALL MY LIFE. HE MOLESTED KIDS, THREW AWAY HIS MONEY, CHEATED MANY MANY OF HIS STAFF AND WAS DISTANT FROM PEOPLE AROUND HIM AND WAS JOKED UPON AND MADE FUN OF AND NOW EVERYONE IS CRYING AND MOURNING HIM, GIVE ME A BREAK

**Justice**
Farrah Fawcett died and went to heaven, she met God and he gave her 1 wish. She asked for all of the children of the world to be safe. So God killed Michael Jackson, that sick mother fuc*er!!!

**Allie**
Sure he was a great entertainer, but underneath he was just another child molester. Farah died and went to heaven and told God she wished he'd protect children, a few hours later Michael Jackson died. There IS a God!

**Blipdr**
WHEN HE SANG "BILLIE JEAN IS NOT MY LOVER" IT WAS BECAUSE HE REALLY LOVED LITTLE BILLY THE 3RD GRADER. BURN IN HELL PEDOPHILE

**Ickster01**
At least the mortician will have an easy time...Michael come pre-embalmed with all of the make-up. While I loved his music, I will remember the pedophile and the plastic surgery. What a whack-o

**Blipdr**
NO PROBLEM FOR THE UNDERTAKER, HE'S LOOKED DEAD FOR YEARS

**MrMorn2**
He was a great talent, but the old song goes, what have you done for me lately?? He was on pain killers big time!! And I hear his nose goes on E Bay for auction this afternoon!!!

**HeAtHeRiFiC88**
.....MJ WAS A CHILD MOLESTER PERVERT WHO ONLY SUNG SONGS WHEN HE WAS 10-25 wow......LAME......ON A SCALE 1-10 WHICH AGE IS MJ'S BF? LOLLLLLL

**Kingman46**
We are the World, I was a sicko, I had little boys **** ** penis. Now I am dead and good riddens.

**Zj513**
i hear they goin to turn wackos body into playdo. So the children can still play with him

**Kingman46,**
How ironic an Angel and a Devil dying on the same day.

**Aesnead2**
He died of food posioning, the doctors found two eight year nuts in his mouth.

**ZatCK**
he was a creep. he may have been the king of pop and all that but he molested young children for christ sake dont let the man off that easy. when charles manson dies are you gonna say it was a long time ago? i think not. his music was great but as a person he was horrible.
troy
Just heard Mcdonalds is coming out with the McJackson burger, A piece of 50 year old meat between two 10 year old buns

**Tom**
Have you ever been raped by an adult? How could you think anyone as sick as Jackson had any shred of decency. You must be a child molester also... SICK SICK SICK!!!

### Les

He was made of 99% plastic so they made legos out of him. Now the kids can play with him for a change.

### Gator

Al Sharpton and The Rev. Jesse Jackson praised and called Michael a GENIUS, He was so great, he was a world ICON. He was a leader in the Black Communities acrosshe World... But... They failed to mention the true MichaelJackson, THE PETIFILE. They didnt mention all the young children he has molested. I guess Michael was Black so that part of him should be overlooked...

### Tarado

Rumors are already spreading that M.J. is NOT dead. That this is the GREATEST faked death in history. That it was staged because he was $500 million in debt and all the commerce generated...downloading songs etc. is all part of a huge scam to work his way out of debt and that he is already hiding out in Dubai.

### JOE B.

YOU MUST FACE THE TRUTH,YOU CANT HANDLE THE TRUTH. HE WAS A PEDFILE.WE KNOW CASES IN PUBLIC,HOW MANY DO WE DONT KNOW ABOUT ? IF YOU DONT BELIEVE SO. IF HE WAS ALIVE TODAY WHY DONT YOU LET YOUR CHILD DRINK SOME WINE,WITH MICHAEL 7 HAVE SLEEP OVER THAT WAS NOTED IN I OF HIS LAWSUITS.

### cuppycake

I am so sick of hearing how Michael Jackson is everybodys hero and their number one. He was a freak of nature, and a child molester. Grown men don't sleep with little boys, grown men don't dangle infants out windows, and no amount of money should make that ok. Anybody who makes this man their idol or hero, is just as sick as he was. He children are better off without him.

### Barb

Let's get real people. Did the President die, did the Dalai Lama die, did the Pope die?? Maybe a national recognition for these worthy people may be in order, and #1 on the list should be our fallen soldiers, who we convienently always seem to forget. But Michael Jackson?? His father must be doing the same drugs MJ did.... MJ was a singer, great, that's it. He slept with little children, molested them, had the money at the time to buy the families off, took drugs, damaged the pschyies of his "own " children by covering their faces for years and making them as paranoid as he was. Have you noticed they are WHITE ??? They are not his biological kids. The real mother should get them, so the Jackson's cannot reap any of the money if earned that would naturally be handed down to the children. National treasure, national memorial, i would puke if this happens, and his family, Al Sharpton and Jesse Jackson should all hang their heads in shame for trying to turn Wacko Jacko into a hero.

**Frasier**
Trying to fathom how someone like Michael Jackson could be $500 million in debt is unreal. Let's all take a step back, breath, and look at the whole picture. This person was a sick individual - not by his choice (hopefully) - but the environment he grew up in. Sorry to say, he was a nut case and there are offspring involved. Why does the nation have to try and make him a hero?! Anyone else in this case wouldn't be looked at twice!

**dan**
Yeah a 10 year old,show me yours, I'll show you mine.
Oh , found not guilty, so was OJ, and Robert Blake. Poor Michael was raised wrong, so was Jeffry Domner. He may have made good music, but he was still a child molester. Why else would you pay 20 million for someone not to testify?? I saw a clip where he was at a concert in France , with a small boy in his lap, they should have arrested him right then !! And Joe?? Yeah, my boy died, by the way I've started a new buisness . What a idiot !!

**chris**
So tired of hearing how great MJ was, he was a child molester, do you people have any idea the serious impact of being molested by an adult does to a child, it destroys trust, intimacy and causes all kinds of psychological damage. MJ was a mentally ill man, I pity him. I don't care how talented

he was... he was ill and should have been punished. Children come first always. Poor Michael Jackson, I do hope he is at peace now. He was abused as a child and he carried the torch to other children...

**arminh**
jacko the sicko is dead and now no more little kids need to worry about being molested by the sicko. he is gone like a plague, leaving behind brokenness and stink. You are what you live, he is sick, what a shame, he could have done so much good, but he chose the devils road. Eternity will be very long for him

**big papa**
wacko jacko was and always will be a damn child molester!!! The ONLY reason he didn't go to jail and rot like he should have is because he bought his way out of it. How the hell can a chil.d describe pigmentation s of his skin on that sicko's genitals IF wacko didn't do anything with or to the kid?? What grown adult in their right mind flashes his private body parts to a child?? He was a sick s.o.b. and Ihe should rot in hell fpor the things he's done. He's a sick piece of shit!

**Beeker D**
MJ WAS A "MESS" PERIOD!
Only the MENTALLY ILL should feel compassion for a: YEAR OLD PAJAMA CLAD PEDOPHILE! Where's the same compassion for his VICTIM'S?
For those that SQUAWK & CLUCK the "IT THING" MJ was not found GUILTY ,remember"IT" wasn't found INNOCENT either! OH YEAHrdb
I was in high school when MJ was going to the top with his music. I played his songs all the time, I even Memorized the thriller video and danced the routine.
When he was accused of child molestation (the first time), I said "NO WAY". But when I heard that he paid $20 million for the accusation to go away, that action made up my mind. If you are innocent, you don't pay for it to go away. He had plenty of money to go to court and fight for his innocence. But he paid to make it go away = guilty.
From then on I refuse to listen to his music and I burned everything I had of his music. Now he is dead I couldn't care less. Did you know he

tried to buy royalty? When Sir Anthony Hopkins was knighted by the Queen for his work in film, MJ asked the Queen for a Knighthhood. She refused and MJ tried to bribe her. Now if he can't be royalty, he will start it for himself. Why do you think he named his son "Prince". - Pathetic. If you want to worship him like a god, go ahead. But to me he is an unfit father (dangling your son out of a 3rd story balcony), addicted to drugs, deep in debt ($400 million). Why didn't he just sell of that stupid ranch of his ?

Now his fans want to make his childhood home into another "Graceland". How stupid.

Like it or not, that's just my opinion.

# EXTRA SWEET

**David,**

I miss and love you Michael....

Rest in peace, Michael. Watching your memorial was one of the most touching moments in my life. I wish I could have been there... I think I was, and you were here, everywhere. Part of me still hopes that this has all been a very bad joke and hope for some magical resurrection. Losing you, someone, who is supposed to be invincible, who is supposed to be, in many ways, above us is really not something I could ever imagine. I loved your music, your dance, and as much as I could get to know you, I loved you as a person... so innocent, so kind, so loving, so caring and so special. Thank you for all the happy moments, when I listened to your music and made me smile... made me feel good... made my day. I'll never let you part... for you're always in my heart. I know I'm not original, but this is very simply the most beautiful way to say what I'm feeling. Love you, Michael, forever.

**Tina G,**

I shead some tears today... Forever my Billy Jean...you will be greatly missed. Keep smiling

**claire,**

"The surprise is not that we lost him but rather that we ever had him at all" G.Greer I will always regret the untimely death of Michael Jackson. If only the world could have seen him perform in front of his fans one more time... just once. I remember that Dangerous was the first album I was ever given by my mam and I listened to it constantly, uninterrupted, for months on end. I wasn't even ten yet but 16-ish years later and I listen to the songs I remember how I felt when I heard them for the first time. I never stopped loving him after then. I only regret that for the last 15 years he was subject to such torment and ridicule - if only the world could have said all these lovely things about him once in a while when he was still with us. I truly hope he is somewhere where he can see what his death has meant to the whole world.

**James,**
true gentleman—Michael, your music has touched and inspired so many of us and your message of love, peace and commitment through your music and actions will continue to conquer all human barriers now and forever, you may no longer be with us in person but your memory and legacy shall live on to inspire and educate the youth of the future, Love is the message. May you now rest in peace michael with the angels and thank you for all you have done . love james

**Kimberly L, School of Dance,**
At that moment... When we got the sad news of MJ passing with the rest of the world, we were rehearsing for our dance nationals in Lake Tahoe. I am a dance teacher from Phoenix and one of our routines was to "Smooth Criminal". we were actually running that EXACT routine for the gala that night to compete one last time when we got the news. we all had chills, even the kids. That night we saw our dancers take the stage and they performed like never before and Michael would have been proud!!! at the end of the routine. they all got up touched their little hearts and screamed in unison REST IN PEACE MICHAEL and threw the peace sign. We ended up winning Grand Champs with that routine and if possible i would like you all to see it. please let me know how.

**Dave,**
shared his life....I first want to say thank you god for the gift you gave to all of us and the world.I grew up listening to mike and was in awe at the way he controlled his life, even when thing's seemed out of controll around him, he showed us all that equality came in more than just color ...but in the heart, and color was no barrieor that was an issue.In our darkest hour a master, a icon, a "LEDGOND" has parted our physical world and enterd into a world that many of us work through our live's to

graduate to ..some to early and some far to late, but from all corners of the world we shed tear's not of just sorrow but of joy ...the joy of knowing that out king live's on and shine's a light of hope that we now know has a name ...[Micheal Joseph Jackson]...As the world come's together for one, we join our heart's for one last concert and join hand's in hope's of making it a better place in the name of Jesus ...keep us safe as Micheal's light shine's on and the angel's now enjoy the company from a person that taught us the meaning of what life was really supossed to be ...Magical ........thank you god ...and thank you Micheal for all the joy and memorie's you gave and left us with R.I.P mike your music will keep us smiling..y. all for your time. ..

**Rita,**
A Pure Heart & Soul - Love you MJ!—Michael Jackson brought people together. Even today people are clapping together all over the WORLD in sweet memory of MJ and his many, many talents. We were so blessed to experience his talents. I believe MJ had a pure heart & soul and would never harm anyone. I understand his love of children as children are innocent and say whatever they think and are true. Thank you Michael for sharing yourself! You will always remain in our hearts and souls! You touched us forever & ever! God Bless Michael Jackson, his children, and his family.

**gina,**
My true love and inspiration...was and IS Michael Jackson! There are no words to describe the adoration i held for this human being! I absolutely loved his style, his moves, his music, and his message! I don't think there will ever be another individual to walk this earth and become as great of an international icon as Michael was! It is not fare what he had to endure, not fare what he had to go through, and not fair that he had to leave us so untimely! I am saddened at the thought of the dance moves, I will never seem him do/create, and all the beautiful songs I will never hear him sing, and the concerts i will never get to go to! He meant so much to me and I can't help but feel a piece of my childhood...a piece of myself and how I identified myself has died with Michael Jackson. I pray you are finally at peace!! I will miss you greatly! You always inspired me to be myself no matter who is judging me, and to follow your heart! I love you Micheal!

**Steven,**

He will be missed—I choose to remember Michael as the greatest entertainer the world will ever see. I can't think of anyone else who could have done what he did. It is important to remember that this was a kind and generous man who gave away over 300 M to charities. He truly sought to change the world and he will be missed. We love you Michael.

**Kathy,**

Hopefully you can finally be at peace—To see Michael perform was just magical. I regret that I will never see that in person but will continue to get goosebumps when I watch videos. God bless his child-like innocence. Much respect for his charity. Michael, may you finally be at peace..

**DAVID R,**

I will see you again in Heaven Michael—Words cannot express my shock and grief. I still think I will wake up tomorrow from a bad dream and find this not to be real. How can someone with so much God given talent be taken away from us so soon. What is God's reason for this? I wish I understood. I will miss him so much. Someday soon I will see you again in Heaven.

**Beth,**

Good Bye Sweet Prince—I have been a MJ fan since the age of 7. I would anxiously await "ABC" laying on my bed at 6 PM every evening for weeks. Our local AM station played it everyday and it was the highlight of my day. As I grew up, so did Michael and when he was out singing about "Off the Wall" I was dancing to it at the local disco with my friends. As I watched him moonwalk for the first time across the stage I was delighted and anxious for him. He will always be in my heart and his music in my head and I will always be grateful for all the wonderful times I had while listening to him. I believe he was a tortured soul who never had the chance to be a young child so when he got older and could afford to do so that is what he did. I do not believe and never will believe that his love of children was anything more than just that. A young soul in a grown man's body who still longed to be a carefree, loving, and caring child. I only hope his children will remember him as the loving Dad he appeared to be. I will miss him.

**Alison,**
YOUR MEMORY WILL LIVE ON FOREVER
As we grow, learn and try to establish ourselves as decent human beings there are few that we can look to. Michael Jackson you were one of the few that could be looked up to. My four year old daughter had just had her fourth birthday when she skated to you song WE ARE THE WORLD it was so beautiful and pure and she loved the song so much we found it hard to get her off the ice.
We have watched the footage over and over and over again and every time we hear the song it has such special meaning. My daughter loved the song so much that as she skated to the song in her program she started clapping to the song and she wasn't supposed too!! You made this special to us. We will never forget you and nor will our children. God bless and guide you and your family forever.

**Lynnette,**
I had to be 7 or 8 when I first Saw Micheal Jackson on television with that cute face; it was just too much for my little heart to handle and I wanted so much to be on that t.v. with them. My cousin & I did the bump off that song "Dancing Machine", and slow dancing to "Got To be There" at the basement parties. Sitting here with my children, and them not knowing Michael till the 80's, they will never know the Michael I knew. I loved you so much Michael and you will be missed and loved and cherished forever. Love Always

**K. E. White-Warner,**
Childhood memories of Michael Jackson—I know that this will sound so funny, but when I was little and my girlfriends and I played house, each of us would always pretend that Micheal Jackson was our husband. Once I argued with a childhood friend that we both couldn't be married to him so I made her go home.... I also remember that the walls of my room were covered with Michael Jackson posters from Right-On magazine. I remember my father coming in one day to ask me "is there any other singer you like"? My response was NO because "he's the best one out here" and my dad was a great fan of his too. We both loved Ben his first single and I remember watching Mowtown 25 with my enitre family when I was 21 and seeing that moonwalk for the very first time!!!

Incredible!!! I WILL LOVE YOU FOREVER MICHAEL!!! REST IN PEACE!

**caroline v.,**

MICHAEL JACKSON ALWAYS...GOD BLESS YOUR FAMILY, FRIENDSAND ALL OF US FANS. MICHAEL CHANGED MY LIFE FOREVER. LIKE MOST OF YOU YHAT GREW UP LISTENING TO THE JACKSON 5 AND LATER ON MICHAEL THE KING OF POP I WASN'T INTRODUCED TILL MUCH LATER. IT WAS IN THE NINETIES I WAS GOING THROUGH A ROUGH TIME IN MY LIFE AND I HEARD MICHAEL FOR THE FIRST TIME ON THE RADIO SINGING 'YOU ARE NOT ALONE' I FELT HIS SINCERETY IN MY HEART AND AT THAT MOMENT I FELT LOVE FOR MYSELF AND WAS ABLE TO TURN MY LIFE AROUND. THANK YOU MICHAEL FROM THE BOTTOM OF MY HEART. I WILL MISS YOU. RIP

**daniel,**

There will be no one like you...FOREVER. I COULD NEVER IMAGINE HOW DID YOU GET ALL YOUR INSPIRATION TO MAKE THE GREATEST SONGS THAT HAVE NEVER BEEN IN THE WORLD. I LIKE YOUR SONGS BECAUSE, THEY CARE ABOUT UNIVERSAL LOVE, LOVE TO EVERYONE WHETHER THEY 'BLACK OR WHITE', CHRISTIAN OR NON-CHRISTIAN, ETC. YOU ARE THE BRIDGE OF THE UNIVERSAL PEACE. YOU ARE THE SYMBOL THAT WILL BE NEVER FORGOTTEN BY EVERY HUMAN BEING ON THE EARTH. I LOVE YOU MICHAEL.

**Joshua C,**

Make this a better place...

Because of you Michael, the world is a better place, and now it is "our" jobs to keep up what you started...to love, to share, and to never give up hope that we can make a change! Thank you Michael for what you stood for, that you did it, and no1 will ever be able to fill your shoes brother!!!!! You will be missed but I'm only going to smile because I know that you are somewhere where there is no pain, and that you are soaring higher than you ever could have under these earthly constraints!!! I am a better person because of you Michael!!!July 7th

**kewlguitar,**
A wonderful date and a wonderful song
In 1983, I went to a club in GA with a beautiful girl who was visiting some friends of mine. It was a Tuesday night, and the club was sparse. This girl was a great dancer, and she dragged me up there for most of the songs. The band then played "Human Nature," and I got the shivers. I don't remember 'how' we danced to that one, but I remember being in a trance by how good the band played it (esp. the drummer). I watched how he really got into that one, and that was the only time I took my eyes off of Laurie! She then told me how they produced the echo and effects for that song (and I thought I knew everything!) We went again to the same club on Saturday and had an even better time! I do know where she is after all these years, but a lot has changed for me. Anyway, thank you..guys of Topper (the band) for doing justice to a great song and providing me with a great memory. My Thriller album got lost in one of my many moves. Michael, you did that song, Human Nature, real justice. Mama's Pearl was the first song you sang that the knocked me out; Human Nature is still my favorite. I miss ya, man.John Williams,

**A Darker Universe,**
The universe will be a darker place without the bright star who was Michael Jackson. The man, the musician, the dancer, the humanitarian, the son, the brother, and a father. May he rest in peace and long live his legacy.

**Big Dave,**
somebody special
This was a man of messianic quality. He sang of love and indifference. He sang of sadness and sorrow. But, most of all he sang of hope for tomorrow. For now we know that we are the world. For without us, (it's children), there is no brighter day! As with any man who has tried to open the eyes of the persecutor, he was tormented. No matter how much he tried to show us to love one another. Whether we be big or small or brave or withdrawn. We all have a voice! We all have a place on this giant rock floating through this wonderful universe. He reached deep inside of

us and gave us hope. He took a rare opportunity and expounded upon it! He gave his life for us! For the message of LOVE. People will say he was a freak. That he wasn't natural. The reality is we are all natural. What he did he did for the effect. And it worked! He gave me hope, joy, laughter, and tears. Great things have/should come of this man's life work. For all who feel that all is lost...remember that Michael would want you all to go on and do wonderful things with your lives. He and Paul McCartney once said; "people are the same wherever you go. There is good and bad in everyone. We learn to live when we learn to give each other what we need to survive, together alive!"

**Viktor,**
I'm sorry that you left to early—When I were younger and got my first CD I remember I had your song: Smooth Criminal on it. It was the greatest song I had ever heard. Ever since I heard it I have admired your work, both as an artist but also as a person. I know you had a though period where you faced lots of problems, but somehow I always knew that you would come back. Come back and show the world how great you are! I am truly sorry that you didn't get to finish "This is it!". I am sure it would have been an amazing show. I hope you'll amaze and entertain everyone who's in heaven, just like you have amazed and entertained all of us on earth.

**Karman,**
MJ forever—Over 6.6 billion people live on this planet.
And all of them will never forget you. You may be gone, but you will live on forever.. for eternity in our hearts. May god bless your soul. We love you Michael Jackson! Always did, always will

**Dee,**
Roller skating to Billie Jean—I remember roller skating to his music in the 80's but I literally grew up listening to his music. I'm 43. 40 years of his music will always be instilled inside of me. Every time I hear his music, I am brought back to my youth and those were the best times of my life.

**sheila,**
Being optimistic—Micheal you will forever live in my heart may you

rest in peace. May God bless your mother, father, siblings and most importantly your children. Your legagcy will continue on. I know that you are up in heaven smiling down on us. Although your dreams of "healing the world" has not totally been achieved, but be proud and happy that your death has gotten us as a nation closer than we ever been. Many nations are mourning your death and because of you we'd united at least for two hours and fifteen minutes (your memorial service).

## TJ JOSLIN,

I will miss michael and remember him forever
I can remember Michael Jackson since i was 6 years old. Me and my older sister use to dance to all his music. I'm 32 now. my sister and i would go across the street from our house when we were little, were there was a open field and we would put a bunch of leaves in a pile. we would lay under them and play the song thriller. and we would play out the whole thing as the song would play. when i was 7 i had his red jacket, his black hat, his white glove, and leather pants and i would break dance to most of his songs. like beat it, billy jean, and others. I could even moonwalk. Michael gave my sister and me a lot of good times as we watched his music videos, listened to all his music as we grew up and we had a lot of laughs. Michael Jackson will be very missed to both me and my sister and we will love him very much. god bless you Michael. now your with my dad. And I know you like my dad will be happy for ever and for ever.

## Catherine,

Heaven is not a bad place to be!!!
I would like to thank the Jackson family for such a wonderful display and honor to this legend and how he broke boundaries for all of the human race how he gave himself to all of us!How he live his life with love for us all. How he show his kindess and love for life not only in his music but how he gave to all what ever the need. How wonderful it was to watch this KING to be honor for a kind and loving man as a person as a father the love he showed his children.The love he showed to the common people his talent will never be match or will no one ever excede his greatness how he open the doors to prove anything was possible I believe he broke threw the boundies of this world I feel he made anything possable threw his actions of kindness caring understanding and love with him in our lives I believe he made it possible for our country to grow .And in that

growth we a African American President there is alot to be thankful for .How blessed are we all that GOD gave us one of his loved ones to learn from. God Bless his family in this time and know that the footsteps in the sand will carry us all threw this time.And everyday we will all let him live in our hearts. GOD BLESS the JACKSON FAMILY for sharing his GREATNESS with us all. And HEAVEN IS NOT A BAD PLACE TO BE !!Thank you and GOD BLESS YOU ALL

**Miss Rose,**
Rest In Peace
Michael Jackson was a person who used his heart, mind, & energy for GOOD in the world. Such a pure example of what one human being can do when they realize the power inside of them, & act to their highest potential. We should not only admire this, but aspire to do the same. Love & blessings to Michael, his family, and all the other fans. What a beautiful soul... he will live forever.

**Nathan, J. J,**
Gone too soon
My name is Nathan I'm 20 and i'm from paris. When MJ left i was really in a sad mood and i asked myself "why am i so sad about this i didn't even known him he's not part of my family?" so i thought about this and i understood.here is my answer. How could i not be upset about the death of someone who has always made me happy with his songs and dances into the best and the worst moments of my life listening to billie jean remember the time bad man in the mirror workin'day and night she's out of my life you rock my world black or white rock with you earth song and so so much other songs , someone who deeply believed in the peace on earth and fought for it. So for all the support and the joyful moments he gave to me by his talent i want to thank him. There is no day without thinking of him.

**D Al Garcia,**
love you forever and ever—Michael I have no words to describe their loss. I had the pleasure of being present in its beautiful golden years. Years of success and change.
I can only admire the great work that you left us, EÇO God to comfort your children, because they said you were a father irreplaceable. I thank

God for giving us a joy of us can take for 50 years. So I did not cry his death, but I celebrate his life, beautiful life that is fantastic and deservedly worthy of being admired and recognized by all our children and children of our children..And unfortunately the saying was:The good die young.. Michael is with the angels..Go in peace

**Jenny,**
YOU ARE FOREVER MISSED & ALWAYS IN OUR HEARTS.
you have brought the world so much inspiration. the incredible things you have done will be remembered & cherished in our memories. no matter what obstacles you come across you still held your head up high & continued to give the world your special gift of musical talent. thank you for all the good things you have done for the world and for making such extraordinary music. you are truly a legend & the king of pop. rest in peace michael jackson. we will always be with you. i thank your family for sharing such an amazing memorial service. much love.

**Anna Ashley,**
Miss you most...
I will never forget you. You were my first celebrity crush. You were my idol and your music touched me in ways that words cannot justify. I will always remember the day I met you. You were shy, sweet and a true superstar. Thank you, Michael. Thank you for all you have given to the world. You were a talented genius who will forever, be remembered, loved, cherished, idolized... but, never duplicated. You are in a better place and making that place even better than it was before you got there.

# POEMS FOR MICHAEL

**Justin**
how i feel torn inside
never the chance to see you fly
we loved you michale you where our thing
your music your mind made us sane
goose bumps and shivers when i seen you dance
you where always the worlds best man
now that your gone i'm torn inside
never the chance to say goodbye
with thease words i bid farewell
to a fallen king you music lives in your hearts
as it did from the start.

**Ana P. B.,**
true colors...
You with the sad eyes
Don't be discouraged
Oh I realize
It's hard to take courage
In a world full of people
You can lose sight of it all
And the darkness inside you
Can make you feel so small
But I see your true colors
Shining through
I see your true colors
And that's why I love you

So don't be afraid to let them show
Your true colors
True colors are beautiful,
Like a rainbow
Show me a smile then,
Don't be unhappy, can't remember
When I last saw you laughing
If this world makes you crazy
And you've taken all you can bear
You call me up
Because you know I'll be there...
be finally happy Michael... wherever you are...

**D. S. Quake,**
His Heart
He not only dances.
He not only sings.
He not only smiles.
He not only lives.
He dances with His heart.
He sings through His heart.
He smiles from His heart.
He lives with loving in His heart.
God bless Sir Micheal Jackson.

**DEANDRA,**
just wanted to let you know.....
you went through
and the lasting memory
of the loss of your loved one,
who died serving
our great country
and fellow Americans
grips this parent's heart,
so very much that
words fail to capture
what truly yours must feel.
I see the little one

with those innocent bright eyes
and bis sunshine happy grins
giving those adoring big hugs
out of pure, unconditional love...
even now as an adult.
Misty eyes, followed by the tears,
cannot be hidden,
knowing a parent's blind love
of their child can only be expressed
in memories past,
looking upwards Above in prayer,
sharing words with loved ones and friends,
and somber visits to the grave.
And while there will always be
that tremendous pride
in valiantly being there
for country, fellow citizens, and you...
nothing can ever replace
seeing your little one grown,
walking through the door
and giving you

**eLeon,**
M. ichael you are the greatest
I. will always love you
C. come back to us
H. e captivated millions
A. icon for everyone
E. very one never stopped caring
L. oved by your family, friend, and fans
J. ust a normal person
A. mazing to everyone
C. an't be stopped
K. nowing power and strength to help people around the world
S. o exciting and willing
O. h my God is what they would say when we see you
N. ever left because your spirit lives on forever reese,

*Juja D.*

**ROSSANA,**
FOREVER
Heal The World
Make It A Better Place
For You And For Me
And The Entire Human Race
There Are People Dying
If You Care Enough
For The Living
Make A Better Place
For You And For Me

**Kayo,**
He's out of my life,
I don't know whether to laugh or cry,
I don't know whether to live or die.
And it cuts like a knife-
he's out of my life.

**L Zimmerman,**
God called Michaels name...
Graced upon this world was a legend,
touching hearts from near and far
a speck of hope in a dark hour
shining the brightest one single star
with so much to lose he gave us his all
the only way it seemed he knew
through song and dance our hearts he romanced
and enticed our bodies to move
a lover of children a child himself
his innocence made some afraid
his eyes were sad, but what a life he had
it took his all yet still he gave
an angel walking upon the ordinary
though we couldnt see his wings
we watched as he flew in and out of our lives
leaving behind so many things
memories and hope, but mostly

truth that love can conquer all
he made this world a better place
and he is one star that will never fall
though our legend, our angel has gone
God has seen his beautiful ways
and he has seen how he struggled
throughout many of his last days
and I beleive he was sent for a purpose
just as he has been taken for the same
to walk beside the Lord in Heaven
yes.. it was God who called Michaels name.

# REAL EXPERIENCES WITH MICHAEL JACKSON

**Vivian C**
I am 10 yrs older than Michael Jackson, in 1967 I was graduating from Roosevelt High School in Gary. We use to stop in fron of 2300 Jackson st and listen to the music and singing coming from that house on Jackson st. The Jackson 5 performed at our Sr. High-y talent show. He stood out and was a super dancer doing then what we use to call "The James Brown". He will be missed but the music, videos, etc will last forever. Sweet Dreams Michael Jackson, sleep with the real King!!!!!

**jimbo**
I'm sorry for what I said. I am just a bit jealous because I wanted him to violate me in a dark room. I went to neverland but he didn't want to have anal intercourse with me. I apologize for everything. I just wanted to lose my anal virginity to Michael Jackson.

**AarON J**
thank u MicHeal jackson for everything u have done for us u maded me think that everything would be alright when I listen'd to your music...I aaron jamison has 2 thriller jacket's..all ablums..signed albums by micheal him self..I remember when I was little and went to one of his concerts and he walked over and touched my hand...I made'd my own video to his song "who is it"...SO I'm HOpeing I can go to his veiwing to say good bye ..well really not good by cause I can just put a dvd in and see him again... well LOve U Micheal and your always in my heart

**Jonar**
When i saw you ! The first time I saw you, Michael, was the only thing I

could say wow. After that it was only Michael Jackson in force. I listened to your music all the time. I tried to dance like you, I pretended that I was on the scene and were you. My grandmother sewed the same clothes as yours. My aunt bought your discs for me. Then when I became older, so I started listening to hip hop. But now when you died, I have taken the star you were, and has again begun to listen to you. And still can not believe you have gone away I can not get it in the head. According to me, you have been a hero who can not die. I love you Michael, rest in peace.

**Taryn**
DEEPLY HURTING—GONE TOO SOON!!!! You have touched this world in a very special way. We won't ever be the same without you. You cared. I can't stop crying. My heart hurts so bad, I wish that you were here to see all of the love this love. You were the music to my life for 42 years. you were in my life musically since I was 7, I saw you at the Uptown and I was hooked. You will be a part of me forever. I loved you more than I ever knew. I will always miss you, forever. All my prayers and Blessings to the Jackson Family May GOD hold you and keep you in this time and always.

**MR SRIPAJAM**
Michael Jackson was bigger than Life itself. Immense talent, cotroversies sure, but what an ENTERTAINER.
I saw him 4 times. You just wanted to go right back to the next show. That's TALENT.

**Janessa**
Billie Jean. I was too young to experience the hype that surrounded Michael Jackson of the 1980s but I believe that anybody who saw him perform at Madison Sq Gardens in 2001 will agree that we got a taste of it. The best performance of the evening was by far 'Billie Jean' because he played it up so well and the crowd got really hyped. When he slapped his suitcase down on the stool and piece by piece assembled his iconic outfit for the song the place was alive and buzzing with excitement. There's nothing quite like it, and seeing him dance is one of the greatest experiences anyone will ever have.

**Danielle**

Live on Michael...There are so many MJ memories... When I was a little kid, I remember going to the movies to see MJ's movie and crying my eyes out. I really loved Michel then and conitnued to love him till today... My closest encounter was being in NYC hanging out with friends and seeing fans running toward a hotel in the city to see MJ and Lisa Marie Pressley waving to fans from a window... Of course you couldn't really get a great look, but it was good enough for many of us waving back:) Rest in Peace Michael, you have been an inspiration to so many and will continue to live on through your music and your actions... My family has come together to see and hear you, there's been much laughter and joy in my life due to your music. God had blessed us with your unique and extra-ordinary abilities and for that we are greatful. Though gone too soon, we know that you will be performing in heaven as you continue to bless others with your presence.

**Luke**

i saw him live in london at his bad, dangerous and history tours. the memories and emotions i had will live with me forever and i feel priveledged to have witnessed such a musical icon in all his greatness. i know he had his fair share of bad press and no one will truely understand the enigma that was michael jackson but no one can take away te fact that he made great music over five different decades. no other artist will ever compare to the king of pop and he will live on in his music and my memories forever.

**Yilin**

1993 I was 11, and ur concert was AMAZING

I just want to tell you, watching u from the cheapest ticket, and being at the stadium where u performed, watching u LIVE.. and your Dangerous Tour being the first concert I had ever attended was the most exciting day of my life! You brought me great joy as a child and even now. Thank you for being brilliant at what you do.

**Ursula**

Friend—It was a pleaseure knowing Michael. The wonderful times taking him to dancing lessons and coming over to our house, spending time with the brothers. They were very special times. Michael was amazing with my children and was so kind to them. Thank you! Michael, you will be missed beyond words. I know that now you will be at peace. God Bless!

**Fred**

Met him at grand opening of Mirage's Secret garden with Steve Wynn-great picture. My only personal visit was at the Grand Opening of the Secret Garden exhibit at the Mirage Resort in Las Vegas. From a tip by the security guard, I had my camera ready for an excellent picture of Michael, looking at me, and Steve Wynn coming out of the exhibit by the pool. He was staying at his Suite at the Mirage and both Michael and Steve greeted me and let me take a great picture. He was kind and they spoke of his new song created for Seigfreid and Roy's performance. My wife and I saw the show and witnessed his debut of the song "Seigfreid and Roy". I will treasure the picture forever, which I had enlarged and framed.

# A WORD FROM BRUCE SWEDIEN

A friend, co-creator and a five-time Grammy Award winner, Bruce Swedien is the author of *In the Studio with Michael Jackson*. Together with Jackson and Quincy Jones, they formed the magic trio responsible for the revolutionary sound of Jackson's records, records that "galvanized the world." The following passages are direct quotations from Swedien's book:

"Michael Jackson is the most professional and the most accomplished artist I have ever worked with. And I have worked with the best the music industry has to offer.

... Doing vocals with Michael is an absolute joy. He's got ears for days and his pitch is incredible."

"...when we record a vocal on a song, Michael vocalizes with his vocal coach Seth Riggs, for at least an hour before he steps up to the microphone to record. I don't mean that Michael vocalizes just once in a while. I mean that he vocalizes every time we record a vocal! To me that is real dedication. One of the most fascinating things about Michael Jackson is the boundless passion that he has for his music. His enthusiasm for the project at hand is like no one else I have ever worked with."

"Michael is so professional, so wonderful to work with. I have never run into anybody that works with Michael and doesn't regard it as a pleasant experience.

...MJ's Musical standards are incredibly high."

"Michael is a gentle soul. He is very polite and kind. He will say, "Can I hear a little more piano in the earphones, please? I turn up the piano in his cue mix and he'll say, "Thank you." This is an industry where you don't hear those words a whole lot. So for that reason I totally respect Michael and his musical integrity is so astounding"

"What I truthfully say is that, first and foremost, Michael is an absolute joy to work with. I can't think of another way to express my experience in working with him. There is no one I would rather work with."

# AFTERWORD

It is time to set aside all judgment, rumors, and opinions and ask ourselves what the truth about Michael Jackson is. To answer this question honestly, we simply need to remember that your truth and my truth combined does not make THE WHOLE TRUTH. All we have is an opinion.

Did Michael Jackson fulfill his dream to "Heal the World" and unite the people of this planet? We do know this: through his life and death, he did unite millions of people around the globe, whether in mourning, celebrating his legacy, or in their harsh criticism. What humanity declares, as this book clearly documents, is "WE ARE NOT INDIFFERENT! WE DO CARE!"

# ABOUT THE AUTHOR

Juja D, PhD is a published author in Bulgaria, EU. She was the creator and host of 96 apisodes of the TV show "Aerobic Gymnastics" in the 80's, which continued airing regularly for 10 years after she immigrated to the U.S. When she had everything—the status and power of a celebrity and the appreciation and love of her colleagues and fans, Juja D left Bulgaria and immigrated to the U.S. with no English, $50 in her pocket and two teenage boys. She started from scratch, working at Ringling Brothers & Barnum and Bailey Circus as a vendor selling cotton candy and popcorn. Remembering the joy of detachment from public life and the feeling of freedom away from the spotlight, the most comforting thought she had at that time was, "I am so glad nobody knows me here!" The author lived the rewards and pleasures of public life, but also paid the true price of fame, a price that takes a toll on one's total existence.